"Want an introduction to theology that combines biblical texts, what people have said across history, and that alludes to works of contemporary culture that show how people look at such themes? *Exploring Christian Theology* is a wonderful doctrinal primer that teaches theology in a way that will engage you and cause you to reflect. Study and learn which texts lead to which views and why. A great way to get acquainted with key biblical theological themes."

Darrell L Bock, Executive Director of Cultural Engagement,
Howard G. Hendricks Center for Christian Leadership
and Cultural Engagement, Senior Research Professor
of New Testament Studies, Dallas Theological Seminary

"There has never been a more urgent need, because of the times in which we live, to have a biblically based statement of Christian theology. Holsteen and Svigel are both qualified to write such an exploration since their lives have been shaped by biblical teaching, and it is this teaching that prompts others to the hope only God through His Word can provide."

Mark L. Bailey, President, Dallas Theological Seminary

"The church is always in need of mature, faithful, biblical theology. And that's exactly what you should expect to find in this volume. This new book is a very important consideration of the church, the Christian life, and the end times. And Christians in all walks of life will find this book to be particularly helpful."

—Dr. R. Albert Mohler Jr., President of The Southern
Baptist Theological Seminary

EXPLORING CHRISTIAN THEOLOGY

THE CHURCH, SPIRITUAL GROWTH, AND THE END TIMES

General Editors
NATHAN D. HOLSTEEN AND MICHAEL J. SVIGEL

Contributing Writers
Douglas K. Blount, J. Lanier Burns,
J. Scott Horrell, and Glenn R. Kreider

Part One: Nathan D. Holsteen
Part Two: Michael J. Svigel

BETHANY HOUSE PUBLISHERS
a division of Baker Publishing Group
Minneapolis, Minnesota

Published by Bethany House Publishers
11400 Hampshire Avenue South
Bloomington, Minnesota 55438
www.bethanyhouse.com

Bethany House Publishers is a division of
Baker Publishing Group, Grand Rapids, Michigan

Printed in the United States of America

Library of Congress Cataloging-in-Publication Data

Exploring Christian theology : the church, spiritual growth, and the end times / writers, Nathan D. Holsteen and Michael J. Svigel ; contributing writers, Douglas Blount, J. Lanier Burns, J. Scott Horrell, and Glenn R. Kreider ; general editors, Nathan D. Holsteen and Michael J. Svigel.

pages cm

Includes bibliographical references and index.

Summary: "Dallas Theological Seminary professors make basic theology accessible for everyone. Included are key doctrines on the church, spiritual growth, and the end times"— Provided by publisher.

ISBN 978-0-7642-1129-4 (pbk. : alk. paper)

1. Church—Biblical teaching. 2. Eschatology—Biblical teaching. 3. Spiritual formation. 4. Theology, Doctrinal. I. Holsteen, Nathan D. II. Svigel, Michael J.

BV600.3.E97 2014

230—dc23 2013034251

Cover Design by Brand Navigation

The authors are represented by The Steve Laube Agency.

14 15 16 17 18 19 20 7 6 5 4 3 2 1

Contents

Introduction

For some people, the word *doctrine* summons yawns of tedium, shudders of trepidation, or frowns of suspicion. Dogmatic preachers exasperate them, feuding denominations weary them, and droning scholars bore them.

When people hear *theology*, the condition sometimes worsens. They picture massive tomes packed with technical discussions, less-than-crucial data, and incomprehensible footnotes—unusable information to distract them from God rather than drawing them nearer.

Most people seeking to grow in their faith want practical principles, not theoretical concepts. They want to *know* God, not just know *about* Him.

Yet the fact is that we can't experience real spiritual growth without solid spiritual truth. We can't know the true God without knowing God truly.

In that case, where do we start? How do we begin to harvest in this fruitful field without getting caught in the tangled underbrush of mere opinions and idiosyncrasies? How can we sort through what seem like countless contradictory theories to find the essential truths necessary for strengthening and living out our faith?

Exploring Christian Theology will offer introductions, overviews, and reviews of key orthodox, protestant, evangelical tenets without belaboring details or broiling up debates. The three *ECT* volumes, compact but substantial, provide accessible and convenient summaries of major themes; they're intended as guidebooks for a church that, overall, is starving for the very doctrine it's too long avoided.

Each volume includes primary biblical texts, a history of each main teaching, relevant charts and graphs, practical implications, and suggestions for literature that you might want to have in your own library. And one of our goals for this work is to offer help to those who haven't read much in the way of theology. So we've included a glossary of terms—the unusual and the significant. If at any point you see an unfamiliar word or wonder about a definition, consider taking a moment to check that list. In a similar vein, you can look at the table of contents for a straightforward and organized glimpse of what's to come.

Further, each part or section (e.g., this volume has two parts) can stand alone—be read or referenced on its own. Or you can study through all the sections related to one "region" of theology and walk away with a handle on its biblical, theological, historical, and practical dimensions. In other words, these books can be used in a number of ways, suitable to your particular needs or interests.

Exploring Christian Theology differs from other mini-theologies in that it strives to present a broad consensus, not a condensed systematic model of one evangelical teacher or protestant tradition. Thus you might use these volumes for discipleship, catechism, membership training, preview or review of doctrine, or personal reference. Like the evangelical movement itself, we seek to be orthodox and interdenominational within a classic consensus.

Treat each volume as a simple primer that supplements (not supplants) more detailed treatments of theology—that complements (rather than competes with) intermediate and advanced works. As such, regardless of denominational or confessional commitments, these books likewise can be used by ministry training programs, Bible colleges, or seminaries for students preparing to undertake in-depth study. Whatever your background, degree of interest, or level of expertise, we hope this volume won't be the end of a brief jaunt but the beginning of a lifelong journey into—or a helpful aid alongside your ongoing immersion into—the exciting world of Christian theology.

Nathan D. Holsteen and Michael J. Svigel
General Editors

ACKNOWLEDGMENTS

We want to acknowledge the helpful contributions of several individuals who pitched in during the planning, research, and writing of this volume.

Our colleagues in the department of Theological Studies at Dallas Theological Seminary deserve recognition. They are all far more than colleagues—they're brothers, advisors, mentors, and friends.

Luke Hatteberg, Garrick Bailey, Nathan Peets, and Ben Lowery, interns, assisted with research and exhibited a passion not only for biblical, historical, and systematic theology but also for sharing evangelical theology with a church in desperate need of doctrinal nourishment.

Rev. Dean Zimmerman and Pastor Arnold Robertstad helped me (Mike) stay balanced and fair in my presentation of legitimate evangelical views that I don't hold but they do.

My (Nathan's) wife, Janice, deserves thanks. She always keeps me grounded and reminds me to ask constantly, "What does this mean where the rubber hits the road?" I thank God for her partnership.

I (Mike) also want to thank my wife, Stephanie, for her patient support and for her constant encouragement to write a book she can actually use.

We want to thank our agent, Steve Laube, for helping us massage this project; Tim Peterson for his tireless efforts in the editing and publishing process; Christopher Soderstrom for his invaluable insights and suggestions; and the editorial and marketing team at Bethany House for their behind-the-scenes work.

The Christian Story in Four Acts

Do you remember this story?

The young nephew of a rugged moisture farmer grows up under the stifling rays of Tatooine's twin suns. But more oppressive than the heat of that desert planet is the smothering grip of the boy's aunt and uncle, who've fostered his naïveté and kept him busy calibrating machines, cleaning droids, and repairing equipment. Anything to keep him from asking about his past, complaining about his wretched condition, or dreaming about a destiny that could drive him far from home. Still, deep in his heart, young Luke Skywalker senses a larger world "out there," beyond the bleak horizon, past the blazing suns, and across the distant stars of that galaxy far, far away.

Ever since the film's original release in 1977, the *Star Wars* phenomenon has continued to resonate with young and old alike, trading in universal themes of fall, struggle, self-sacrifice, and redemption. Most storytellers admit that the movies reflect something profound about the human experience, touching something deep within the soul. George Lucas, the creator of the *Star Wars* franchise, quite intentionally cast his narrative in a time-tested form, drinking deeply from the wells of ancient mythology and incorporating themes that repeatedly appear in epic poems, plays, legends, myths, and religious beliefs of various world cultures.[1]

Lucas utilized what storytellers often call "the hero cycle."[2] With this pattern, authors grasp and hold their audience by tapping into universal experiences—elements common to most or all individuals and cultures:

- an experience of personal conflict between good and evil
- frustration with the present world
- anxieties about the future
- a sense of having a greater purpose and meaning
- the conviction that this world isn't the way it's supposed to be
- the hope that things will one day be better than they are

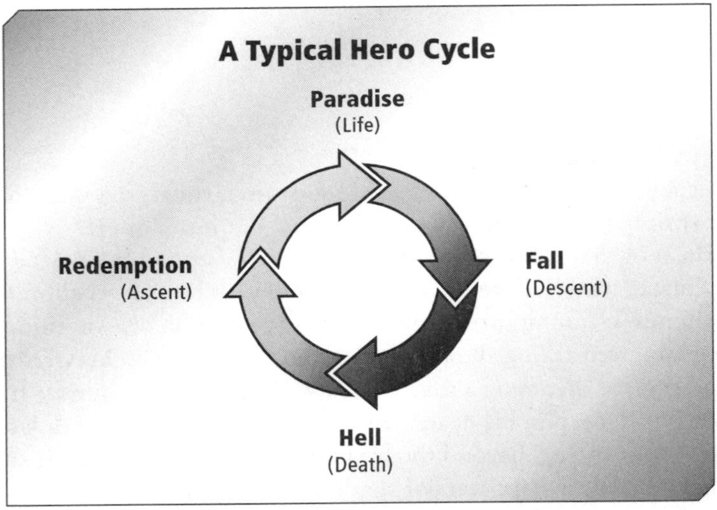

Our well-known stories of initiation, fall, struggle, testing, redemption, and ultimate victory put into words, portray on stage, or project on screen the unconscious realities we feel in our hearts. Our favorite movies or books are "favorites" because they touch on themes related to this cycle that resonates with our experiences. They "speak" to us, inviting us to enter into a larger story that transcends our lonely individualism and our deteriorating world.[3]

Reminiscent of the hero cycle (with some astonishing twists), the chronicle of the classic Christian faith is a captivating account that can be summed up in four acts: Creation, Fall, Redemption, and Restoration.

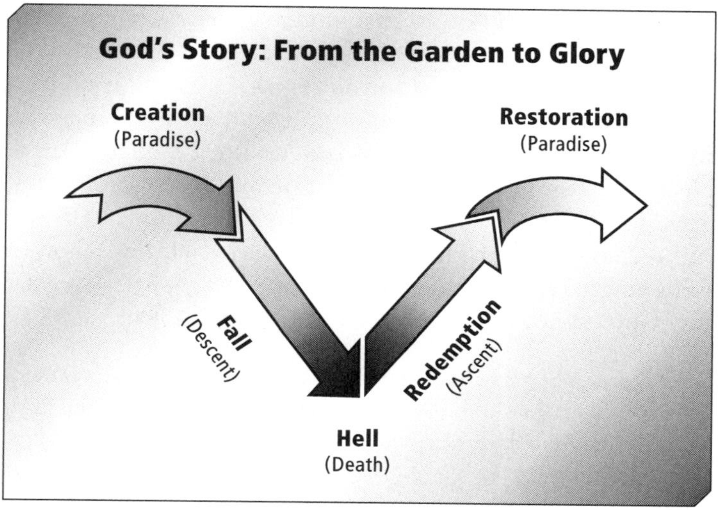

Act I: Creation

If a composer were to write a score for the Old Testament, what kind of motifs would he or she employ? Gentle harps and melodic strings? Majestic trumpets? Delightful woodwinds or pounding drums? Through whatever means, the theme would probably *begin* with a burst of symphonic grandeur, followed by a flourish of interwoven melodies signifying the creation of heaven and earth in glorious perfection.

As this bold overture resolved into a blissful ballad, however, a dark and ominous minor chord would slither into the melody, eventually turning the key from major to minor. Perhaps oboes and bassoons would replace flutes and piccolos; enter bass drums for xylophones; cellos and basses for violins and harps; tubas for trumpets. We'd hear harsh, discordant notes.

Even so, amid this cacophony, hints of the original beauty, majesty, and power would occasionally break through, promising to reemerge and eventually, ultimately, to triumph.

What, in words, is the theme of the Old Testament? *The tragic fall of a perfect creation followed by judgment and the promise of final redemption.*

Genesis 1–2 stunningly depicts the original creation of the heavens, the earth, all living things, and humankind. The story begins not with competing deities or an absolute nothingness but with *God*: "In the beginning, God created the heavens and the earth" (Gen. 1:1). God, through His eternal Son and Spirit, created everything that exists—whether things in heaven or things on earth, "things visible and invisible."[4] The triune God is the Author, Producer, Director, and leading Actor in the story of creation and redemption. And, as Master Storyteller, He has made himself known through His works (Ps. 19:1–2) and through His Word (2 Tim. 3:16). He both shows and tells His power, His plan, and His purpose. Simply put, the great and mighty God is knowable and has made himself known:

> Long ago, at many times and in many ways, God spoke to our fathers by the prophets, but in these last days he has spoken to us by his Son, whom he appointed the heir of all things, through whom also he created the world.[5]

As the crowning work of His creation, God made humans, male and female, co-regents over what He had made with a mandate to "be fruitful and multiply and fill the earth and subdue it" (Gen. 1:28). God desired to share the stage of His production with creatures He formed from mud, transforming dust into stars (Ps. 8:3–6). They were created in the image of God—that is, reflecting His glory and character and destined to rule as His representatives over creation (Gen. 1:26–30). As God's image-bearing envoys, humans were to work in the Paradise of Eden, cultivating it and ultimately extending its borders to cover the entire uncultivated earth (2:7–25).

Act II: Fall

Alas, that state of pure innocence would not last. As intelligent creatures given free will, the first humans succumbed to temptation and turned their backs on their Creator, forfeiting their role as His rulers over earth and falling victim to sin and death (Gen. 3). The blast wave of this disobedience resounds forward through all human history, its devastating effects illustrated in Genesis 4–11: murder, anarchy, destruction, and then rebellion against God. Everybody today will admit that something is wrong with the world and with the people in it. As Ecclesiastes says, "Surely there is not a righteous man on earth who does good and never sins" (7:20), and "The hearts of the sons of men are full of evil and insanity is in their hearts throughout their lives" (9:3 NASB).

Thus half the story cycle is complete—from Paradise and life, through tragic fall, to an earthly state of living condemnation and then universal death.

Act III: Redemption

If we were to commission the same composer to score a New Testament sequel to the Old Testament part of the story, what kind of themes would we want? How does the continuation of His-story in the New Testament relate to its beginnings in the Old?

The sequel's score would probably look like a mirror image of the initial themes. From darkness to light, from fall, judgment, and promises delayed to promises fulfilled, mercy and grace extended, and redemption realized. Discordant notes and chords would be replaced by a symphony of instruments and voices singing praises to our God and King. The nearly forgotten opening scenes of the prequel would be restored and then surpassed.

What, then, is the theme of the New Testament? *The long-awaited redemption of a fallen creation followed by the restoration and fulfillment of all God's promises and purposes.*

God did not abandon humankind to hopelessness. Already in Genesis 3, after the fall of Adam and Eve, He pledged that the offspring of the woman would bruise the Serpent's head, ultimately destroying sin and evil (v. 15). He then advanced His plan of redemption through the calling of Abraham (Gen. 12), to whom He promised that a particular offspring would mediate blessings to the world (Gen. 13:15; Gal. 3:15–16). After this promise passed from Abraham through Isaac and Jacob to the tribe of Judah, it then narrowed to the dynasty of King David. In Isaiah's famous prophecy this same promise of a Redeemer is narrowed to an individual coming king, the Messiah:

> The people who walk in darkness
> Will see a great light;
> Those who live in a dark land,
> The light will shine on them. . . .
> For a child will be born to us, a son will be given to us;

> And the government will rest on His shoulders;
> And His name will be called Wonderful Counselor, Mighty God,
> Eternal Father, Prince of Peace.
> There will be no end to the increase of His government or
> of peace,
> On the throne of David and over his kingdom,
> To establish it and to uphold it with justice and righteousness
> From then on and forevermore. (Isa. 9:2, 6–7 NASB)

The redemption plan continued to be revealed throughout the Old Testament Scriptures. Despite human failures—even of those to whom He'd given amazing guarantees of His presence and love—God remained faithful, ultimately sending the promised Offspring—His own divine Son (John 3:16).

When God's Son was to enter the redemption story, God sent the angel Gabriel to confirm that this child, born to a poor family from an insignificant village, was the One through whom the ancient promises would be fulfilled:

> You will conceive in your womb and bear a son, and you shall name Him Jesus. He will be great and will be called the Son of the Most High; and the Lord God will give Him the throne of His father David; and He will reign over the house of Jacob forever, and His kingdom will have no end. (Luke 1:31–33 NASB)

As the plot unfolded, though, God's narrative took a world-shaking turn. Instead of following the cycle's upward path—the Hero passes through various trials, endures setbacks, and overcomes failures while pressing on toward His reward—God's Chosen One *retraced the descent*, surrendering His life to the executioner. The only being in human history that deserved never-ending life with God voluntarily suffered a brutal death (Phil. 2:5–8).

Even this ironic fate had been foretold in the prophecies of Isaiah:

> Surely our griefs He Himself bore,
> And our sorrows He carried;
> Yet we ourselves esteemed Him stricken,
> Smitten of God, and afflicted.
> But He was pierced through for our transgressions,

> He was crushed for our iniquities;
> The chastening for our well-being fell upon Him,
> And by His scourging we are healed.
> All of us like sheep have gone astray,
> Each of us has turned to his own way;
> But the LORD has caused the iniquity of us all
> To fall on Him. (Isa. 53:4–6 NASB)

Nevertheless, for God's matchless Hero, death was not the end. Against all expectations—including those of His despairing followers—Jesus of Nazareth was raised from the grave and stepped out of the tomb more than alive—He was *glorified*. Having died in a mortal body susceptible to sickness, pain, and death, He was raised in a physical but immortal body, incapable of illness, impervious to hurt, and overflowing with eternal life.

Furthermore, through Jesus Christ, God began writing His-story's final chapter. Those people who became united with Christ by placing their faith in Him could now partake of His glory, sharing the Hero's reward, and surpassing even the original purpose for humankind that God had established ages ago in Eden.

The Hero's victorious reentrance into the halls of heaven opened a new chapter in God's unfolding drama. After the resurrected Savior's ascension, and prior to His in-the-end return as Judge and King, He sent His Spirit to stir the hearts of His former enemies and call them to His cause. Countless converts from every nation, tribe, people, and language have been and still are flocking to His side (Rev. 7:9–10). Through spiritual union with their King, this kingdom-in-the-making also experiences a shared spiritual communion in the church. Through this spiritual-physical community of the life-giving Spirit, centered on Jesus Christ's person and work and focused on the glory of God the Father, members of Christ's body grow in faith, hope, and love. Together they become more and more like Jesus their King, the Spirit working in them to carry out the Father's redemptive mission in this still-fallen world.[6]

Act IV: Restoration

That brings us to the final resolution, the future restoration of the original creation. In the beginning, humans were expelled from Eden, unable to experience immortality in a Paradise free from suffering, frustration, fear, and death. At the present time God, through Christ and by the Spirit, is calling to himself a people who will participate in His drama's final chapter. When Jesus returns and renews all things, creation's groaning will be turned to glory as the entire earth is transformed into a new, even better Eden, and all those who've been united with Christ will be made like Him (1 John 3:2).

Revelation 21:3–4 describes the glorious coming reality:

> Behold, the tabernacle of God is among men, and He will dwell among them, and they shall be His people, and God Himself will be among them, and He will wipe away every tear from their eyes; and there will no longer be any death; there will no longer be any mourning, or crying, or pain; the first things have passed away. (NASB)

Thus, between Genesis and Revelation—from the Garden to Glory—God's unparalleled story unfolds. Every person and event moves history and humanity *forward* toward a final goal—restoration. God's grand narrative of creation, fall, redemption, and restoration truly satisfies our restless longings for purpose and meaning and also fulfills our heart's desire for acceptance in meaningful relationship. As Augustine once prayed, "You have made us for yourself, and our heart is restless until it rests in you."[7]

The timeless story also provides an ultimate answer to human injustice and inequality, as Christ's kingdom will be an eternal golden age of peace and prosperity for all (Isa. 11:1–9). Likewise, it offers vital, unshakable hope to those who now are hurting, and lonely, and lost. The concrete promises and detailed visions God has preserved for us throughout the Scriptures provide healing hope to those struggling with anxiety, fear, despair, and depression. When a person's gaze is drawn from his or her temporary groaning to the certainty of future everlasting glory through resurrection and restoration, the words of the apostle Paul ring true:

> I consider that the sufferings of this present time are not worthy to be compared with the glory that is to be revealed to us. For the anxious longing of the creation waits eagerly for the revealing of the sons of God. For the creation was subjected to futility, not willingly, but because of Him who subjected it, in hope that the creation itself also will be

> set free from its slavery to corruption into the freedom of the glory of the children of God. For we know that the whole creation groans and suffers the pains of childbirth together until now. And not only this, but also we ourselves, having the first fruits of the Spirit, even we ourselves groan within ourselves, waiting eagerly for our adoption as sons, the redemption of our body. For in hope we have been saved, but hope that is seen is not hope; for who hopes for what he already sees? But if we hope for what we do not see, with perseverance we wait eagerly for it. (Rom. 8:18–25 NASB)

The good news about God's story is that anyone can become a part of it. Jesus of Nazareth is truly God in the flesh; He truly died and was raised from death, and He truly offers a new identity and new future for all who trust in Him alone for salvation. And those who embrace in faith the Hero of this story will have a share in the restoration of all things.

> He who sits on the throne said, "Behold, I am making all things new." And He said, "Write, for these words are faithful and true." Then He said to me, "It is done. I am the Alpha and the Omega, the beginning and the end. I will give to the one who thirsts from the spring of the water of life without cost. He who overcomes will inherit these things, and I will be his God and he will be My son" (Rev. 21:5–7 NASB).

You Are *Here*

The two parts of this book take us up to the ultimate chapter of God's story. Here we move from the fall and the work of redemption . . . through the intermediate mission of the church . . . to the eventual effects of restoration.

In Part One, "Created in Christ Jesus: Church, Churches, and the Christian Life," we discover the rescue operation of the church and the Spirit's ongoing work of remaking the members of Christ's body into the image of their King. This transitions us from redemption in the theoretical and historical to redemption in the practical and present.

In Part Two, "When He Returns: Resurrection, Judgment, and the Restoration," we will come to understand the major contours of God's plan for final consummation. His redeemed people as well as this fallen creation both have an incomprehensibly wonderful future in His plan and purpose.

As we explore the biblical, theological, and historical foundations of ecclesiology, sanctification, and eschatology, we'll be able to look back at the entire sweeping narrative of creation, fall, redemption, and restoration, and join the heavenly chorus praising God for the great things He has done . . . and will yet do:

> "Hallelujah! For the Lord our God the Almighty reigns. Let us rejoice and exult and give him the glory, for the marriage of the Lamb has come, and his Bride has made herself ready; it was granted her to clothe herself with fine linen, bright and pure"—for the fine linen is the righteous deeds of the saints. (Rev. 19:6–8)

PART ONE

Created in Christ Jesus

Church, Churches, and the Christian Life

BY NATHAN D. HOLSTEEN

High-Altitude Survey

Spy novels have gripped me for as long as I can remember.

I inherited a love of reading from my parents, and as a young man I cut my teeth on novels written by authors like Alistair MacLean. I read everything I could get my hands on. I even read *H.M.S. Ulysses*.

But nothing in MacLean prepared me for my first Robert Ludlum novel: *The Bourne Identity*. You may remember the basic story: a man found floating in the Mediterranean regains consciousness after he's pulled up by fishermen. But he has amnesia and so cannot remember who he is—in fact, he can't remember anything about his life. The men take him to a doctor, who finds a piece of microfilm surgically implanted in his hip. That leads him to a secret bank account in Zurich. And so the tale begins. As the man follows one clue to his identity after another, he's drawn deeper and deeper into a danger-everywhere existence of which he has no memory.

That thriller's intricate plot line simply blew me away. I still remember my head spinning as I tried to assess and assimilate all the info, seeking to figure out, right along with Jason Bourne, *who in the world IS this guy*?

Unlike that masterpiece of espionage, the book you now hold in your hands is not a mystery. You won't have to wade through multiple shootouts or miraculous escapes before discovering the essence of ecclesiology (the study of the church) and sanctification (developing a life of holiness). In the pages to follow we're going to explore these two major areas of theology, and I won't be trying to persuade you that my personal views on either or both are precisely correct. Yes, I have personal views that I teach and preach, but for this book our goal is to introduce you to the unity and diversity of evangelical perspectives. (Again, if you're unfamiliar with these words or others, remember there's a glossary of terms in the back.) In the book's first half, I want not only to share a taste of the uniqueness of various views but also to draw you back to the center of evangelicalism by highlighting the principles that bind together the different strands of our diverse tradition.

In yet another departure from the *Bourne Identity* pattern, I also want to clue you in right up front to our major themes. You already know that in Part One we'll focus on ecclesiology and sanctification; I'd like to prepare you for the actual claims you're going to encounter.

First, an orientation to ecclesiology.

To many Christians, the doctrine of the church does seem mysterious, perhaps approaching opaque. Even some professional theologians shy away from venturing too far into this realm. But I believe it can be presented in a fairly simple fashion once we've acknowledged the appropriate starting point. And just as for Jason Bourne, that starting point is to ask, "Who am I?"

Bourne began to assemble a comprehension of his lost identity by observing his own skill set and by trying to ascertain how the people around him helped clarify who he was. We're going to do something like this in approaching the doctrine of ecclesiology, and when we do we'll find that all aspects of our spiritual skill set—and every spiritual relationship we have—point always, only, inexorably, to one person: Jesus Christ. This means the way to start wrestling with ecclesiology is to stop wrestling. Every datum points to Jesus. To put it another way:

> *Who I am can only be determined in relation to who Jesus is—the God-man, our Redeemer, my Savior.*

Now, that statement points to the central principle for all protestant evangelical ecclesiology. This principle, while clearly related, is distinct:

> *There is no authentic ecclesiology apart from a saving relationship with Jesus Christ.*

As we all know, the nature of that saving relationship is that it's invisible—no one can "see" someone else's genuine faith. No bright halo hovers above the heads of authentic saints. There's no tiny blue

LED planted in a believer's ear to show that he or she participates in a saving relationship with Jesus. And which congregation or denomination a person belongs to doesn't yield the answer either—genuine Christians participate in some pretty dead churches, and non-Christians hang out in some vibrant churches. One of my heroes, John Calvin, made this same observation when he taught that "every church is a mixed body."[1]

You may have heard it said that "Christianity isn't a religion, it's a relationship." Sometimes people use this cliché to dismiss the visible church from their lives and focus just on their personal, private, individual experience with the cool Guy named Jesus. But that misuse—or even abuse—shouldn't deter us from something nevertheless true about the cliché. While it isn't an excuse to dismiss the visible church as irrelevant, our invisible spiritual relationship with Jesus Christ is what makes the visible church eminently relevant.

Ecclesiology: A Community Son-Centered and Spirit-Formed

It may sound overly simplistic, yet I believe the following observation provides a high-level overview of ecclesiology: the study of the church, properly speaking, must start with the invisible saving relationship between the Redeemer and the redeemed. That is, the community of the redeemed is Son-centered. Jesus Christ is the center and source of the church, which is the community of the redeemed under His headship. With this basic statement, all evangelical Christians would agree.

But there's more that unites evangelicals with respect to the doctrine of ecclesiology. The community is definitely Son-centered, and it's also Spirit-formed. The Holy Spirit of God forms the church of Jesus Christ. (This, we'll see, is the message of Scripture and the consistent affirmation of evangelicals throughout history.) As a result, the church finds its unique identity as the community of the redeemed because of an invisible relationship with Jesus Christ. Then we recognize that only because of the Spirit's ministry do we have invisible union with our Savior and visible unity with His people.

These are the emphases of an evangelical ecclesiology:

The church is Son-centered and Spirit-formed.

Sanctification: A Life Son-Centered, Spirit-Formed, and Community-Minded

As to providing a high-level overview of the doctrine of sanctification, the convenient truth is that it starts in much the same place as ecclesiology. To return again to Jason Bourne, once he began to answer "Who am I?" he also began to formulate an answer to "What do I do now?" Only when we realize the former can we offer a reasonable approach to the latter.

This is precisely why the principle that undergirds ecclesiology also undergirds sanctification: *the study of sanctification, properly speaking, must start with the invisible saving relationship between the Redeemer and the redeemed.* Once again, this is the starting point, precisely because no one can even dream of living the Christian life unless he or she is already united to Christ in salvation. That is, authentic sanctification flows out of genuine justification. (By the way, we look at justification in much more detail in another volume in this series; for now, we'll focus on the relationship between justification and sanctification.)

Sanctification is not me-oriented, it's *we*-oriented. Its focus is Christ, by the power of the Spirit—but its *purpose* is community-oriented.

And I don't mean a geographical community; I mean the body of Christ. Sanctification, as the growth in holiness of individuals who are in a saving relationship with Jesus Christ, has as its purpose the strengthening of His body, the church. As justified individuals grow in fellowship with Christ and with one another through the work of the Spirit in the context of their local church communities, the worldwide body of Christ also grows in holiness, magnifying Christ's name and bringing glory to God the Father.

That's it. That's our high-altitude overview. All that remains is to work out the consequences of these two basic affirmations:

- *The study of the church, properly speaking, must start with the invisible saving relationship between the Redeemer and the redeemed.*
- *The study of sanctification, properly speaking, must start with the invisible saving relationship between the Redeemer and the redeemed.*

Passages to Master

It hasn't always been easy to define exactly what makes a person, a church, or a ministry "evangelical." However, one prominent feature has been an insistence on "the paramount place of inspired Scripture as the final authority in matters of faith and practice."[1] Scripture's pride of position in "doing theology" is no recent invention of desperate leaders to establish stable authority in a world gone mad. Reliance on the Bible as the sole inspired source of divine revelation has been part of the Christian tradition for millennia.

Augustine summed up the belief of the early church around AD 420 when he said that the Bible "has paramount authority . . . to which we yield assent in all matters of which we ought not to be ignorant, and yet cannot know of ourselves."[2] Similarly, the great medieval scholar Anselm of Canterbury wrote around AD 1100, "If I say anything which plainly opposes the Holy Scriptures, it is false; and if I am aware of it, I will no longer hold it."[3] And, in the Reformation era, we ought to observe Martin Luther's bold stand on the Word of God as the final authority in matters of Christian conviction: "Unless I am convinced by the testimony of Scripture or by clear reason . . . I cannot and will not recant anything."[4]

The patristic, medieval, Protestant, and evangelical commitment to inspired Scripture as the final, unimpeachable, uncorrectable authority in all matters of faith and practice shouldn't surprise us. Paul himself said, "All Scripture is breathed out by God and profitable for teaching, for reproof, for correction, and for training in righteousness" (2 Tim. 3:16). So in every doctrinal inquiry, we turn to Holy Scripture as the starting point and center point of our theology, because therein we hear God's own voice on the matter.

> **Scripture Memory 1**
>
> ***Acts 1:4–5***
>
> 4 And while staying with them he ordered them not to depart from Jerusalem, but to wait for the promise of the Father, which, he said, "you heard from me;
> 5 for John baptized with water, but you will be baptized with the Holy Spirit not many days from now."

The following thirteen New Testament passages form the foundation and structure for Christian ecclesiology and sanctification. Numerous additional passages could be included, but by mastering these you'll be able to establish your own understanding of the Christian community and the Christian life with a firm footing. Along with a basic discussion of the points of agreement and disagreement among various Bible-believing Christians regarding the meaning of these passages, you'll also find verses to commit to memory.

(1) *Acts 2:* The Day of Pentecost and the Holy Spirit's Coming

When I was growing up I became enthralled with all things World War II. I devoured books and entire encyclopedias on the subject, even pondering hypotheticals like *what would have happened if the German pocket battleship* Bismarck *faced off against the giant Japanese battleship* Yamato? Somewhere amid this fascination I encountered the concept of a turning point. In what Americans called the Pacific Theater, the Battle of Midway stands identified as a turning point—a confrontation where the momentum changed from favoring the Japanese forces to favoring the Americans. In that one clash the Japanese fleet lost four aircraft carriers. The sinking of the *Akagi, Kaga, Hiryu,* and *Soryu* not only took the lives of more than two thousand unfortunate sailors but also crippled the Japanese Navy's ability to maintain an effective air war in the Pacific.

While historians still debate Midway's exact effect, another kind of turning point altogether stands astride any biblical discussion of the church: a defining moment in the ministry of the Holy Spirit that we call the day of Pentecost. The central passage is found in Acts 2.

To understand the change in the Spirit's ministry, it's important to get a running start with Acts 1. Before Luke tells of the post-ascension works of the apostles, he recounts how Jesus told them to wait in

Jerusalem for "the promise of the Father," which, Jesus said, "you heard from me" (1:4). He further identified this thing for which they were to wait in saying, "You will be baptized with the Holy Spirit not many days from now" (1:5).

It seems in the text of Acts that the disciples immediately understood this prediction of the Lord to refer to a turning point, for they connected this prophecy with the promise of a restored kingdom in Israel (1:6). But what would occur was not exactly as they'd expected. Instead of restoring the kingdom to Israel in an immediate and literal fashion, the turning point involved a new ministry: the baptism of the Holy Spirit.

While different traditions within evangelicalism see the import of the Spirit's baptism in different ways, it's clear that Acts affirms the following:

1. The ministry of the Spirit that appears on the day of Pentecost must be called the baptism of the Holy Spirit.
2. The baptism of the Holy Spirit is something promised by the Father and affirmed by Christ.
3. The baptism of the Holy Spirit is therefore something new; it is a turning point in the ministry of God's Spirit.
4. The baptism of the Holy Spirit is foundational for the subsequent mission of the apostles and the existence of the New Testament church.

The first affirmation is easily seen by observing the correlation between Acts 1:5, Acts 2, and Acts 11:15–16. In 1:5, Jesus himself predicted an occurrence He described as being "baptized with the Holy Spirit." For some, this creates discord with the textual description of the day of Pentecost in Acts 2, for there we find the Spirit's effect on the disciples described as their being "filled with the Holy Spirit." But this apparent distinction need not trouble us. Peter, himself a hearer of Jesus' words and a recipient of the Spirit's ministry on Pentecost, identified (see 11:15–16) this *filling* with the promise of Spirit *baptism* that Jesus uttered in Acts 1.

Acts 11 recounts the story of Peter and the Gentile believers told in Acts 10, when the Lord worked miraculously to show the apostles that Gentiles were also included in this new undertaking of the Holy Spirit. In a nutshell, God taught Peter through a vision that things formerly unclean (to God's people) were, after the turning point, clean. As a result, Peter went with some Jewish companions to the house of Cornelius, a Gentile, in Caesarea. While there, the gift of the Holy Spirit fell upon the Gentiles who were listening to Peter speak. This amazed the Jewish believers "because the gift of the Holy Spirit was poured out even on the Gentiles" (10:45).

What's more, Peter quickly equated the Spirit's ministry to these Gentiles with the ministry he himself had experienced on Pentecost. He said, "Can anyone withhold water for baptizing these people, who have received the Holy Spirit just as we have?" (10:47). This account implies something else significant: from this time on, non-Jews (Gentiles) would no longer find salvation by turning to Judaism, but rather by turning in faith to Christ (see more on the fourth affirmation below).

One additional act in this vignette draws our attention. When Peter returned to Jerusalem and explained to the Jewish Christians what had happened in Caesarea, he restated the same conviction: what had happened to the disciples on the day of Pentecost had now happened to Gentile believers in Christ. But this time he took his conviction one step further: he identified the "reception" of the Holy Spirit (described in Acts 10) as the Spirit's "baptism": "I remembered the word of the Lord, how he said, 'John baptized with water, but you will be baptized with the Holy Spirit'" (11:16).

Now we've come full circle. The very event that Christ predicted is seen to be the baptism of the Holy Spirit. The coming of the Spirit on the day of Pentecost is the Spirit's baptism. And the event that solidified the position of Gentile believers in this fledgling movement is the baptism of the Holy Spirit.

Having identified the central event—the baptism of the Holy Spirit—in this biblical turning point, let's proceed to the event's significance, which is depicted in the second, third, and fourth affirmations numbered above.

Second, the baptism of the Holy Spirit is something promised by the Father and affirmed by Christ. This is exceedingly non-controversial, as it's simply a restatement of what Acts 1 says, and very few evangelicals will quibble over it. But matters get more interesting as we move into the final two affirmations.

To the third: the baptism of the Holy Spirit is thus a new turning point in the Spirit's ministry. While this affirmation is not found explicitly in Acts, to many readers it is absolutely inescapable, seemingly entailed by what the text does explicitly state. For example, is any other conclusion more plausibly drawn from Jesus' command? When He told the disciples to wait in Jerusalem for what the Father had promised, it seems unlikely He was telling them to wait for something that had already happened. His directive seems to entail the observation that something new was about to take place, something related to a promise given by the Father. Beyond this, in Acts 2, Luke strongly implies that the baptism of the Spirit was new. The experience of the disciples and Peter's defense of that experience in his speech to the people gathered in Jerusalem leave other understandings in an awkward position.

The fourth and final affirmation regarding this vital turning point is that the baptism of the Holy Spirit is foundational for the apostles' mission and the New Testament church's existence. In fact, it seems the Spirit's baptism is the foundation for the rest of the book, for everything the apostles did in the remainder of Acts was predicated upon and driven by it. Beyond this, the baptism of the Holy Spirit drives the identity of the fledgling community of the redeemed. No longer is the covenant community restricted to Jews—it's now open to *all who believe in Christ*. The equal reception of the Spirit dramatically demonstrated the equality of all who place their faith in Jesus.

Evangelicals agree on the crucial place this passage holds in an understanding of the church. George Smeaton, a representative voice from nineteenth-century Scottish Presbyterianism, provides one perspective on the decisive nature of this turning point:

> The Church of Christ, in the days of His flesh, did not, properly speaking, exist, though His word had found entrance into individual souls. It was at Pentecost that the Lord, by the power of His Spirit, welded into a Church the souls on whom the word had exercised a saving efficacy. The Holy Spirit, at the commencement of what is called His "mission," collected the disciples into a living unity; and this great work of the Spirit is called the Church, the kingdom of God, the body of Christ, the temple of the Spirit, the habitation of God in the Spirit (Eph. ii. 22), a conquest from the kingdom of darkness and death.[5]

Acts 2, then, establishes a firm basis for a key starting point, namely, *the focus of ecclesiology is found in a relationship between the believer and Jesus Christ.* That relationship is marked by the baptism of the Holy Spirit.

Although among evangelicals there is broad agreement on the momentous import of the Spirit's ministry in defining the church, significant disagreement persists over exactly how to understand the boundaries of the church. For instance, should we consider those who came to God in faith before the revelation of the Spirit's baptism to be part of the church? Some evangelicals say yes, because the key thing is being rightly related to God, and even those saints before Christ's first coming can only be saved on the basis of His shed blood, so, being the people of God, they are members of the church. Others say no, because the church's distinguishing mark is its peculiar relationship with Christ as seen in the new "turning point" ministry of the Holy Spirit. Such evangelicals don't deny the salvation of saints in previous ages; they simply see that salvation in a different light.

This raises one of the most-discussed questions in protestant evangelical ecclesiology: *When did the church begin?* The following chart shows three different responses:

VIEWS OF THE BEGINNING OF THE CHURCH

View	Representative	Reasoning
The church began with Adam.	R. B. Kuiper[6]	All people ever saved are saved through one Savior and one way of salvation—faith in Christ. OT saints, then, are saved through faith in Christ as prophesied in the OT. Thus, all OT saints are members of the one church, the body of Christ. The logical beginning of this saving faith is found in Adam and Eve, who thus constituted the first church.[7]
The church began with Abraham.	D. Douglas Bannerman	Due to the significance of the biblical role Abraham played, and the nature of the promises God gave to him (which turn out to be corporate in nature), it may be said that "the Church of God, built upon the Gospel and the covenant of grace, was distinctly and visibly set up in connection with God's dealings with Abraham."[8]
The church began on the day of Pentecost.	Millard Erickson	The way the term *ecclesia* is used in the NT, and the way Jesus speaks of His church as yet future in Matthew 16, along with the significance of the gift of the Spirit in Acts 2, allows one to conclude that the church began at Pentecost.[9]

Though we can read Acts 2 in slightly different ways, at the same time, evangelicals have major points of agreement. The church is defined by a saving relationship with Christ, and that relationship was radically changed by the coming of the Holy Spirit on the day of Pentecost, a "turning point" in God's plan of redemption.

(2) *Romans 11:* The Olive Tree, Israel, and the Church

Near the end of 2012, the world became fascinated with the Mesoamerican Long Count (more popularly known as the Mayan) calendar. According to some interpretations, it finished on December 21 of that year, the end of a 5,125-year cycle. This fueled a number of speculations—some serious, some humorous—about a "Mayan apocalypse." My personal favorite was a Dan Piraro cartoon portraying two ancient Mayans, one of whom presents his latest carved circular calendar and says, "I only had enough room to go up to 2012." The other replies, "Ha! That'll freak somebody out someday."[10]

> **Scripture Memory 2**
>
> ***Romans 11:19–21***
>
> 19 Then you will say, "Branches were broken off so that I might be grafted in."
> 20 That is true. They were broken off because of their unbelief, but you stand fast through faith. So do not become proud, but fear.
> 21 For if God did not spare the natural branches, neither will he spare you.

It soon became obvious the doomsayers were wrong—but it's still a legitimate historical question to ask: "What did it all mean, anyway?"

The same might be asked of our next significant passage regarding ecclesiology, for in it we again find areas of agreement and disagreement—areas that revolve around the interpretation of an image the text presents. Paul uses an olive tree to illustrate the relationship between Israel and the church.

The imagery shows up in Romans 11 rather suddenly. Paul compares Gentile believers to branches "cut from what is by nature a wild olive tree, and grafted, contrary to nature, into a cultivated olive tree" (v. 24). Along the same lines, he portrays the people of Israel, who've rejected Christ, as branches broken off a cultivated olive tree "because of their unbelief" (v. 20).

This raises a question that has vexed many a Bible student: what does the tree itself represent? If Christ-rejecting Israel is depicted as natural branches broken off of the tree, and Christ-believing Gentiles are depicted as wild branches grafted into the tree, *what is the tree?*

The suggested answers are numerous, but two seem to receive the most attention: (1) the tree represents Israel, and (2) the tree represents a position of covenant blessing. Those who opt for the first believe that the image presents the church as the "new" (or the "true") Israel. In this view, the image of the tree itself seems best identified as "Israel," for Israel is the heir of God's promises to Abraham.[11] This, for instance, is how one prominent evangelical arrives at the statement "those who are united to Christ [i.e., the church] are united to Israel. They are Abraham's seed, members of the commonwealth of Israel, fellow-citizens with the saints, God's covenant people."[12]

Other evangelicals think the nature of the image rules out that option,[13] so they arrive at the second—that the tree represents the place of divine blessing (or the state being in right relationship with God due to faith in what He has revealed). Thus, even though many Israelites (the natural branches) were not participating in their own covenantal promises due to their unbelief, one day "all Israel will be saved" (v. 26); that is, at a future time, all of Christ-rejecting Israel will be brought back into obedience through God's grace.[14] Option 2 therefore leads to the conclusion that the church is somehow distinct from Israel—a conclusion not shared by many who favor option 1. As a result, Romans 11 will always represent a bone of some contention.

Before we write Romans 11 off as entirely "disputed territory," though, we should notice the agreement that arises from both views of the olive-tree imagery. Either way, the church and Israel are indeed united in at least one significant sense: both partake of the "nourishing root of the olive tree" (v. 17) by faith. Both, to be living and vital, depend on a life-giving relationship with the one gracious God. Again we see ecclesiology's foundational principle: the church's true identity rests on a saving relationship with God through Christ.

(3) *1 Corinthians 12:12–31:* Christ's Body and Its Members

Recently I was browsing through the guide on our TV service—a scrolling slate of myriad offerings on seemingly hundreds of channels. (Plus, channel after channel just for shopping!) Overall I was struck by the number of shows whose main stock-in-trade relates to body image. *Project Runway*, *America's Next Top Model*, and many others parade our cultural vision of the ideal human form, and for those more recliner-riveted than runway-ready, *Insanity Workout*, *Beauty Report*, and the like are there to whip us into shape. The TV provides more than ample evidence that ours is a body-obsessed culture.

It all reminded me of the elf in Santa's workshop who was packing a Barbie doll in a gift box when his manager came over and demanded, "What do you think you're doing?"

"It's okay," the elf said. "This girl is on the naughty list, and Santa wants to give her something that will challenge her self-esteem!"

Anyway, with all the attention we give our own bodies, it's ironic that we've missed one of God's most important messages—that Christians *ought* to be body-conscious, ought to devote such attention to the body . . . of Christ.

This teaching leaps out from the text of 1 Corinthians 12, which begins with a discussion of spiritual gifts. The church, Christ's body, exhibits a number of different gifts that all come from the same sovereign source: the Holy Spirit. So with respect to giftedness, the body of Christ displays God-intended unity amid diversity. This same principle—unity and diversity—carries over into the main body of the chapter. Beginning in verse 12, Paul repeatedly emphasizes that while every believer is unique, every unique believer is part of the same body. What's more, this is precisely the result intended by God's Spirit, whose work it is to baptize all believers into the one body of Christ. No physical body could ever work effectively if it were composed of only one part, reduplicated billions of times. This is the import of Paul's observation: "God arranged the members in the body, each one of them, as he chose. If all were a single member, where would the body be? As it is, there are many parts, yet one body" (vv. 18–20).

Scripture Memory 3

1 Corinthians 12:4–7

4 Now there are varieties of gifts, but the same Spirit;
5 and there are varieties of service, but the same Lord;
6 and there are varieties of activities, but it is the same God who empowers them all in everyone.
7 To each is given the manifestation of the Spirit for the common good.

The text reemphasizes the point made in Acts 2: the Spirit's distinct work since Pentecost is to "baptize" believers into the church. The invisible spiritual reality undergirds authentic membership in the community of the redeemed. Paul clearly calls this incorporation into the gift-sharing community, in which spiritual growth occurs, being "baptized" by the Spirit (1 Cor. 12:13).

Furthermore, the truth about the members and the body—the diversity and the unity—leads to another very practical end: "That there may be no division in the body, but that the members may have the same care for one another" (v. 25). The upshot is that each member of Christ's body ought to view and treat every other member with honor and compassion—authentic community life plays out in the local church in which we're to be committed, participating members, and not for ourselves, but for one another.

(4) *1 Peter 2:4–10:* The Church as a Royal Priesthood

With this brief but powerful passage, we again find a pattern of agreement and disagreement: some evangelicals see the church as becoming the recipient of Old Testament promises that had been given to Israel, whereas others see Old Testament citations (in the New Testament text) as illustrative in helping the inspired New Testament author make his point about the nature of the church.

> **Scripture Memory 4**
>
> ***1 Peter 2:5, 9***
>
> [5] You yourselves like living stones are being built up as a spiritual house, to be a holy priesthood, to offer spiritual sacrifices acceptable to God through Jesus Christ. . . . [9] But you are a chosen race, a royal priesthood, a holy nation, a people for his own possession, that you may proclaim the excellencies of him who called you out of darkness into his marvelous light.

In this case, Peter uses a number of Old Testament passages to show that the church is a community of individual "living stones" being built up "as a spiritual house" to be a holy priesthood and "to offer spiritual sacrifices acceptable to God through Jesus Christ" (vv. 4–5). On this point there is firm agreement among Bible-believing interpreters. Here the Old Testament symbolism paints a powerful picture, for the mental images of the temple and sacrificial system sharply illuminate the author's plan to explain the nature of the church.

In cutting through the differences that swirl around the question of the relationship between Israel and the church, Peter's emphasis seems fairly straightforward: God is doing something in the church that is connected to Israel but was never fully accomplished in Israel's case. To be specific, He is doing even more in the church than He did with Israel, though there are similarities in the patterns according to which He made the two. For example, Peter calls those who belong to Christ "a chosen race, a royal priesthood, a holy nation, a people for his own possession" (v. 9). All these terms come from Old Testament descriptions of Israel, but now, with reference to the church, we see that God has revealed His grace in a new way. The grace of God in Christ has made the church something that Old Testament Israel never became but was supposed to have been (a royal priesthood, a holy nation).

This brings us back to the central focus of all ecclesiology: the saving relationship between Redeemer and redeemed that comes by grace, through faith, wrought by the Spirit's miraculous work. Scot McKnight put it well:

> The church is an exclusive and a privileged community because it is a saved community. It is not a social organization, structured to provide its participants with opportunities for social interaction. It is not organized in this sense at all; rather, it is a group of people who have been called by God to trust in him, obey him, and associate with others that have the same calling, trust, and obedience. Any church today that does not immediately "advertise" itself in this way does not understand what it means to be "in the church." From beginning to end, the church desires salvation through Christ and through the attending work of the Holy Spirit. It preaches that salvation begins with a "new birth," continues through the ministry of the gospel, and climaxes at the final day when that praise, honor, and glory are expressed. Whether it stems from the fear of sounding dogmatic or from a desire for respect, any church that denies its calling to announce salvation in Christ alone is denying its primary God-given mission.[15]

The point, again and again, is that the church *is* the community of the redeemed. It starts with a saving relationship that comes by grace through faith, and it proceeds along the lines of obedience created by that relationship. Yes, the redeemed are ushered into a real community of fellow saints for sanctification, but this communion of saints *begins* with the work of the Spirit in an eternal relationship with God through Jesus.

(5) *Galatians 6:15–16:* The Church as the Israel of God

While I'm no film critic, I think one of *the* classic movie lines comes from *Mrs. Doubtfire.* I don't claim much objectivity on this either, for not only is the sound of a Scottish accent music to my ears—and Robin Williams did a surprisingly good job with it—but also because the humor he usually brings to his roles tweaks my funny bone. Anyway, in the scene I have in mind, "Mrs. Doubtfire" chucks a lime at his ex-wife's new boyfriend. When the man turns to find out who lobbed it, he/she bellows, "Oh sir! I saw it! Some angry member of the kitchen staff—did you not tip them? Oh, the terrorist, he ran that way—it was a run-by fruiting!"[16]

> **Scripture Memory 5**
>
> ***Galatians 6:15–16***
>
> 15 For neither circumcision counts for anything, nor uncircumcision, but a new creation.
> 16 And as for all who walk by this rule, peace and mercy be upon them, and upon the Israel of God.

Well, a similar "event" in the text of Galatians has theologians and scholars turning to and fro, scratching their heads, wondering who threw the fruit. The reason this passage, near the end of the letter, has fostered so much discussion is that Paul mentions—and only mentions—"the Israel of God."

If you're wondering how much trouble these four words could stir up, the answer is, more than you might think. But the trouble was already lurking just beneath the surface, for different groups within protestant evangelicalism have already settled upon differing ways of understanding the relationship between Israel and the church before they address this passage. As a result, in its own right, this textual "run-by fruiting" doesn't provide enough information to confirm or refute strongly held views.

For example, some teach that the church—or, more specifically, Christ, with all who are His—is itself the "Israel of God." This reading of Galatians 6 fits well within any theological system maintaining that the church is the present manifestation of God's people that has existed from generation to generation since God gave His covenant promises.[17] Others teach that Paul's "Israel of God" refers to those within ethnic Israel who believe in Jesus, their Messiah. This reading fits well within a theological system holding that the church and Israel are distinct.[18]

In fact, as those on both sides of this discussion should admit, the real scriptural bases for the principles germane to this discussion are elsewhere. However, we can justifiably pause at this point and make a key observation. Once again we find unquestioned agreement on one point: the church is composed of those who are both Jew and Gentile, for "in Christ Jesus you are all sons of God, through faith" (Gal. 3:26).

(6) *Ephesians 2:11–3:13:* The Church and the Mystery of Gentile Inclusion

When I was in high school, I went to a Halloween costume party at church. At the time our youth group was small enough that one could easily get to know everybody else by name. So it was rather trivial to identify each person, no matter what kind of getup each had donned for the occasion.

But the "best costume" contest was suddenly "wrapped up" when someone walked in completely concealed in aluminum foil, draped in such a way as to hide any distinguishing characteristics. This person also had gone to the trouble of borrowing work boots that provided no clue, and didn't speak or make idiosyncratic movements that would give away his or her identity. Even the eyes were shrouded in darkness behind specially crafted holes. No one knew who this mystery guy/gal was until he chose to reveal himself, and he easily walked off with the prize.

Scripture Memory 6

Ephesians 2:19–21

19 So then you are no longer strangers and aliens, but you are fellow citizens with the saints and members of the household of God,
20 built on the foundation of the apostles and prophets, Christ Jesus himself being the cornerstone,
21 in whom the whole structure, being joined together, grows into a holy temple in the Lord.

Chapters 2 and 3 of Paul's letter to the Ephesians explain a similar situation with respect to the church. It was a mystery, and until God chose to reveal this truth through the body of Christ, no one knew it. Which truth is this? *The gracious inclusion of the Gentiles in the church.*

Prior to the New Testament era, most Gentiles were not included among the people of God. They'd been "separated from Christ, alienated from the commonwealth of Israel and strangers to the covenants of promise, having no hope and without God in the world" (2:12). In their former situation, Gentiles were not a normative part of God's people and did not share in what He had promised.

But the finished work of Jesus and the coming of God's Spirit changed all that. Paul articulates the revelation of this mystery: God the Son and God the Spirit have made the two formerly opposing parties into one. Before, only Israel could claim to inherit God's covenant promises; now, "in Christ Jesus through the gospel," Jew and Gentile can be "fellow heirs," "partakers" in God's gracious blessings and "members of the same body" (3:6).

Like most central texts on ecclesiology, Ephesians 2–3 yields overwhelming agreement within the ranks of evangelicalism, and it's found in the passage's central point: all peoples are now able to partake of the promises of God in Christ. Because of what Jesus did on the cross (2:16), and because of the ministry of the Holy Spirit in incorporating all who believe into Christ's body (2:18), Jew *and* Gentile can be "fellow citizens with the saints and members of the household of God" (2:19).

(7) *1 Corinthians 11:17–34:* The Lord's Supper

This text is often considered the prime authorization for the church's practice of the Lord's Supper. Whereas the gospels of Matthew, Mark, and Luke portray the acts of our Lord at the Last Supper in a way that could be considered merely *descriptive*, 1 Corinthians 11 clearly indicates that He meant the observance of the bread and wine to be a frequent practice in the gathered community (vv. 20, 26, 33–34). The Last Supper wasn't simply a meal Jesus had with His disciples in the past; it's a meal His followers were to have in memory of Him from that time forward.

This passage also had as its original audience—the church in Corinth—a gathering of primarily Gentile believers (no doubt with some Jewish believers present), and as a result the questions that might have been raised against the *prescriptive* nature of the gospel accounts are resolved here. "I received from the Lord what I also delivered to you," Paul says (v. 23), connecting the Lord's authority with the continuing practice of the Lord's Supper in the church. On this all Bible-believing Christians agree, which is something beautiful, a glorious realm of virtual unanimity gracing the evangelical world.

We may have different names for the practice (e.g., Communion, Holy Communion, the Lord's Supper, the Lord's Table, the Blessed Sacrament, the Eucharist, the Body and Blood of Christ); we may practice it with varying frequencies (e.g., weekly, monthly, quarterly); we may observe it in diverse ways (e.g., leavened or unleavened bread, grape juice or wine, open to all believers or only to church members); we may believe different things about the relationship between the elements and Christ's presence (e.g., "real," "spiritual," or "memorial"). Nonetheless, all evangelicals maintain that the Lord's Supper is an essential mark of a properly constituted church community. To restate the principle that arises from this passage: *The practice of the Lord's Supper is an authoritative ordinance or sacrament for all churches in the Christian tradition.*

Scripture Memory 7

1 Corinthians 11:23–26

23 For I received from the Lord what I also delivered to you, that the Lord Jesus on the night when he was betrayed took bread,
24 and when he had given thanks, he broke it, and said, "This is my body which is for you. Do this in remembrance of me."
25 In the same way also he took the cup, after supper, saying, "This cup is the new covenant in my blood. Do this, as often as you drink it, in remembrance of me."
26 For as often as you eat this bread and drink the cup, you proclaim the Lord's death until he comes.

(8) *Matthew 28:18–20:* Baptism

This passage, often called "the Great Commission," serves as a potent ending to the gospel of Matthew and presents the basis for the ordinance or sacrament of water baptism. Again there is virtual unanimity among orthodox protestant evangelical churches who regard these post-resurrection, pre-ascension words of Jesus as the authority on its practice:

> All authority in heaven and on earth has been given to me. Go therefore and make disciples of all nations, baptizing them in the name of the Father and of the Son and of the Holy Spirit, teaching them to observe all that I have commanded you. And behold, I am with you always, to the end of the age.

The command's clarity is compelling: our task is to make disciples, to baptize them and teach them to do what Jesus requires of us. Yes, there has always been diversity regarding the most appropriate candidates (only those who profess faith, or also the children of believers), the best mode (immersion, sprinkling, or pouring), and the specific words and actions associated with the rite (e.g., personal testimony, confessing faith in Christ's person and work, a Trinitarian creed). However, as with the Lord's Supper, evangelical Christians of every stripe believe that water baptism is a prescribed ordinance or sacrament in Christ's church.

New Testament Passages Related to Baptism

Though churches and denominations differ on whether all of these refer to water baptism or to Spirit baptism, the following passages are generally regarded as key texts that inform a Christian understanding of baptism.

Matthew 28:18–20	Romans 6:3–4
Mark 16:16	Ephesians 4:4–6
Acts 1:4–5	Ephesians 5:25–26
Acts 2:37–41	Colossians 2:12
Acts 8:14–16	1 Peter 3:21–22
Acts 10:44–48	Hebrews 9:13–14
Acts 18:8	Hebrews 10:22
Acts 22:16	

(9) *Romans 6:6–14:* Regeneration, Sin, and the Believer

If we're saved not by works but by grace through faith, as all in the orthodox protestant evangelical tradition hold, then can't we live it up, go hog-wild . . . really, do anything we want? Doesn't God's infinite grace give us a license to kill—morally speaking? If you haven't heard this confused line of argument from young or immature believers yet, you will. But the notion isn't new. In fact, it's as old as the good news of God's grace itself.

Romans 6 is a central passage on sanctification because it asks and answers a key question regarding the life of the believer: "Are we to continue in sin that grace may abound?" (v. 1). Paul's immediate answer is emphatic:

Scripture Memory 8

Matthew 28:18–20

18 And Jesus came and said to them, "All authority in heaven and on earth has been given to me. 19 Go therefore and make disciples of all nations, baptizing them in the name of the Father and of the Son and of the Holy Spirit, 20 teaching them to observe all that I have commanded you. And behold, I am with you always, to the end of the age."

"By no means! How can we who died to sin still live in it?" (v. 2). And in developing this response, the apostle Paul offers a perspective on sin and grace that has shaped every evangelical understanding of the doctrine. The basic concept here is that God's grace in regeneration has brought to the believer a freedom from sin *and* the ability to live a life of righteousness. That is, *regeneration is the basis for sanctification.*

Paul makes this affirmation by first considering the fact of Christ's death and resurrection along with its application to the believer in justification. The death of Christ has become our death because of our identification with Him: those who've been "baptized into Christ Jesus were baptized into his death" (v. 3). Similarly, not only is His resurrection *our* hope of bodily resurrection in the future (v. 8), it's also the pattern of our present life after our conversion: "Just as Christ was raised from the dead by the glory of the Father, we too might walk in newness of life" (v. 4).

What's more, Paul doesn't leave this affirmation in the abstract but, in verse 11, transitions from the doctrinal truth of Christ's death and resurrection to the practical truth associated with life as a follower of Jesus. Specifically, he goes on to answer the question many readers might ask at this point: What, then, should I do about this?

His imperative is in the first instance a command to reckon, to consider, to take as truth the simple affirmation that the believer, through identification with Christ, is "dead to sin and alive to God in Christ Jesus." The consequence of this reckoning is a fourfold moral imperative (vv. 12–13):

- *Do not let sin "reign in your mortal body."*
- *"Do not present your members to sin as instruments for unrighteousness."*
- *"Present yourselves to God."*
- *Present "your members to God as instruments for righteousness."*

The very presence of these requirements undergirds the suggestion made earlier, that the ability to do these things and the freedom from sin upon which they are predicated comes to the believer as a result of the grace of regeneration. The idea of "walk[ing] in newness of life" brings quickly to mind the normative evangelical understanding of regeneration.

So, returning to our basic observation from Romans 6, *regeneration is the basis for sanctification*. While this concept finds broad acceptance within the evangelical world, we'll soon see that there's debate over exactly *how* regeneration forms this basis. As this is where a most fundamental question for any evangelical perspective on sanctification arises, perhaps the best way to introduce it is to turn to that stellar example of all things theological: Dr. Seuss's wildly influential *The Cat in the Hat*.[19]

You probably know the story. Two kids are left at home on a rainy day; Mother is gone, Father isn't even mentioned. With nothing to do because of the weather, the two are bored beyond description. But then, suddenly, a cat strolls through the front door, and he's not some mangy feral feline trying to escape the downpour—this one's dressed like a gentleman!

The Cat spearheads all kinds of fun (and potentially trouble-inducing) activities, causing widespread disorder along the way. The family's fish, in the role of moral compass, continually says the kids should make the Cat leave. After a while, the Cat brings out a big red box, from which emerge two little beings—Thing One and Thing Two—that, beginning with the indoor flying of kites, proceed to turn the substantial mess into an absolute disaster.

Then, amid all manner of Thing-caused-chaos, we catch a glimpse of Mother returning. Even if I weren't a trained engineer, I could guarantee that the scope of the mess prohibits it being cleaned up in the amount of time she would take to traverse the sidewalk and come through the front door. However, the Cat in the Hat has one last trick up his sleeve: a massive, multi-armed, automated cleaner-upper machine! In the nick of time, the house is clean and the Cat flees the scene. As the book ends, Mother steps into a clean home with two well-behaved children sitting just as they were when we first met them.

I'd like to rewind a bit and highlight Thing One and Thing Two. The tale's climax of maximal fun (joined to maximal domestic damage) coincided with their arrival, the moment they appeared and started "helping." This image can help us recall the range of evangelical perspectives on the process (and progress) of sanctification. Herein we all see two "things" involved.

Scripture Memory 9

Romans 6:12–14

12 Let not sin therefore reign in your mortal body, to make you obey its passions.
13 Do not present your members to sin as instruments for unrighteousness, but present yourselves to God as those who have been brought from death to life, and your members to God as instruments for righteousness.
14 For sin will have no dominion over you, since you are not under law but under grace.

Thing One might correspond roughly to sanctification's divine element—the work of God in bringing about spiritual growth. Thing Two might parallel the human element—our own striving in the pursuit of holiness. Both "Things" are involved. Very few evangelicals would dream of ascribing the entire work of sanctification to *only* Thing One or *only* Thing Two; they must somehow play together.

Even strong proponents of predestination typically affirm that the work of sanctification involves *some kind* of responsible participation of the human will with the will of God, even if the description of roles must be finely nuanced. Anthony Hoekema, a respected representative of Reformed theology, writes,

> We may define sanctification as that gracious operation of the Holy Spirit, involving our responsible participation, by which He delivers us as justified sinners from the pollution of sin, renews our entire nature according to the image of God, and enables us to live lives that are pleasing to Him.[20]

The point is this: evangelicals all agree that divine work (Thing One) and human work (Thing Two) both occur in the process of sanctification. But they disagree on just how the two fit together and which, if either, predominates.

(10) *Romans 7:14–25:* The Believer and the Battle With Sin

In this controversial passage, Paul depicts a person at war within himself: "I do not do what I want, but I do the very thing I hate" (v. 15). Beyond this, "I have the desire to do what is right, but not the ability to carry it out. For I do not do the good I want, but the evil I do not want is what I keep on doing" (vv. 18–19).

Every reader agrees: this situation is troubling. But *who* is this person?

Some commentators suggest the subject is a believer—either Paul or a hypothetical person who has already experienced regeneration and now faces the battle of living the Christian life. In this view, the Christian life is something a believer wants desperately to fulfill, but something inside causes him/her to do what he/she doesn't want to do.[21] Instead of living in obedience, the believer finds that he/she actually engages in the evil he/she doesn't want to carry out.

On the other hand, some evangelicals insist that this is far too bleak a picture to represent a regenerate (saved) person. Rather, this must be an unregenerate (unsaved) person who can't seem to do what's right because he or she doesn't have the life-giving Spirit dwelling inside.[22]

Both perspectives run into difficult questions. For those who say Romans 7 describes a believer, one might ask, "Wouldn't this give far too much credit to the power of sin? Doesn't it make the power of God in Christ look too weak?" For those who think Paul portrays an unbeliever, the question becomes, "How can it be said that an unbeliever delights in the law of God? [see v. 22]. How would this be possible for an unregenerate person?"

In whatever way we answer the question regarding Romans 7 itself, other texts (like Galatians 5, discussed below) *do* indicate that the authentic Christian life involves struggle against sin . . . even for (or, perhaps, *especially* for) the Spirit-led believer.

The following chart summarizes some different views on the singular personal pronouns *I* and *me* in Romans 7:14–25.[23]

WHO IS "I"?

Romans 7:14–25 as believers	Paul is describing his present experience as a Christian struggling with sin, thus this is applicable to all believers.
	Paul is rhetorically placing himself in the shoes of Christians who must be delivered from their immaturity or "carnality" to live victoriously in Christ.
Romans 7:14–25 as nonbelievers	Paul is vividly recalling his past experience in struggling against sin before becoming a Christian; hence this is typical of all unbelievers who try to live completely moral lives.
	Paul is figuratively placing himself in the shoes of non-Christian Jews who struggle with sin, those who know God's Law but cannot succeed in living by it.

(11) *Galatians 5:16–26:* The Holy Spirit and Our Battle With Sin

This classic passage gives vivid hue and texture to the relationship between the Holy Spirit's ministry in the believer's life and the challenging process of progressive (ongoing) sanctification. "Walk by the Spirit," Paul says, "and you will not gratify the desires of the flesh" (v. 16). Once again, he portrays this battle as a conflict between the desires of the Spirit and of the flesh—between the divine will and human unwillingness. In this case, though, he goes further and gives numerous examples that contrast "the works of the flesh" and "the fruit of the Spirit." The former include sexual immorality, enmity, strife, jealousy, fits of anger, envy, drunkenness, and the like; the latter includes love, joy, peace, patience, kindness, goodness, and the like.

Most evangelicals agree that this text provides one of the most detailed and accurate descriptions of a life lived under the Spirit's direction. Once more: *sanctification is directly related to the ministry of the Holy Spirit*. Small wonder, then, that many use the term *the spiritual life* in broad equivalence to *sanctification* or *the Christian life*. The disagreement that does exist comes primarily as believers seek to answer this question: How does one actually *do* this thing Scripture describes as *walking by the Spirit*?

Scripture Memory 10

Romans 7:22–23

22 I delight in the law of God, in my inner being,
23 but I see in my members another law waging war against the law of my mind and making me captive to the law of sin that dwells in my members.

At this point Thing One and Thing Two reemerge from the box into which we've tried to keep them stuffed. Remember, those characters represent the two emphases of divine work and human work in sanctification. In a strongly Reformed view on the matter, the grace of God in Christ—the grace of salvation—predominates the process. Progress, then, ultimately depends on God's work, even though this work shows up in the life of the believer as he or she works in making use of the means of grace God has established.

Conversely, for instance, some in the broader Holiness tradition maintain that the human element is determinative, as regards Things One and Two. That is, God comes to the aid of willing hearts. Others speak in terms of a mysterious "cooperation" (synergy) between God's will and the will of regenerate hearts.

So what gives?

To help us understand the toe-to-toe stand-off between two extremes (and the various perspectives in between), let me draw another analogy, this one from "The Zax," a brief, lesser-known Dr. Seuss story in which two odd-looking creatures—a North-going Zax and a South-going Zax—meet on the prairie of Prax. Instead of easing even one inch to the right or left to let the other pass, these opposites on the "Zaxdom" spectrum face off forever, unable to relent.[24] Not that theologians are frowning, furry who-knows-whats with folded arms, always refusing to budge. *However*, the two factors of divine sovereignty and human responsibility will always stubbornly assert themselves in any consideration of sanctification. The reason is that both contribute essential elements of a mysterious truth held in tension. Though some traditions might emphasize one more than the other, and some seek to balance the two tendencies, the tension will always remain.

Scripture Memory 11

Galatians 5:22–23

22 But the fruit of the Spirit is love, joy, peace, patience, kindness, goodness, faithfulness,
23 gentleness, self-control; against such things there is no law.

TWO EXTREMES AND A TRUTH IN TENSION

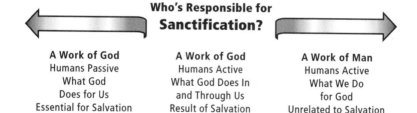

Who's Responsible for Sanctification?

A Work of God	**A Work of God**	**A Work of Man**
Humans Passive	Humans Active	Humans Active
What God Does for Us	What God Does In and Through Us	What We Do for God
Essential for Salvation	Result of Salvation	Unrelated to Salvation

(12) *Ephesians 4:* The Believer and Progressive Sanctification

This text in Ephesians has occasioned some debate because it contains an ambiguity rooted deeply in Greek grammar. While we won't go into the delicacies represented by infinitives of indirect discourse,[25] we note that most major translations make the same choice—namely, they render "to put off," "to be renewed," and "to put on" in the form of apparent commands (e.g, *do* this—"*put* on . . ." and "*be* renewed . . ." and "*put* off . . ."). The alternative is to translate them as simple statements of fact: "you were taught that you have put off your old self . . . you have been renewed in the spirit of your mind . . . and have put on the new self."

The effect of this decision is immediately obvious: if these words are commands, then what we have here is a sort of summarization of the recipe for living the Christian life. And most evangelicals do indeed take this view.

Once again the pesky pranksters, Things One and Two, enter the scene, for this text seemingly would be telling every believer that while the new life available to him in Christ is absolutely and entirely a gift of God, the living-it-out portion depends on effort, or obedience, in *putting off* the old self, *being renewed* in the spirit of the mind, and *putting on* the new self (vv. 20–24). In other words, the emphasis would be on human responsibility.

Scripture Memory 12

Ephesians 4:20–24

20 But that is not the way you learned Christ!—
21 assuming that you have heard about him and were taught in him, as the truth is in Jesus,
22 to put off your old self, which belongs to your former manner of life and is corrupt through deceitful desires,
23 and to be renewed in the spirit of your minds,
24 and to put on the new self, created after the likeness of God in true righteousness and holiness.

Now, this understanding would dovetail well with the following context, in which we receive several practical moral directives (vv. 25–32):

- Speak the truth.
- Be angry, but don't sin.
- Do honest work.
- Don't speak in corrupt ways.
- Avoid actions that destroy close fellowship.
- Promote a spirit of gentleness and forgiveness.

But just as we then find ourselves siding with Thing Two (personal human obedience in the process of sanctification), suddenly Thing

One resurfaces and asserts that there's only one reason we would will and do anything good: God is working in us to obey!

> Therefore, my beloved, as you have always obeyed, so now, not only as in my presence but much more in my absence, work out your own salvation with fear and trembling, for it is God who works in you, both to will and to work for his good pleasure. (Phil. 2:12–13)

Suffice it to say that it's no wonder the evangelical tradition has been home to a number of theories and models of sanctification that attempt to address the tensions in different ways.

(13) *Philippians 3:20–21:* The Hope of Final Sanctification

Where's the perfect place to conclude a whirlwind tour of key passages on sanctification? *At the end*, of course! Whatever angst the presence of Things One and Two may have generated in our thinking about sanctification, Philippians 3 is the cleaner-upper machine that resolves our internal wrangling in expectation of God's decisive act. All our struggles with the process and progress of becoming like Jesus, all our battles with sin, all our disappointment in acts of disobedience that we wish we hadn't done—*all* of these, one day, will be swallowed up in a victory that is *solely God's doing*.

Most evangelicals affirm that this life—the Christian's walk aimed at pursuing holiness—is a constant struggle for the simple reason that sin is still with us. But Philippians 3 establishes a guarantee, a certain future. This hope is rooted securely in a deed that has nothing to do with human effort. The power of God in Christ *will* one day change us. He will transform us—again. His death on the cross broke sin's *power*; the transformation He will bring when He returns will leave sin out in the cold. Finally, we will be freed from its very *presence*.

> **Scripture Memory 13**
>
> ***Philippians 3:20–21***
>
> [20] But our citizenship is in heaven, and from it we await a Savior, the Lord Jesus Christ, [21] who will transform our lowly body to be like his glorious body, by the power that enables him even to subject all things to himself.

This text gives rise to what we call "final sanctification," because the holiness every believer will experience then will be compared to the sinless, glorified body of our resurrected Lord. The doctrine of final sanctification brings our discussion from ecclesiology (the God-given community of spiritual growth) through sanctification (the mysterious but practical process of spiritual growth) to eschatology, the Bible's teaching on last things. We'll resume that discussion directly in the second part of this book.

THE CHURCH AND THE CHRISTIAN LIFE IN RETROSPECT

"We believe in one, holy, catholic, and apostolic church."[1] These words of the Council of Constantinople (AD 381) sum up the basic biblical and theological boundaries that historically have defined orthodox ecclesiology.

- The church is *one* because the Holy Spirit unites believers to Christ and therefore to one another. This invisible spiritual unity should therefore manifest itself in unity among the brethren.
- God's Spirit makes the church *holy* by sanctifying individuals as they gather corporately and participate in the life of the church.
- Under the headship of Christ, each local congregation should understand itself as part of a larger whole, the church "universal" or *catholic*. This ought to foster cooperation and community not only among churches spanning the globe, but with other churches spanning history.
- Finally, the church is *apostolic* as her doctrines and practices conform to the standard the apostles established and set forth in their writings.

Together these boundary lines—unity, holiness, catholicity, and apostolicity—have served as bellwethers of the church's health in any given era. Yet too often the church has tended to sacrifice holiness for the sake of unity . . . or abandoned charitable relationships with other churches by emphasizing idiosyncratic hobbyhorses that isolated and set them apart. The balancing act necessary to maintain these four markers has never been easy.

Throughout history, orthodox ecclesiology also has defined the church as "the communion of saints," indicating that true churches should be composed of the truly redeemed—those spiritually and invisibly united with Christ through the Holy Spirit. Yet this likewise has created tensions. Some have emphasized the invisible, spiritual church (the "saints") to the neglect of the visible, physical church—those gathered locally for worship and instruction. Others have stressed the physical church to the point of neglecting genuine conversion and spiritual life among its members and even its leaders. Further, this has led to discussions on how sanctification is to be accomplished:

- Individually or corporately?
- Passively or actively?
- Through personal methods or by corporate means?

As we begin to survey the history of ecclesiology and sanctification through the patristic (AD 100–500), medieval (500–1500), protestant (1500–1700), and modern (1700–present) eras, we will highlight uneasy tensions between the visible/physical and invisible/spiritual realities of the church. The following narrative will demonstrate that the church has not always consistently held these two distinguishable but inseparable components of a healthy, balanced ecclesiology in careful equilibrium.

The Patristic Period (AD 100–500)

I've been a Dallas Cowboys fan for most of my life. I cheered them on in the days of "Dandy Don" Meredith, through the reign of the iconic hat-crowned Tom Landry. You can imagine my excitement, then, when Jerry Jones bought the franchise and within seven years won three Super Bowls in a span of four seasons. Yes, the cost was significant—in particular, Landry was let go inauspiciously. Still, Jones had the Cowboys on an exceedingly wonderful trajectory, playing some of the most dominant football in its storied history.

In retrospect, however, the beginning of the Jerry Jones era is a mixed bag. It brought championships, sure. Yet what we didn't see during those heady days was the onset of a dark, dark illness: the owner's continued insistence on playing the part of general manager—a role for which he was, and is, and evermore shall be, ill-suited.[2]

Let me draw an analogy between the Dallas Cowboys with the Jerry Jones administration and developments in the patristic era. While that epoch of church history, spanning about four centuries, witnessed a number of epic "championships" in the defense of apostolic teaching, amid that heroism were planted and cultivated the seeds of a dismal coming harvest:

- a weakening of the fourfold marks of unity, holiness, catholicity, and apostolicity
- an imbalanced focus on the visible church compared to the invisible company of the redeemed
- an increasingly institutionalized approach to sanctification

The early church fathers' era will always be celebrated as a victorious time, largely because they often echoed the very emphases that they received from the apostles themselves. Yet simultaneously one can detect in this period the seeds of a growing institutionalism. During seasons of persecution and threats of heresy, various assemblies looked to individual church leaders as the very emblem of the church. Ignatius of Antioch (c. AD 110) wrote, "Let everyone respect the deacons as Jesus Christ, just as they should respect the bishop, who is a model of the Father, and the presbyters as God's council, and as the band of the apostles. Without these no group can be called a church."[3] And, "Let no one do anything pertaining to the Church apart from the bishop. Let that be held a valid eucharist which is under the bishop or one to whom he shall have committed it. Wherever the bishop shall appear, there let the congregation be; even as where Jesus may be, there is the catholic Church."[4]

In response to heresy, Ignatius understandably was calling his readers to faithfulness to their orthodox leadership. Though this strategy averted the crisis of false teaching, his strengthening of these offices put down roots that would bear unintended fruit in later centuries. As Earle Cairns has stated,

> [Ignatius] was the first to place the office of the bishop in contrast with the office of the presbyter and to subordinate the presbyters or elders to the monarchical bishop and the members of the church to both. The hierarchy of authority in the church is, according to him, bishop, presbyter, and deacon. However, Ignatius did not exalt the bishop of Rome as superior to other bishops even though he was the first to use the word *catholic*.[5]

A little later, Irenaeus of Lyon (c. AD 180) successfully buttressed the holiness of the church's apostolic and catholic teaching by emphasizing the physical, visible unity between churches and by appealing to an unbroken succession of bishops connecting those churches to the apostles themselves:

> We are in a position to reckon up those who were by the apostles instituted bishops in the Churches, and [to demonstrate] the succession of these men to our own times.[6] . . . It is a matter of necessity that every Church should agree with this Church [at Rome], on account of its pre-eminent authority, that is, the faithful everywhere, inasmuch as the apostolic tradition has been preserved continuously by those [faithful leaders] who exist everywhere.[7]

Whether or not Irenaeus intended it, his defending of orthodox truth by appeals to the succession of bishops and their shared unity did plant seeds of an institutionalism that would dominate ecclesiology in later centuries.

Around AD 250, Cyprian of Carthage watered these seeds. In his case, however, the challenge was not to protect orthodox teachings concerning the triune God and the person and work of Christ; it was to defend the visible, organizational unity of the church's leadership in the face of fragmentation caused by responses to persecution.[8] J. N. D. Kelly notes of this shift that "the criterion of Church membership is no longer, as for Irenaeus, acceptance of the teaching guaranteed by the episcopate as apostolic, but submission to the bishop himself."[9] Cyprian's emphasis on the church's visible unity *centered on the bishop* downplayed the invisible nature of the church manifested in holiness (purity of doctrine and practice) and apostolicity (conformity to the apostles' faith and teachings).[10]

This greater emphasis on the church's visible unity began to forge an increasing complexity in its hierarchy. From the New Testament's twofold leadership of elders (or "overseers") and deacons, we see the rise of the single bishop in each local church presiding over the presbyters (later called "priests"), assisted by the deacons. Eventually, archbishops over bishops, subdeacons, and various other ecclesiastical offices become normative.[11] Further, throughout the fourth and fifth centuries, the bishop of Rome began to claim primacy as the chief bishop over the entire church worldwide, a claim resisted by the bishops of other parts of the church—especially in the East, where bishops never did accept Rome as the head of the church universal.[12]

In a similar vein, this overemphasis on the visible church and her institutional unity affected the church's view of salvation and sanctification, especially as they relate to the sacraments. The two most famous of Cyprian's sayings fit here:

> As the birth of Christians is in baptism, while the generation and sanctification of baptism are with the spouse of Christ alone, who is able spiritually to conceive and to bear sons to God, where and of whom and to whom is he born, who is not a son of the Church, so as that he should have God as his Father, before he has had the Church for his Mother?[13]

> There is no salvation outside the church.[14]

If the visible church is seen as the sole conduit of God's saving and sanctifying grace, the visible church, defined as the institutional church united with Rome, is seen as the standard of membership in the invisible church.

So it shouldn't surprise us that patristic leaders placed an increasingly stronger emphasis on participation in the church's sacramental life as the sole means of spiritual growth toward salvation. Baptism originally marked a person's conversion to Christ, confession of faith in the triune God, repentance from sin, and admission into the church. It also admitted a believer to participation in the spiritual blessings centered on the Lord's Supper (or the Eucharist). Eventually, however, the church would emphasize baptism as the means by which justifying grace is received, the Spirit is imparted, and forgiveness is attained—not only to believers but also to their children.

The church also began increasingly to think of the Lord's Supper more in terms of a spiritual sacrifice and to believe in the real presence of Christ's flesh and blood in the elements of bread and wine. Participation in these sacred rites, the church thought, brought about more than merely spiritual blessing: the sacraments *transmitted* saving grace. As the patristic period progressed, the sacraments—including a third, penance, for those who committed grave sins after baptism—continued to play a central role in the church's identity as a visible unity centered on particular practices.

With Augustine (d. ca. AD 430), we see further indications of the visible church's monopoly on the sacraments of saving and sanctifying grace:

> There is one Church which alone is called Catholic; and whenever it has anything of its own in these communions of different bodies which are separate from itself, it is most certainly in virtue of this which is its Own in each of them that *it, not they, has the power of generation.* For neither is it their separation that generates, but what they have retained of the essence of the Church; and if they were to go on to abandon this, they would lose the power of generation. *The generation, then, in each case proceeds from the Church, whose sacraments are retained, from which any such birth can alone in any case proceed*—although not all who receive its birth belong to its unity, which shall save those who persevere even to the end. Nor is it those only that do not belong to it who are openly guilty of the manifest sacrilege of schism, but also those who, being outwardly joined to its unity, are yet separated by a life of sin.[15]

We can characterize the church's first four hundred years as an age of major change and development. The earliest leaders more or less maintained the balance of unity, holiness, catholicity, and apostolicity. They regarded the church's spiritual (invisible) and physical (visible) aspects as necessary components, but gradually shifted the emphasis from spiritual unity to institutional unity—including an increasingly complex hierarchy—even to the detriment of doctrinal and pragmatic holiness. Ignatius's original sense of the word *catholic* changed from the idea of the whole body of churches spread throughout the world under Christ's headship to the physical organization throughout the world under the Pope's headship (in the Western Roman Catholic Church) or under the leadership of the bishops whose authority was manifested through several church councils (in the Eastern Orthodox Church).

During this era we also witness the strengthening of the role of the single bishop, first over each local (city) church, then over regional churches. In that development of episcopal governance, the priests ("presbyters" or "elders") were to submit to the bishop's rule, and the laity became increasingly irrelevant to the true church's essential constitution. The church began to be viewed less in terms of the "communion of saints," as was reflected in the second-century Apostle's Creed, and more in terms of the institution's rites, laws, and offices. Attempting to achieve and maintain worldwide institutional unity, after the Emperor Constantine made Christianity a legal religion (in AD 313), bishops of larger cities began to wrangle with each other over territorial jurisdiction, doctrinal matters, and authority in the church.

And, the Roman Catholic bishop, called the "Pope," claimed superiority over all others; in contrast, the bishops of Eastern churches said all bishops shared equal rank and that only ecumenical councils—official gatherings of bishops from around the world—had final ecclesiastical authority.

Finally, the doctrine of sanctification was never fully developed during this era. Generally, salvation began to be seen as a process that began with conversion at baptism and continued throughout a believer's life. Justification and sanctification were never clearly distinguished in the early church, nor were salvation and sanctification regarded as something distinct from the church's sacramental system. Baptism—either of new believers or of believers' infant children—and the Lord's Supper were upheld as the main means of saving and sanctifying grace. To these two major sacraments the church would add other practices—particularly penance and confirmation—believed to apply sanctifying grace to the lives of faithful members.

The Medieval Period (500–1500)

Up to the sixteenth-century Reformation, the church and sanctification never received extensive and complete treatment in Christian theology.[16] In many ways these two doctrines were joined at the hip, for as the medieval Catholic Church viewed its sacramental system as *the* means of both saving *and* sanctifying grace, its leaders would speak of the church's nature and function and offices in increasingly loftier terms. Also, after Christianity grew from persecuted and illegal to the empire's official religion, transitionally it began to amass power, prestige, wealth, and political clout, which affected how the church viewed itself and its place in the world. As R. E. O. White puts it:

> [The concept of sanctification] hardened, in the medieval church, into asceticism (a dualistic misapplication of Paul's athleticism). This involved a double standard: "sanctity" and "saintliness" came to be applied only to the "religious" person (priest, monk), whereas a lower attainment, compromising with the world, was tolerated in the "ordinary," "secular," or "lay" Christian.[17]

The aforementioned seeds of institutionalism, planted in the early church and sprouting thereafter in the patristic period, ultimately grew during the Middle Ages into a massive, impenetrable forest. Both ecclesiology and sanctification focused heavily on the *visible* church—its institutional unity and worldwide uniformity—and downplayed the *invisible* church, its life as the communion of saints devoted to apostolic teaching and to holiness of faith and practice. The first half of the medieval period (c. 500–1000) witnessed several major developments:

- the progressive rise of the papacy and its attainment of wealth and political power
- numerous monasteries founded to revive waning spirituality
- increased use of images, incense, and fixed liturgies in worship
- the church's influence on political powers to fight off the advance of Islam through the Crusades

All had profound impact on the institutional church, threatening its holiness and apostolicity. Yet a cataclysmic blow to unity and catholicity fell in AD 1054, when the bishops of Rome and Constantinople condemned each other as heretics, thus severing the Western Latin-speaking church from the Eastern Greek-speaking churches. Though it had gestated for centuries, this official East/West break marked the historical birth of the Roman Catholic Church's claims to be the exclusive representative of Christianity in the world and, through its sacramental system, the exclusive means of salvation.

Thereafter, the Roman Church continued to grow in power. Popes pushed the visible institutional unity achieved in the earlier centuries toward absolute uniformity of belief and practice. Whereas the Eastern Orthodox churches continued to function with some degree of "unity in diversity," the Western Roman Catholic Church strived for "the Roman ideal of discipline and uniformity."[18] With this emphasis came the codification of what became known as "canon law"—a body of rules and regulations that governed the spiritual and ecclesiastical life of the Roman hierarchy and all her works. This period also witnessed the founding of universities across Europe where scholars attempted to synthesize and monopolize all knowledge—especially philosophy and theology—for the sake of the kingdom of God, that is, the Catholic Church. More and more religious orders were founded, cathedrals and monasteries built, and wars fought to protect Christendom's wealth and prosperity. The lines between Church and State blurred; the distinction between the secular world and God's sacred kingdom became meaningless.

For a sense of the developments in ecclesiology and sanctification toward the visible, institutional church, consider the assertions of the Fourth Lateran Council, which convened in 1215. It dictated that all baptized Christians must participate in the sacraments of confession and penance at least once a year. It also dogmatically affirmed transubstantiation—belief that the bread and wine of the Eucharist were miraculously but imperceptibly transformed into Christ's literal body and blood upon the priest's consecration. The council also asserted the supremacy of the Roman Church over all other churches around the world, and for the first time the seven sacraments were clearly listed as the only means by which a person receives saving and sanctifying grace.[19]

A TALE OF FIVE POPES: THE RISE OF PAPAL POWER

Gregory I (590–604)	Under his benevolent, sincere leadership, the Roman Church filled a political vacuum created by Rome's fall to the Goths. Attempted to unite all the Western churches by asserting Roman jurisdiction and commissioning missionaries.
Leo III (795–816)	Crowned Charlemagne "Emperor" of the Holy Roman Empire; the first papal installation of a secular king would be seen as the kingdom of God's final triumph over human kingdoms (the Church appeared to be sanctioning the State).
Gregory VII (1073–1085)	Claimed that the Roman Church was *the* one true church that never erred and that the Pope has authority to crown and depose kings.
Innocent III (1198–1216)	Claimed that the Roman Church had absolute supremacy over all temporal powers; called on crusaders to reclaim the Holy Land by force; dogmatized the system of seven sacraments at the Fourth Lateran Council (1215).
Boniface VIII (1294–1303)	Asserted full papal authority over all councils, kings, and churches—salvation depended on submission to the supreme Roman pontiff. The one, holy, catholic, and apostolic church was *only* that visible institution headed by the Pope.

By the end of the fifteenth century the scale had shifted from a balance between the invisible and visible church to a decisive emphasis on the Roman Catholic Church as the one true church, without which no one could be saved. In fact, Boniface VIII, in his decree known as *Unam Sanctam* (1302), claimed, "We declare, state, define, and pronounce that for every human creature to be subject to the Roman pope is altogether necessary for salvation."[20] That is, the Pope alone was the visible head of the one, holy, catholic, and apostolic church. What he taught must be believed; what he instructed must be obeyed.

Throughout the medieval period voices of dissent could be heard, though their cries of protest were muffled by suppression or met with persecution and even execution. In the ninth century, Gottschalk of Orbais (c. 804–868) insisted that the true church was invisible—consisting of the elect within the visible church—and that the sacraments of Baptism and the Eucharist were only actually effective for them.[21] About the same time, Ratramnus of Corbie, a monk, wrote *On the Body and Blood of the Lord*, a treatise that argued against what would later be dogmatized as the doctrine of transubstantiation.

As the darkness of the Middle Ages deepened, other challenges to the institutional church's claims came from bold reformers like the

Englishman John Wycliffe (1320–1384) and the Bohemian John Hus (1369–1415), both of whom wrote works entitled *De Ecclesia* (*On the Church*). Wycliffe's views heavily influenced Hus, and each held that the invisible church of the elect establishes the authenticity of any visible expression of the church. Thus, even the Catholic Church's leadership—including the Pope himself—could well be infested with unsaved frauds while average peasants could constitute the true spiritual church within the Church. Such beliefs—while seemingly consistent with the earliest apostolic and patristic emphases—usurped the Church's authority structures and so were met with strict condemnation. For example, the Council of Constance (1414) called Hus to defend his views, pledging safe passage to and from the proceedings. After he obeyed the summons, the council condemned him as a heretic and burned him at the stake.

Incidentally, this same council had to resolve what became known as the "papal schism," in which no fewer than three popes claimed to be the one visible head of the one visible church. Such a fracturing of unity undermined the claims of the Roman Church's supreme authority, with even the papacy itself subject to division and confusion. Ironically, when the Council of Constance succeeded at removing the competing popes from office and finally electing Martin V as the Church's one head, that council-appointed leader "denied that a general council was superior to the pope," apparently not realizing that such a decree would technically invalidate his own election.[22]

Needless to say, toward the close of this period we can discern several significant developments and differences from the apostolic and early patristic eras. These included, among others, the ascent of the bishops' power, the rise of the papacy, the fixing of liturgical worship, and the evolving and addition of sacraments as means of saving grace. Political and moral corruption were threatening to destabilize the whole Christian world.

The Council of Constantinople (AD 381) had confessed belief in the "one, holy, catholic, and apostolic church."[23] Now, as Euan Cameron notes,

> every traditional epithet applied to the Church, "one, holy, catholic, and apostolic," had been somehow put in doubt in the fifteenth century: unity by schisms, holiness by moral failings, catholicity by lack of general agreement, apostolicity by doubts about individual popes.[24]

Number of Sacraments Throughout History

Early Churches: Many "signs" were "sacramental"—that is, mysterious in pointing to spiritual truths—but Baptism and the Eucharist held central places as the rites of initiation and continued consecration; in some places penance began to be practiced for admitting wayward baptized Christians back into the fellowship of the Church.

Medieval Church: Seven sacraments of saving and sanctifying grace began with Baptism, included the Eucharist, and grew to include a system of Penance, Confirmation of those who'd been baptized as infants, Marriage to expand the Church physically, Orders (or ordination) to expand the Church spiritually, and Unction (or anointing) in preparation for death.

Reformation Church: Baptism and the Lord's Supper (or Communion) were restored as the visible church's two sacraments, or ordinances; other activities were seen as means of grace for sanctification. Many practices such as confirmation, orders, and anointing are maintained in some traditions but not usually with sacramental status.

Modern Evangelical Churches: Baptism and the Lord's Supper are generally upheld as the sacraments or ordinances; other activities are practiced as means of testimony or spiritual growth.

The Protestant Period (1500–1700)

We've traced an unhealthy overemphasis on the visible, physical church over against the invisible, spiritual reality of Christ's body, from its innocent and mostly harmless seeds in the early patristic period—through the saplings of institutional unity and almost mechanical means of sanctification—into the dark, deep-rooted forest of Christendom's forced uniformity and man-made hierarchy under the Pope's secular-and-sacred authority. As we transition from these centuries, though, the few sparks that had ignited isolated beacons of reform in figures like Wycliffe and Hus will explode into an all-consuming reformers' fire in those like Martin Luther, Ulrich Zwingli, and John Calvin.

One major aspect of the explosion that ended Roman Catholic dominion was the Protestant insistence that the invisible elect, not the institutional church, take precedence and give legitimacy to the church's visible manifestation on earth. In this reemphasis on its invisible nature, reformers like Luther and Calvin attempted to restore balance to ecclesiology, drawing heavily on biblical teaching, patristic foundations, and the definition of the church in the Apostles' Creed. Jaroslav Pelikan explains:

> This confession of the reality of the church as the communion of saints he [Luther] set over against the institutionalism he attributed to Roman Catholic doctrine and over against the individualism he took to be implied in at least the more radical versions of Protestant doctrine.[25]

Similarly, Timothy George notes,

> In the perspective of the Reformation, then, the church of Jesus Christ is that communion of saints and congregation of the faithful who has heard the Word of God in Holy Scripture and which, through obedient service to its Lord, bears witness to that Word in the world.[26]

Whether or not in a given realm they met with success, these reformers and others strived to restore a balance without going to either extreme of neglecting the visible church by overemphasizing the invisible (individualism) or neglecting the invisible by overemphasizing the visible (institutionalism).

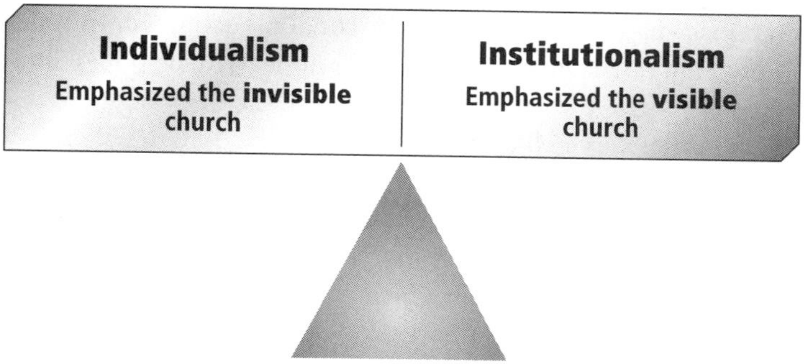

The main Reformation traditions shared this renewed emphasis on the church's spiritual, invisible dimension that they believed had been forsaken for centuries. Specifically, the view of the Calvinist Reformed tradition, Louis Berkhof observes, is similar to the Lutheran perspective on the matter: "Both agree that the real essence of the Church is found in the *communio sanctorum* [communion of saints] as a spiritual entity, that is, in the invisible Church."[27]

THREE HISTORICAL MODELS OF CHURCH ORDER

Episcopal	Presbyterian	Congregational
• Church authority rests with the "bishop" (*episkopos*).	• Church authority rests among the "elders" (*presbyteroi*).	• Church authority rests in the congregation of voting members.
• Roman Catholicism, Eastern Orthodoxy, Anglicanism, Episcopalian, Methodism, and some Lutherans	• Presbyterianism, Reformed churches, and many local independent (often described as "elder-led") churches	• Anabaptists, Puritan, Congregational churches, and many "low" or free churches (including most Baptists and Brethren churches)

The Protestants insisted that Catholicism's monopoly on salvation and sanctification was a grave deviation from the apostolic norm, yet the Reformation didn't yield complete agreement on details of ecclesiology or sanctification. As to church governance and order, a number of traditions would develop out of the turmoil. When the institutional church's visible uniformity was decisively challenged by reemphasis on the invisible church, the new Protestant churches had to ask, and answer, "Who, then, is to lead the local congregations? How should they be organized?"

Some, like the Church of England, the Methodists, and some Lutherans retained many vestiges of the episcopal model, in which regional bishops maintained authority over local priests (with no pope). Others, growing from the Calvinist Reformed movement, developed a presbyterian model in which authority rested in local, regional, and even national councils or "synods"—that is, a plurality of leadership sharing governance. Finally, in reaction to both models, Congregationalists sought to establish autonomous local churches, free of governmental and hierarchical domination, in which final authority rested in the local congregation of voting members. Today these various traditions—episcopal, presbyterian, and congregational, with various shades in between—continue within orthodox protestant evangelicalism.

Likewise, the Protestant Reformation produced a number of competing views regarding the sacraments. Though they more or less agreed the Roman Catholic seven-saving-sacraments system was inherently flawed, the Reformers never came to a consensus on the precise nature and function of the sacraments of Baptism and Communion. However, they all agreed that these two were to be maintained in the life of the church.

The following chart compares some of the most prominent views:

Proponent	On Baptism	On the Lord's Supper
Roman Catholicism	Baptismal regeneration removes the guilt and power of original sin; an initial infusion of saving and sanctifying grace. For adults/unbaptized infants.	Sacrament of saving grace; cleanses and strengthens baptized, confirmed Catholics after confession and penance. (Doctrine: transubstantiation.)
Martin Luther (German Lutheranism)	Removes guilt of original sin; sign and sacrament of saving grace, validated when later confirmed by personal faith. For adults/unbaptized infants.	Sacrament of sanctifying grace that strengthens faith. For baptized, confirmed believers in good standing. (Doctrine: consubstantiation.)
Ulrich Zwingli (Swiss Reformed)	Outward sign of initiation into the new covenant community; an act of obedience, pledging a life of faith toward God as a member of His church. For adults/unbaptized infants.	Outward sign, testimony of continued faith and of fellowship with Christ. Commemoration brings spiritual blessing. For baptized believers in good standing. (Doctrine: symbolic presence.)
John Calvin (Swiss Reformed)	Outward symbol of inner reality, of initiation into new covenant community (as circumcision was of the old covenant); validated when later confirmed by personal faith. For adults/unbaptized infants.	Outward symbol of inner reality and means of sanctifying grace. For baptized, confirmed believers in good standing. (Doctrine: real *spiritual* presence of Christ at the observance by the power of the Spirit.)
Menno Simons (Anabaptism)	Outward sign, testimony of faith in Christ; act of repentance and obedience, valid when preceded by faith and confession. For willing believers only.	Outward symbol, testimony of continued faith and obedience. For baptized believers in good standing. (Doctrine: symbolic presence.)

The Modern Period (1700–Present)

The modern story with respect to ecclesiology is one of fragmentation. The Roman Catholic Church simply re-entrenched in the view that the visible church is *the* source of grace and authority. In fact, its position may have become even more rigid after the Reformation than before.[28] Other traditions, meanwhile, followed a variety of courses—some maintaining the emphases of the Reformers, some following hybrid paths. The one thing that may safely be said is this: the evangelical tradition, regardless of the denominational connections that exist within it, typically traces its pedigree to the Reformers with regard to their various views on church governance (episcopal, presbyterian, or congregational), the sacraments, or sanctification.

Perhaps the most significant points of diversity that began to fray then, and continued fragmenting into the modern era, are the competing models of sanctification. Because the major thrust of the protestant period was that the invisible church gives life to the visible church, within a few generations came developments in the doctrine of sanctification that emphasized the practical effects of the invisible (and often individual) relationship between the Redeemer and the redeemed. As the various strands of the Reformation found the nature of the church in this invisible relationship, each began to wrestle with the next logical question: what is the relationship between justification and sanctification? In their answers, the period after the Reformation became a veritable flower garden, with numerous models of sanctification sprouting up and finding a place in the diverse bouquet we call modern evangelicalism.

While definitions of modern evangelicalism are notoriously difficult to defend, it may be reasonable to suggest that the following is one way to *describe* it: evangelicalism is the collection of those from every strand of the Reformation who cling to the authority of Scripture and the consequent centrality of the work of Christ, resulting in an affirmation of the need for personal conversion.[29] With this in mind, it seems incumbent upon any introduction to evangelical doctrine to present the various ways in which modern protestant traditions see the shape of sanctification.

Regarding how to slice and dice those arising from the Reformation, the first two are simple—we must list the Lutheran tradition (arising from the teaching of Luther) and the Reformed tradition (arising primarily from the teaching of Calvin). But what to do next?[30] In the treatment that follows, I will proceed according the assumption that one's place in the evangelical spectrum of views on sanctification is largely determined by the following factors:

- view of the relationship between justification and sanctification
- view of the Holy Spirit's role in sanctification
- view of how a believer engages the Spirit in order to pursue sanctification

I believe that constructing a list of major evangelical perspectives leads us to the following list: Lutheran, Reformed, and Wesleyan/Holiness views.[31]

Lutheran Views of Sanctification

The central point of Lutheranism on sanctification is most often found in the traditional phrase *simul iustus et peccator* ("at the same time righteous and a sinner").[32] Many Lutherans unpack this by holding that the most decisive act on a sinner's behalf is God's declaration of acceptance before Him—the divine pronouncement of righteousness, or "justification." Sanctification, viewed from the human perspective, is nothing more than the state of being justified—sanctification *is* justification; justification *is* sanctification. David Scaer notes, "Sanctification describes the same reality as does justification but describes the justified Christian's relationship to the world and society. Justification and sanctification are not two separate realities, but the same reality viewed from the different perspectives of God and man."[33] Similarly, Francis Pieper says, "Scripture teaches that wherever the Holy Ghost works faith in the Gospel in a man, He immediately works also sanctification and good works in that same man through that faith. . . . It is therefore correct to say that where there is no sanctification, there is also no faith."[34]

Because of the tight justification/sanctification bond in Lutheran thought, and because of its all-pervasive emphasis on justification by faith alone, some have accused Lutheran sanctification of being antinomian—or *against good works*. That flies in the face of Lutheran

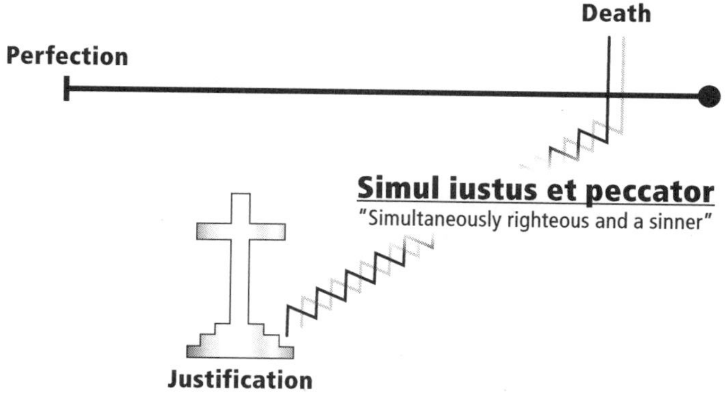

teaching. Rather, the Lutheran says, with conviction: justification is by faith alone, apart from works, and yet the believer *must* do good works because Scripture does not leave it to the individual's discretion whether he/she will or will not do good works.[35]

Reformed Views of Sanctification

The Reformed approach, greatly resembling the Lutheran view, starts from the same place, namely, justification by grace through faith alone. Yet in the Reformed tradition these two aspects of God's saving work are not so seamlessly united, and the two are distinguished (though not separated). What differentiates Lutheran and Reformed views of sanctification seems to be (1) the Spirit's role and (2) how the believer participates in the Spirit's work.

First, the Reformed tradition normally sees the Holy Spirit as the primary agent of sanctification, and the grace of sanctification is categorically distinct from the grace of justification. As Johannes Wollebius (c. 1600) wrote:

> Sanctification differs from justification (1) in genus: the righteousness of the former belongs to the category of quality, that of the latter to the category of relation; (2) in form: (a) in justification faith is regarded as a hand grasping the righteousness of Christ, in sanctification faith is regarded as the principle and root of good works; (b) in justification sin is removed only as regards liability and punishment, in sanctification it is gradually abolished as regards existence; (c) in justification Christ's righteousness is imputed to us, in sanctification a new righteousness inherent in us is infused into us; (3) in degrees: justification is an individual, perfect happening, alike to all; but sanctification is a successive act, gradually tending to perfection and, according to the variety in the gifts of the Holy Spirit, more shining in some, less so in others.[36]

Reflecting the modern era, Herman Witsius said sanctification is "that real work of God, by which they, who are chosen, regenerated, and justified, are continually more and more transformed from the turpitude of sin, to the purity of the divine image."[37] But the Reformed tradition is agreed that the work of God in sanctification is primarily the work of the Holy Spirit. Berkhof representatively says that "sanctification may be defined as *that gracious and continuous operation of the Holy Spirit, by which He delivers the justified sinner from the pollution of sin, renews his whole nature in the image of God, and enables him to perform good works.*"[38]

Second, as to how the believer engages the work of God's Spirit, in the Reformed tradition there is responsible participation of the regenerate person empowered by the Spirit from within. The focus of the believer's work is on the twin elements of *mortification* and *vivification*, gleaned from Ephesians 4: "Put off your old self . . . to be renewed in the spirit of your minds, and to put on the new self." While the commands, often characterized as mortification and vivification—or putting to death and making alive—make plain that the Christian life will contain "ups and downs," the general direction is toward maturity in Christ. Even so, perfection can never be achieved until death.

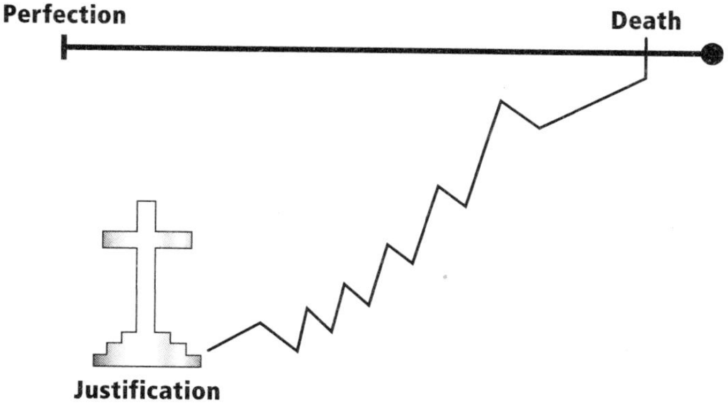

Wesleyan/Holiness Views of Sanctification

Growing out of the Reformed perspective, the Wesleyan view—named after John Wesley (1703–1791)—has had a most profound modern impact on sanctification, especially in evangelicalism. From this standpoint, three affirmations prevail:

1. The law of love is a fulfillment of Scripture's moral imperatives.
2. Believers can comply perfectly with the law of love, leading to "entire sanctification."
3. These first two principles imply a second divine work of sanctifying grace that is completely separate from justification.

This model begins with an innovative observation. Just as Jesus said that the summary of the Old Testament Law is found in the command to "love the Lord your God with all your heart and with all your soul and with all your mind" (Deut. 6:4; cf. Matt. 22:37), John Wesley reasoned that living by a "law of love" was equivalent to fulfilling the moral law. Melvin Dieter remarks:

> [Wesley's] studies of the Old and New Testaments led him to the conclusion that persons who, under grace, fulfill the "royal law of love" as taught most simply and explicitly by Christ Himself in the Sermon on the Mount and subsequently by all of the New Testament writings are also fulfilling the moral intent of the Ten Commandments. Wesley thus relates the fulfillment of the law's moral obligations to the process and end of sanctification rather than to the more objective views of Reformation orthodoxy, which find their fulfillment and satisfaction of the moral law in the act of the believer's justification.[39]

Observing the lives of believers, however, yields the conclusion that many do not experience this compliance with the law of love. As a result, Wesleyans realized that a second work of divine grace is needed for a believer to experience entire sanctification. Kenneth Grider, a respected proponent, writes that the term *second blessing* "underscores the fact that entire sanctification is indeed received subsequent to the time of our conversion."[40]

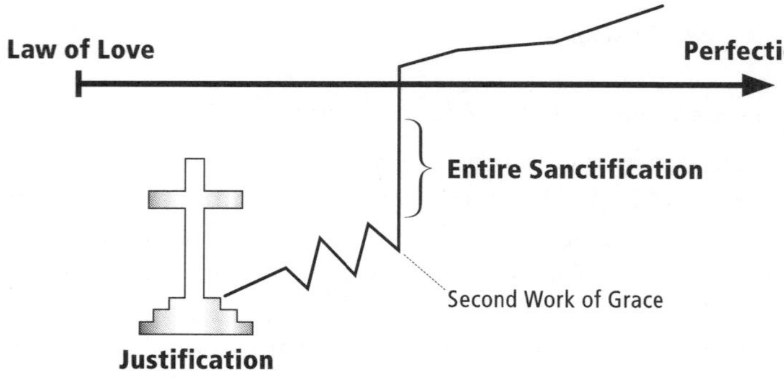

Other similar views also could be classified within the Wesleyan family. In the nineteenth and twentieth centuries, some forms of Pentecostalism, for example, arose from the matrix of the Wesleyan Holiness movement. In some parts of Pentecostal thought, the overall direction of sanctification was the same as described above, but instead of being "entirely sanctified" a person was thought to have also received "the baptism of the Holy Spirit."[41] Further development in the Assemblies of God ultimately resulted in their removing the conceptual link between the baptism of the Holy Spirit and entire sanctification.[42]

THE CHURCH AND THE SPIRITUAL LIFE THROUGH THE AGES

Patristic Period (100–500)	Medieval Period (500–1500)	Protestant Period (1500–1700)	Modern Period (1700–Present)
• Church regarded as spiritual (invisible) and physical (visible), though the visible gradually was emphasized (100–500) • Ignatius of Antioch first uses "catholic" to describe the worldwide church (c. 110) • Threat of heresy leads to strengthening the role of the single bishop (100–500) • Baptism gradually regarded as the means of saving grace (200–400) • Council of Constantinople (381) defines orthodox ecclesiology as "one, holy, catholic, and apostolic" • Gradual rise of Roman claims of worldwide papal authority (250–500)	• Roman Catholic Church exerts authority in the West, pushing for uniformity in doctrine, practice, and organization (500–1500) • The Eastern Orthodox and Roman Catholic Churches officially split, partly over Rome's claims of papal supremacy (1050) • Church organization and power increase with greater role for the church in secular matters (500–1500) • Transubstantiation becomes the official dogma of Roman Catholicism (1215) • System of seven sacraments becomes dogma (1439) • Dissenting voices (e.g., Wycliffe and Hus) are silenced (1300–1500)	• Martin Luther challenges papal authority and sparks the Reformation against illegitimate developments in theology and practice (1517) • The Protestant Reformation results in governance changes, leading to episcopal, presbyterian, and congregational church traditions (1550–1700) • The church fragments into numerous competing denominations, each with its own governance and with some unique doctrines and practices (1500–1700) • Council of Trent solidifies Roman Catholic dogma against Protestant ecclesiology (1545–1563)	• The rise of modern evangelicalism leads to expansion of missions and evangelism (1700–Present) • Controversy over liberal developments in doctrine lead to mainline denominational splits and new denominations and independent churches (1850–1950) • The modern ecumenical movement seeks to establish doctrinal, liturgical, and even organizational unity among diverse churches and denominations (1900–Present) • Diverse and competing models of sanctification proliferate (1700–Present)

Obviously, the doctrines of ecclesiology and sanctification in the protestant evangelical tradition from 1700 to the present day display a foundational unity amid sometimes radical diversity. The unity is seen in the dominant theme in any evangelical ecclesiology: *the invisible church is the foundation of the visible church*. Flowing out of this affirmation is the conviction that the Spirit's work is the key to sanctification.

Still, evangelical churches that make both of these crucial affirmations display a surprising creativity in explaining how aspects of sanctification and ecclesiology fit together. The result? A brilliant world of evangelical traditions hosting numerous orthodox protestant perspectives: from Lutherans to Presbyterians, from Baptists to Pentecostals, from Methodists to Bible Churches, from Anglicans to Anabaptists—unity in diversity . . . the "one, holy, catholic, and apostolic church."

Facts to Never Forget

Not too many years ago, my son played on a Pee Wee Baseball team. The coach was a friend of mine, and I tried to help as much as I could, snagging fly balls, serving as first-base coach, and the like. In batting practice, I can't even guess how many times he had to say, "Keep your eye on the ball!" Kids that age are still developing the requisite hand-eye coordination, and long experience (I think I heard my dad's voice once or twice as a youngster approached the plate) has proven that the first item of business in learning to hit a baseball is indeed to *keep your eye on the ball.*

Having looked at some of Scripture's central passages, and perused the pages of history for an idea of how themes in ecclesiology and sanctification developed, it's time to examine some key principles we've encountered along the way. These are basic to understanding how evangelicals see the doctrines of ecclesiology and sanctification. If we keep our eyes on these principles, we won't strike out when it comes to a proper grasp of the primary doctrines.

Fact 1: The central principle of ecclesiology is a saving relationship with God in Christ.

In the study of theology, one encounters phrases traditionally preserved in Latin. And, I'll admit, sometimes I wonder if the only reason we recite them in Latin is to make things sound more complicated than they really are. But then I'll find one, and then another, that simply demands to be so preserved because the Latin conveys so much more than its English equivalent.

One such expression (at least in my book) is *sine qua non*. Literally translated "without which not," it typically refers to conditions or elements that are indispensable or necessary. To say it another way, *sine qua non* refers to that without which [something] could not exist.

Now, as I struggle to put it into English terms, you see why I think this is one phrase best left alone. But that's not the point of this little section. The point is this: the *sine qua non* of the true church is a saving relationship between the Redeemer and the redeemed. If God did not reach down into our world and enter into a saving relationship with human beings, there would be no church. Yes, there could still be church buildings, church members, church activities, and church programs, but none of these would constitute the true church—the communion of *saints*.

The church is composed of those who've been given spiritual life. The gift of salvation is what results in the church; the invisible relationship gives rise to a visible communion. One passage that shows this is in Ephesians 5, where Paul ties the relationship between Christ and the church to the one between husband and wife. Even when we briefly consider its words, we find one stunning feature: Christ loves the church, and gave himself up for her that He might sanctify her. This seems to imply that the essential nature of the church is that she participates in a saving relationship with God through Jesus Christ.

We have already seen the power of this fact while investigating church history. It seems to be the primary affirmation of the apostolic and the reformation church, and its affirmation or denial forms the central trajectory of this doctrine's history. Finally, as we'll see in the section on dangers to avoid (below), it must be said: affirming, and acting upon, this central principle will protect God's people from many significant perils in the realm of ecclesiology.

Fact 2: The visible aspects of the church must serve, honor, and develop the invisible reality of the church.

Fact 2 is the mirror of Fact 1—its direct consequence, as it happens. The logic is conclusive: if the church exists precisely because of an invisible relationship that itself is a gift of God, then everything about that church ought to serve this relationship's development. To say it backward, if we emphasize the church's visible aspects over the invisible, then we deny the priority of a relationship offered by God and insist that the visible church is the source of salvation. For evangelicals, this simply would not do.

Fact 3: Variety (diversity) in Christ's body is God's design.

I've been shaving my head for about fifteen years. It began as an experiment in view of the imminent arrival of Mr. MPB: Male Pattern Baldness. I said to my wife that when MPB arrived, I did not want the "laurel wreath" haircut but instead would prefer my head completely bald.

Her response surprised me: she gave her blessing to try a "preview." And then *my* response surprised me: it was comfortable.

What's clear is this: I investigated shaving my head precisely because I was trying to save the very top of my body from dishonor. And that's the point of this fact about biblical ecclesiology. The body of Christ is made of many different individuals, all gifted uniquely by the same Spirit that baptizes them into the body. Each person—each part of the body—is valuable (see 1 Corinthians 12).

Further, this is part of God's very design. This diversity is His wisdom and blessing for the church. As a matter of fact, at one point (see Ephesians 4), this variety is portrayed as "gifts" Christ has given the church for building her up.

Nevertheless, from our human perspective, we often see this diversity as a pain in the church. Different people, different perspectives, different gifts, different concerns . . . this all adds up to conflict. To friction. To difficulty.

That's why it's vital we're reminded regularly: *Variety in the church is God's design!* What's more, our response to this variety ought to be to honor one another in compassion while celebrating the unity of the body in Christ.

Fact 4: Scripture is not silent on how we ought to "do" this thing called *church*.

One thing I've never done well is keep track of all the manuals that come into my life. Over the years I've been deluged: mower manuals, humidifier manuals, electronic thermometer manuals, kitchen mixer manuals . . . the list goes on and on and *on*. I feel I've already had more manuals than there are particles in the universe—somewhere around 10^{87} sounds right. I guess I feel justified in not keeping track of them. So why even try to keep them around?

Of two possible answers, I don't know which is more compelling. First, I'm of German descent, and maybe that's all that needs to be said. But if not, then try the second: what if, on the off chance my dog accidentally bumps my son while he's using the mixer, the transverse Planckian armature colloid gets impaired? *Then* what? How will I know if this is a repair I can perform at home (with the right power tools) or if we should kick the mixer to the curb?

However, one "manual" I've endeavored sedulously to keep close at hand is the Bible. Like all true evangelicals, I regard it as God's Word, and recognizing it as such leads me to our fourth fact: We have not been left without instructions on how we "do" this thing called *church*. We've already examined a couple of central passages (1 Corinthians 11 and Matthew 28) wherein we found agreement that churches ought to be practicing the ordinances (or sacraments) of the Lord's Supper and Baptism. If we add to these what we learn from 1 Timothy 4:13 and 2 Peter 3—that the early church read letters from the apostles and wrestled with the contents—we can suggest that sermons ought to be part of our meetings. These elements, along with hymns and prayers (see Ephesians 5), seem to be the primary and indispensable parts of our gathering together.

This also raises a substantial question: do we think we have things *so* figured out that these biblical concepts are no longer authoritative for us? Why would we play with such instructions? We don't have the freedom to do "whatever we want" in church worship. We must obey God's Word, and so every evangelical ought to grapple with the most appropriate and biblically sensitive ways to celebrate the ordinances and to shape our services together.

Fact 5: Sanctification and justification are inseparably bound together.

When my wife and I lived in Scotland, we had the privilege of semiregular visits to Edinburgh, and on one of those trips we encountered the legend of a dog named "Greyfriars Bobby." During the 1800s, as the story goes, a man named John "Auld Jock" Gray, who worked for the city, had a wee Skye Terrier. Gray and Bobby were inseparable—so much so that when Auld Jock died in 1858, Bobby followed him to his grave in Greyfriars Kirkyard. Then, according to legend, Bobby stood guard over his master's resting place until he himself died about fourteen years later.

The townspeople were so moved by Bobby's loyalty that they erected a statue in his honor. First placed shortly after the dog's death in 1872, it can still be seen just across from the graveyard in front of Greyfriars Bobby's Bar.

Bobby's refusal to be separated from his master reminds me of a fact worth focusing on, with respect to another inseparable bond. This one is between two phases (or aspects) of salvation: sanctification is inseparable from justification. Or, put another way, justification implies sanctification, and on this, with perhaps just a few objections, evangelicals everywhere agree. It's what we say next that tends to conjure up the most dispute; so my suggestion is that for now we leave things here. Suffice to say that if God begins the work of salvation in justification, then He most assuredly will continue that work in sanctification and complete it in glorification.

Soon, when we discuss some of the hazards in the areas of ecclesiology and sanctification, we'll find that maintaining the connection between justification and sanctification is crucial.

Fact 6: Sanctification is a work of the Holy Spirit that involves the believer's responsible participation.

This fact might be the most pragmatically important with regard to the doctrine of sanctification. Evangelicals agree doctrinally that both Thing One (the divine element) and Thing Two (the human element) are involved in the sanctification process. Yet even with this recognition, some evangelicals are so zealous to emphasize Thing One that they advocate a view of sanctification that *can* become so lopsided as to end up laying responsibility for a believer's sin at God's feet. On the other hand, some emphasize Thing Two to such an extent that sanctification is no longer seen as the Spirit's work—or that it's a fully optional facet of salvation.

Rather, we'd do well to accept that sanctification, while inseparably joined to justification, is nonetheless distinct from it. We can characterize the distinction in this way: justification is purely the act of God; glorification is purely the act of God; sanctification, in the salvific middle, retains *some* dependence on human action. Thus it's key to hear a Reformed theologian like Anthony Hoekema say that Scripture "also describes sanctification as a process that involves our responsible participation."[1]

Fact 7: Sanctification is a team sport.

I was a member of our high school's gymnastics team. Yes, we had one. No, I wasn't very good. But we had a good time, and as nobody was permanently disfigured, it was a success.

In one of the gymnast's realities, it's a team sport, yet you always perform alone. Every routine, every time—it's you and the apparatus. While your score is added to your team's total, it also remains your own individual mark.

This may be a reasonable way of describing the sport of sanctification. You must work hard, both alone and with your teammates. And your score will affect not only your team but also your own individual accomplishment.

Most of us are well aware of sanctification's "individual aspects." We've heard (in so many words) of mortification and vivification, of the spiritual disciplines, of quiet times and prayer journals and Bible study. And I am absolutely in favor of these! As with gymnastics, the preparation is both individual and teammate-assisted.

But this leads to the part that, for most evangelicals, is less familiar. There are solo elements, yet the overall pattern of sanctification is team-based.

Seven Facts to Never Forget

1. The central principle of ecclesiology is a saving relationship with God in Christ.
2. The visible aspects of the church must serve, honor, and develop the invisible reality of the church.
3. Variety (diversity) in Christ's body is God's design.
4. Scripture is not silent on how we ought to "do" this thing called *church*.
5. Sanctification and justification are inseparably bound together.
6. Sanctification is a work of the Holy Spirit that involves the believer's responsible participation.
7. Sanctification is a team sport.

Even though each individual bears responsibility for his or her growth in holiness (by responsible participation with the Spirit's work), one's growth as an individual *always* occurs in the context of the body of Christ. We train, and grow, as part of the body. Our life as a Christian reflects on the body.

That is precisely why it's *not* okay to forsake our assembling together (Heb. 10:25)—to pursue, as the following section suggests, a "Lone Ranger sanctification." That's also why it's not okay for churches to abandon the arduous process of church discipline. But once we see it this way, things begin to make more sense. Sanctification is a team sport.

Dangers to Avoid

I'll never forget the first time I realized that the symbol so commonly used to identify poison—the skull and crossbones—was also the stereotypical symbol to designate pirates.

This, I think, must be why cannibals never eat pirates.

In all seriousness, our study of ecclesiology and sanctification has skirted deftly past quite a few dangers. Now let's take a little time to carefully apply a *DO NOT INGEST* decal to a couple of ideas. These are concepts, attitudes, or actions that will either harm or poison the church or harm or poison one's own growth in holiness. While I have no firm convictions about exactly *what* would happen if you were to entertain these ideas or act upon these principles, that's not the point. The point is this: when you see the skull and crossbones, you choose not to eat or drink the contents.

Please don't hear me warning about *heresy*, as that term is normally reserved for errors that threaten the very fabric of the Christian faith. The dangers listed here don't belong on a list of heresies but rather are dangers that threaten the church's vitality. I should mention they're not ordered in terms of how unsafe they are but rather, somewhat loosely, by placing ecclesiological dangers first, then sanctification-related dangers second.

Danger 1: Corporation Over Corpus

This risk arises ultimately from a failure to emphasize the foundational nature of the saving relationship with Jesus Christ. As we've seen, the hallmark of an evangelical perspective on ecclesiology is maintaining a balance between the invisible and the visible. The invisible church, composed of all who've entered into an eternal saving relationship with God through Christ by the Spirit, is the true church. Every visible church is an expression of the true, invisible church.

But when we lose sight of the invisible reality that undergirds the visible church, we can end up focusing on the wrong things. For example, we can begin to treat the church on purely visible terms—acting like it's a corporation rather than the body (*corpus*) of Christ. This attitude is absolutely destructive to the church, because the rules of business are brutal, cutthroat. A corporation must thrive to survive. Eliminate the opposition. Jettison weak members. Downsize now and again, perhaps, to maximize profitability.

This is *not* the way a body works. When your lungs are congested, you don't fire them and hire a new pair. The whole body works together for healing, and it suffers until that healing comes. The very idea that the church is Christ's body has implications for how we view it and treat it.

One *possible* danger sign: when the only books leaders are reading come from the corporate world, there may be a problem. Don't get me wrong—learning about leadership is a positive thing, and especially for those who hold leadership positions in ministry. But are church leaders reading books that speak of *shepherding*? of body life? of healing broken relationships? The pattern of Jesus is not the pattern of the corporate CEO. As a result, should we really accept a situation in which the primary paradigm for a pastor is drawn entirely from corporate headship?

There's no clear-cut line of demarcation here. But leadership in the church is not simply business acumen or "getting things done." It may involve those things at times, but leadership in the church absolutely must focus—again and again—on the spiritual relationship between the Redeemer and the redeemed. This is a *spiritual* leadership, and whenever we, as leaders or as members, accept an attitude toward the church that views it as some kind of business, we've lost sight of what's most important.

Danger 2: Growth Over Health

I recently took my son to the pediatrician for his annual checkup, and during the exam I became amazed all over again at the state of today's medical knowledge. Yes, there are many mysteries left to explore, but our understanding of how preadolescent and adolescent bodies grow (for instance) is far more detailed than ever before. And as I write this, I'm very glad we don't measure the growth of children by looking for additional body parts. Thankfully, we measure growth by measuring development in bodies, doing what bodies ought to do. We measure *health*.

The second danger, related to the first, insofar as it too arises from neglecting the foundational element of spiritual relationship in the church, likewise surfaces when we fail to prioritize the invisible over the visible. In a nutshell, the hazard is that by focusing on the church's visible aspects we begin to measure it—and even to measure success in ministry—by looking at what's visible. This error, I perceive, is epidemic in the evangelical world, and it's a denial of our very DNA. We have a rich heritage of maintaining that *the invisible gives rise to the visible*. We have a powerful tradition of insisting that being born again—born from above, as Jesus describes it in John 3—means we have received, by grace, through faith, a divinely bestowed relationship with God through Christ. This is what makes us part of the church.

But then many churches proceed to pursue growth as measured by the number of attendees, or the size of the physical plant, or the dollars in the budget. No matter how we do it, if we prioritize *any* sort of physical growth over spiritual development, we have denied our heritage.

Perhaps our Lord intended more by the metaphor of the church as Christ's body than we typically assume. How does a body grow? Certainly not by obsession with physical stature or the quantification of various parts. A body grows by pursuing health, and that ought to be our focus as well.

This principle—that church growth ought to be considered something spiritual—seems to be supported by a reading of 1 Corinthians 3, in which the apostle Paul speaks of "building the church" (see especially v. 10). The kind of building to which he refers is *growth in the truth*, or *growth in spiritual maturity*—the kind that lays aside divisions and schisms. By the time he reaches the end of chapter 4, the issue has become crystal clear. Paul wants the Corinthian church not to grow in size, number, or budget but to grow by following the proper "guide"—by imitating those who imitate Christ.

So, how do *you* define church growth? If your growth-related focus is on numbers, on power, on assets, on acreage, then you may be an *ersatz evangelical*. On the other hand, if by "growth" you mean development in Christlikeness or discernible increase in holiness, then likely you are the rightful heir of the Reformers and a defender of the apostolic teaching.

Danger 3: Fractured Family

When I was in sixth grade, my entire class was punished for the playground sins of one person. Yes—one person. This, at least for most preteens, is enough to set off the "injustice alarm." But what made the situation nearly intolerable is that the guilty party wasn't even in our class. [S]he and his/her[1] entire class went unpunished, while a couple dozen innocents were indelibly branded as uncouth, lawbreaking brigands.

The third danger has something of this in common. The fractured family is seen when we forget that the church is Christ's body and so forget that church is the place for body life, for addressing body-related issues. When we do this, we slowly begin to tailor our services to cater to some who happen to attend but may not believe or follow Jesus and so are not part of the true (invisible) church.

We begin to change the content of our sermons. Gone are any significant expositions of God's Word—that could be too off-putting for some. Gone are any strong stands on conviction—that would be bone-chilling for many in our "enlightened" culture. Gone are discussions of anything but simple and inoffensive doctrines. All because we've gradually fallen prey to the notion that we must cater to a crowd that's not ready for the truth of God's Word.

I call this the "fractured family" because the actual body of Christ is now left out in the cold. Since services are now aimed at others, where does the body go for feeding, for fellowship, for real family time? In my sixth-grade experience, the party that *needed* discipline didn't get it; in the fractured family, "church" does not meet the church's needs.

Danger 4: Sectarianism's Siren Song

I'm an alumnus of the state school that shows up on my diploma as "Louisiana State University and Agricultural and Mechanical College." So, I guess what most people call "LSU" is really "LSU A&MC."

Hearing this, you won't be surprised that I'm a big fan of college football. Specifically, LSU football and SEC football. And I'm happy to point out that *only* the Southeastern Conference has *real* college football.

Actually, while I am indeed an LSU (and SEC) supporter, I don't really believe other schools and conferences aren't legit or respectable. The point is this: pride can sometimes lead us to conclude that *only* our group has *the* secret recipe for something. It could be SEC football. Or it could be the "real" inheritance of an evangelical Christian faith. Only *our* church knows the truth; lives the truth; teaches the truth.

We evangelicals value highly our birthmark, the truth of God's Word. But sometimes that commitment ends up singing us to our destruction. Like sailors entranced by the song of the sirens, we can become enchanted with the sound of our own voices and come to conclude that only we can adequately represent the body of Christ, or true evangelicalism. We write off other churches as hopelessly misguided or only nominally Christian.

Such sectarianism puts asunder the broader body of Christ. We elevate inconsequential issues to the status of essentials; on the basis of disagreement about these newly defined "essentials," we refuse to fellowship or cooperate with brothers and sisters in Christ with whom we have so much in common. Plus, in so doing, we reinforce stereotypes about the strange, mythical creatures that inhabit "that church" down the street.

Sectarianism's siren song, the danger of sacrificing that unity on the altar of my own tradition's idiosyncrasies, destroys the beauty of a unity that could be based on our common confession of Christianity's central truths. As the Vincentian Canon puts it, we share realities that have been believed "everywhere, always, by all."[2]

Danger 5: Lone Ranger Sanctification

I'm old enough to remember *Lone Ranger* TV episodes. As to why he was known by this name, I imagine that if we surveyed random fans, the most common answer would involve his fighting against crime and injustice alone—after all, this is the enduring inference of the term *lone ranger*. While the truth of the character's name may have more to do with his having been the sole survivor of a massacre involving six Texas Rangers—he being the "lone" Ranger to survive—I'm in no position to battle culturally affirmed connotations. For purposes of this discussion, let's just assume that *lone ranger* means "going it alone."

One of the menaces we must confront, "Lone Ranger sanctification" is the view that my growth in holiness is a realm in which I "go it alone." That is, the local church is not an integral part of my growth; it's an ancillary effect of my personal growth, which largely takes place in isolation from the body. This approach is wrong, it's dangerous, and it harms the body of Christ.

First, the very baptism that identified us with Christ—the baptism that initiated our spiritual relationship with the Redeemer—is also the baptism that made us part of His body, the church. In other words, we were baptized by the Holy Spirit *into* (not out from) the church. How can a relationship that started by being made part of His body continue by ignoring and avoiding that reality? This is the lesson we encountered earlier from 1 Corinthians 12: no part of the body will function well and keep growing if cut off from the body.

I acknowledge that there must be a balance between the corporate and individual aspects of sanctification. As individuals, we pursue intimacy with the Lord and practice spiritual disciplines. But that pursuit and that practice is not in denial of our place in Christ's body; rather, it enhances our place and is aimed at serving the body. This, after all, is the exact flow of thought in Paul's Romans 12:1–2 "individual sanctification" passage.

To listen to most evangelical expositions of this text, one would think the whole point is to individually present our bodies to God as a living sacrifice, a spiritual service of worship. This is one of the elements Paul affirms, but I do not believe a solo presentation is the entire deal. That individual sacrifice, or submission to God, is designed to benefit the body—this is the point of verses 3–13. So, it seems, *even individual sanctification is body-oriented*.

Danger 6: Evangelical Antinomianism

Antinomianism is a concept that erupted in the context of Reformation-era Lutheranism. Precisely because Lutheran thought placed such emphasis on the finished work of justification, questions began to circulate about the believer's consequent attitude toward holy living.

To say it another way, if justification is a done deal for the believer, and that right standing before God is received by faith alone, apart from any works, then why does one need works after he or she has been justified by faith?

This is an honest question, and one the Lutheran tradition quickly sorted out. The answer was, essentially, that justification *is* complete, and based only on faith, apart from works. But justification has implications, one being that every believer is expected to live a life befitting justification. Yes, a holy life is necessary, though that life of holiness never earns justification. Those in Lutheran circles who denied the need for holy living were called *antinomians*.

Much like those folks of old, many of us have missed the point. There is today a rampant illness I call *evangelical antinomianism* among those who sincerely believe in Christ and spout an orthodox doctrine of justification by faith yet nevertheless fail to see that justification does have implications. Failing to live Christ-shaped lives, instead they are completely acculturated. The statistics are everywhere: evangelicals look, think, and act just like the culture around them. We display the same weaknesses, spend our money the same way, and exhibit the same values on marriage and divorce.

Where is the tide of Christian conscience, wrestling seriously with the biblical command "You shall be holy, for I am holy" (1 Peter 1:16)? It seems to have been overcome by evangelical antinomianism, and it's high time for another Luther to take his stand and call the people of God to holy living.

Danger 7: Sanctimonious Self-Improvement

Back in the day, every car had a carburetor, the part of the internal combustion engine that mixed air and fuel in the proper ratios for burning in the cylinders. Fuel injection is now the preferred method of accomplishing the same basic task, but as an old-timer I have to say that something beautiful was lost when cars stopped using the carburetor. To be specific, we lost a part that was itself made up of zillions of other tiny parts.

The first time I took apart a carburetor is etched into my memory. It was on a little four-cylinder engine, and I had to clean it, so I took it off and began disassembling, blissfully unaware of the many risks of doing this without an illustrated parts breakdown. When I had put it back together, I was patting myself on the back for a job well done as I prepared to re-install . . . and then I looked down at the ground and saw a part I'd missed. My heart crashed! One tiny (but absent) piece would keep the carburetor from working properly.

That same problem is reflected in our last "danger." Antinomianism involves a misunderstanding of the right connection between justification and sanctification; *sanctimonious self-improvement* involves a misunderstanding of the Holy Spirit's role in sanctification. Unfortunately, it leaves out a vital part—the Spirit's role—and as a result sanctification simply does not work.

Earlier, regarding Romans 6, I suggested that sanctification is illustrated by Things One and Two in Dr. Seuss's *The Cat in the Hat*. At that time we observed that one trademark of an evangelical view of sanctification is the recognition that both Thing One (divine element) and Thing Two (human element) are involved. The error of sanctimonious self-improvement is a denial of the biblical truth that sanctification is the work of the Holy Spirit with the believer's responsible participation.[3]

Seven Dangers to Avoid

1. Corporation Over Corpus
2. Growth Over Health
3. Fractured Family
4. Sectarianism's Siren Song
5. Lone Ranger Sanctification
6. Evangelical Antinomianism
7. Sanctimonious Self-Improvement

It seems to me that the source of this hazard is the loss of belief that the church is a spiritual organism rather than a collection of individuals. When we lose sight of the reality that the church is the body of Christ, we begin to view it the other way. Then each individual is left to his or her own "Lone Ranger sanctification," with the result that sanctification reduces to self-improvement.

By the way, our culture does not help us in remembering that growth in holiness must come in right relationship with God's Spirit; we're told at every turn that we're the masters of our fate—we are the captains of our soul. But this is just the voice of sanctimonious self-improvement. It's a lie.

Sanctification is part of that invisible relationship between Redeemer and redeemed; as such, it is entirely dependent upon the Spirit's ministry. Don't leave that part out!

Principles to Put Into Practice

The Charge of the Light Brigade, a poem written by Alfred, Lord Tennyson, captures my attention each time I ponder its words afresh. What power leaps off the page! What exquisite skill Tennyson displays as he draws the reader into the visceral experiences of battle!

It's the second stanza that always stops me in my tracks:

> "Forward, the Light Brigade!"
> Was there a man dismay'd?
> Not tho' the soldiers knew
> Some one had blunder'd:
> Theirs not to make reply,
> Theirs not to reason why,
> Theirs but to do and die:
> Into the valley of Death
> Rode the six hundred.[1]

The fighters forever immortalized here found themselves with naught to do but to "do and die," to ride gallantly ahead despite someone else's grave error. Certainly, for me, this is the work's central *pathos*—that keen interplay between nobility and futility.

Perhaps that is, in a lesser way, where we stand now. We've confronted vital principles in their biblical and historical context. We've considered aspects and concepts from the doctrines of ecclesiology and sanctification. Now a question looms intently before us: "What difference does it make?"

To make a difference, we—you and I—must ride nobly forward, encased in the armor and attitude of "do or die." In what direction? What actions do we take as we ride boldly? My suggestion is that we consider carefully how to respond to the following five principles. Though I'm sure many could come up with five equally (or even more) compelling axioms to put into practice, I strongly suspect that to practice these means we'll be part of changing our world for the better.

Principle 1: Pursue the unity of the faith.

In college I had a roommate who was simply exceptional. We got along well, with enough flexibility on each side to deal with the minor misunderstandings that invariably crop up. He was absolutely a gift from God.

He was from New Orleans, and when we stayed at his parents' house he and his friends introduced me to the festivities of Mardi Gras. We took in a number of parades; the crowds were immense; the city was electric but also strange and unfamiliar. My roommate did not have to say—not even once—"stay with me." I was utterly determined not to get separated from him in that situation. My personal well-being, I was convinced, depended on it.

So here's the question: as you look around at the various churches, groups, or bodies that make up evangelicalism, how do you view them? Are they more like the Mardi Gras mobs—people who represent a threat to your well-being? Or are they like my roommate and his friends—the only hope of your well-being being preserved?

You already know where I'm going with this line of thought, so let me just say it. The first principle to practice as we strive to live out a biblical ecclesiology is this: pursue the unity of the faith.

I am so grateful to work at a confessional institution whose doctrinal statement affirms this very dictum, for I believe it is a direct consequence of recognizing that the work of Christ in salvation is the starting point for all ecclesiology. While your affiliation with a visible church does matter, what matters far more is your identification with Christ. That's why I'm thrilled that my seminary affirms that "all believers . . . are under solemn duty to keep the unity of the Spirit in the bond of peace, rising above all sectarian differences, and loving one another with a pure heart fervently."[2]

That's a great place to start! Rising above factious dispute—nonessential differences between, say, the Independent Bible Church and Presbyterian, or Baptist and Episcopal—we love one another fervently with pure hearts. We are brothers and sisters in Christ! Our family relationship *in Christ* far outweighs any temporal labels.

Principle 2: Get involved.

We know that pursuing the unity of the faith follows from placing the proper emphasis on the invisible church—recognizing that all who are *in Christ* are members of His body, the invisible church. This second principle arises from a similar place: placing the proper emphasis on the visible church.

If you're a believer in Jesus Christ—if you are spiritually united with the risen and ascended Son of God—then the thing to do is simply this: get involved in a local church. Your spiritual union with Him and consequent incorporation into His body, the invisible church, entails—requires—your participation in the local, visible expression of that body.

Wrapped up in this principle are several aspects, first among them the admonishment in the letter to the Hebrews: we are to be "not neglecting to meet together, as is the habit of some, but encouraging one another, and all the more as you see the Day drawing near" (10:25). Genuine, ongoing, sustained participation in a local church is nonnegotiable for the believer.

Further, simply attending is insufficient. According to Scripture, God's Spirit has equipped every believer with gifts, talents, abilities, convictions, sensitivities, and more. All of these are intended for the health of the church. Plainly, then, merely "darkening the door" or "making a regular appearance" doesn't measure up.

The mandate here is to strive to use your gifts for the body's benefit; for example, the verse just before the one above says, "Let us consider how to stir one another up to love and good works" (v. 24). So there it is in all its glory: *get involved in a local church in such a way that your gifts are used for its benefit*. If you find this too onerous, then you need to ask: am I humble enough to place the needs of the body ahead of my own desires for comfort? Lone Ranger faith doesn't work.

The Lord commands us to live and grow in harmonious union with the rest of His body; nothing else is *meant* to work.

Principle 3: Practice obedience to those in authority.

Long ago, during my engineering days, I was working on a program that had encountered significant difficulties. As I prepared to brief my customer on the nature of the issues, along with my proposed solution and the time and money needed to complete it, a VP from corporate headquarters visited me. He asked for the whole story, digested the details, and then told me to lie to my customer.

I couldn't believe my ears. I informed him that I would be telling the truth, that I was willing to suffer whatever consequences resulted, and that I was committed to working as hard as necessary to overcome the obstacles facing us. Never have I feared for my job as I did right at that time.

In that instance, fortunately, everything turned out fine. I did tell the truth. The customer appreciated my candor and persistence in making things right. Our whole team worked hard; the program concluded successfully.

This does *not* mean that if you tell the truth everything will turn to gold. That's not what I'm saying. I *am* saying there may be times when those in authority direct us to do something morally unacceptable. In those cases, the believer is responsible to do what's right. *When* there's a conflict, we're to obey God rather than men (see Acts 5:29).

Since we're talking about authority and conformity, let me offer a third principle to emphasize as we pursue excellence through our ecclesiology: *practice obedience to those in spiritual authority.*

Many if not most of us have true difficulty with this. Generally, we're trained from day one to admire those who, with innate grit and a pioneer's spirit, rise up against the odds and by sheer force of independent will achieve success. Isn't this the American way?

The sad thing is it's not the right way—not in the church. By God's plan, His people have spiritual shepherds to help guide them. Pastors. Elders. Overseers. Bishops . . . Whatever terms your ecclesiastical tradition uses, someone has responsibility for your spiritual care and feeding. That's the person I'm talking about, and you need to *obey* that person (or those persons).

Yes, I've heard it all before. "*Obey* is too strong a word!" and "That gives authority figures too much power!" But no, it's not too strong a word; it's a straightforward biblical precept. And they don't have *absolute* authority; they've been placed in *spiritual* authority. You do not have to shortchange your moral principles in the interests of following their lead, yet in matters of spiritual development and church order, we Americans need to learn some old-fashioned obedience. Hebrews 13:17 deserves our attention:

> Obey your leaders and submit to them, for they are keeping watch over your souls, as those who will have to give an account. Let them do this with joy and not with groaning, for that would be of no advantage to you.

Principle 4: Develop the spiritual disciplines.

In junior high I was on the wrestling team for two years. Then I decided the sport wasn't worth it—too much pain involved. There were push-ups and sit-ups by the millions. There were laps around the school by the thousands. There was running in a rubber suit to make you sweat enough to "make weight." And, when you're actually wrestling, there's physical exertion that uses every muscle and sucks *every single drop* of moisture from your body. Your tongue binds to the roof of your mouth like it's stuck to frozen metal in January. Even your eyeballs go all wrinkly like a raisin.

Okay, that last part was exaggeration. But seriously—not worth it. Not for me.

The price we pay in order to garner various accomplishments in life brings us to a consideration of our fourth principle: develop the spiritual disciplines. These are the metaphysical equivalent of push-ups and sit-ups, and Scripture reveals their importance, which likewise has been emphasized by generation upon generation of faithful Christ-followers.

I don't want to get wrapped up in discussing which disciplines are "best," so why don't we just stick with the ones that have stood the test of time: Prayer. Studying God's Word. Meditation (especially on God's Word). Fasting. Memorizing God's Word. Silence.

If some or all of these sound odd or faintly cult-like, you may have lost touch with our faith's rich heritage. So here's the challenge: read up a bit on these disciplines; then begin to try them out. Don't expect to do a thousand sit-ups the very first time—but practice them. Patiently. Consistently.

One word of warning: there's nothing "magical" in any discipline. Just like lots of exercise won't make you a great wrestler (believe me, I know), so fasting doesn't make you a "great Christian." The whole point of each is to help you focus on your relationship with the living God first, and with Christ's body second. Do not let these disciplines isolate you from the body, but rather develop them for the glory of God and the benefit of the body of Christ.

Principle 5: Encourage accountability.

The last principle to practice is really a spin-off of a couple of others. If you're to get involved and practice the spiritual disciplines, then you'll necessarily be developing spiritual relationships characterized by transparency. And that is a very good thing.

Accountability—the kind that benefits both individuals and the body of Christ—happens in at least two places. The first is in personal relationships of honesty and authenticity. The second is in the life of the local church.

Five Principles to Put Into Practice

1. Pursue the unity of the faith.
2. Get involved.
3. Practice obedience to those in authority.
4. Develop the spiritual disciplines.
5. Encourage accountability.

Every believer can benefit from a friend or two with whom there is utter trust and open accountability. This is a huge part of spiritual formation. At the same time, every local church needs to commit itself to accountability—holding each member accountable for words and actions that befit the body. This "organizational level" accountability helps form the church in holiness.

Voices From the Past and Present

One of the most amazing blessings of living in the twenty-first century is the ability to gaze back across the ages and consider the heroes of the faith. What an honor to be able to read the works of Augustine, to contend with the insights of Martin Luther, to marvel at the brilliance of Anselm. Taking regular advantage of this privilege can serve in keeping us grounded, for "standing on the shoulders of giants" assists us in identifying what are truly major issues and also helps us realize how much our thinking has been shaped by those who have gone before.

So what have these giants said about ecclesiology and sanctification? To aid in answering this question, this section offers a selection of quotations related to these doctrinal areas from each major era of church history.[1]

The Patristic Period (c. AD 100–500)

Didache (c. AD 50–70)

"Baptize as follows: after you have reviewed all these things, baptize in the name of the Father and of the Son and of the Holy Spirit in running water. But if you have no running water, then baptize in some other water; and if you are not able to baptize in cold water, then do so in warm. But if you have neither, then pour water on the head three times in the name of Father and Son and Holy Spirit. And before the baptism, let the one baptizing and the one who is to be baptized fast, as well as any others who are able. Also, you must instruct the one who is to be baptized to fast for one or two days beforehand."[2]

Clement of Rome (c. 95)

"The apostles have preached the Gospel to us from the Lord Jesus Christ; Jesus Christ [has done so] from God. Christ therefore was sent forth by God, and the apostles by Christ. Both these appointments, then, were made in an orderly way, according to the will of God. Having therefore received their orders, and being fully assured by the resurrection of our Lord Jesus Christ, and established in the word of God, with full assurance of the Holy Ghost, they went forth proclaiming that the kingdom of God was at hand. And thus preaching through countries and cities, they appointed the firstfruits [of their labors], having first proved them by the Spirit, to be bishops and deacons of those who should afterwards believe. Nor was this any new thing, since indeed many ages before it was written concerning bishops and deacons. For thus saith the Scripture in a certain place, 'I will appoint their bishops in righteousness, and their deacons in faith.'"[3]

Ignatius of Antioch (c. 110)

"Flee from divisions as the beginning of evils. You must all follow the bishop as Jesus Christ followed the Father, and follow the council of presbyters as you would the apostles, and respect the deacons as the commandment of God. Let no one do anything that has to do with the church without the bishop. Only that Eucharist which is under the authority of the bishop (or whomever he himself designates) is to be considered valid. Wherever the bishop appears, there let the congregation be; just as wherever Jesus Christ is, there is the catholic church. It is not permissible either to baptize or to hold a love feast without the bishop. But whatever he approves is also pleasing to God, in order that everything you do may be trustworthy and valid."[4]

"Let everyone respect the deacons as Jesus Christ, just as they should respect the bishop, who is a model of the Father, and the presbyters as God's council, and as the band of the apostles. Without these no group can be called a church."[5]

Justin Martyr (c. 150)

"As many as are persuaded and believe that what we teach and say is true, and undertake to be able to live accordingly, are instructed to pray and to entreat God with fasting, for the remission of their sins that are past, we praying and fasting with them. Then they are brought by us where there is water, and are regenerated in the same manner in which we were ourselves regenerated. For, in the name of God, the Father and Lord of the universe, and of our Saviour Jesus Christ, and of the Holy Spirit, they then receive the washing with water."[6]

"This food is called among us the Eucharist, of which no one is allowed to partake but the man who believes that the things which we teach are true, and who has been washed with the washing that is for the remission of sins, and unto regeneration, and who is so living as Christ has enjoined. For not as common bread and common drink do we receive these; but in like manner as Jesus Christ our Saviour, having been made flesh by the Word of God, had both flesh and blood for our salvation, so likewise have we been taught that the food which is blessed by the prayer of His word, and from which our blood and flesh by transmutation are nourished, is the flesh and blood of that Jesus who was made flesh."[7]

"The wealthy among us help the needy; and we always keep together; and for all things wherewith we are supplied, we bless the Maker of all through His Son Jesus Christ, and through the Holy Ghost. And on the day called Sunday, all who live in cities or in the country gather together to one place, and the memoirs of the apostles or the writings of the prophets are read, as long as time permits; then, when the reader has ceased, the president verbally instructs, and exhorts to the imitation of these good things. Then we all rise together and pray, and, as we before said, when our prayer is ended, bread and wine and water are brought, and the president in like manner offers prayers and thanksgivings, according to his ability, and the people assent, saying Amen; and there is a distribution to each, and a participation of that over which thanks have been given, and to those who are absent a portion is sent by the deacons. And they who are well to do, and willing, give what each thinks fit; and what is collected is deposited with the president, who succours the orphans and widows and those who, through sickness or any other cause, are in want, and those who are in bonds and the strangers sojourning among us, and in a word takes care of all who are in need. But Sunday is the day on which we all hold our common assembly, because it is the first day on which God, having wrought a change in the darkness and matter, made the world; and Jesus Christ our Saviour on the same day rose from the dead. For He was crucified on the day before that of Saturn [Saturday]; and on the day after that of Saturn, which is the day of the Sun, having appeared to His apostles and disciples, He taught them these things."[8]

***Irenaeus of Lyons** (c. 180)*

"The Church, having received this preaching and this faith, although scattered throughout the whole world, yet, as if occupying but one house, carefully preserves it. She also believes these points [of doctrine] just as if she had but one soul, and one and the same heart, and she proclaims them, and teaches them, and hands them down, with perfect harmony, as if she possessed only one mouth. . . . Nor will any one of the rulers in the Churches, however highly gifted he may be in point of eloquence, teach doctrines different from these. . . . For the faith being ever one and the same, neither does one who is able at great length to discourse regarding it, make any addition to it, nor does one who can say but little diminish it."[9]

"It is incumbent to obey the presbyters who are in the Church—those who, as I have shown, possess the succession from the apostles; those who, together with the succession of the episcopate, have received the certain gift of truth, according to the good pleasure of the Father. But [it is also incumbent] to hold in suspicion others who depart from the primitive succession, and assemble themselves together in any place whatsoever, [looking upon them] either as heretics of perverse minds, or as schismatics puffed up and self-pleasing, or again as hypocrites, acting thus for the sake of lucre and vainglory. . . .

"Those, however, who are believed to be presbyters by many, but serve their own lusts, and do not place the fear of God supreme in their hearts, but conduct themselves with contempt towards others, and are puffed up with the pride of holding the chief seat, and work evil deeds in secret, saying, 'No man sees us,' shall be convicted by the Word, who does not judge after outward appearance, nor looks upon the countenance, but the heart. . . .

"From all such persons, therefore, it behooves us to keep aloof, but to adhere to those who, as I have already observed, do hold the doctrine of the apostles, and who, together with the order of presbyters, display sound speech and blameless conduct for the confirmation and correction of others. . . .

"Such presbyters does the Church nourish, of whom also the prophet says: 'I will give thy rulers in peace, and thy bishops in righteousness.' Of whom also did the Lord declare, 'Who then shall be a faithful steward, good and wise, whom the Lord sets over His household, to give them their meat in due season? Blessed is that servant whom his Lord, when He cometh, shall find so doing.' Paul, then, teaching us where one may find such, says, 'God hath placed in the Church, first, apostles; secondly, prophets; thirdly, teachers.' Where, therefore, the gifts of the Lord have been placed, there it behooves us to learn the truth, namely, from those who possess that succession of the Church which is from the apostles, and among whom exists that which is sound and blameless in conduct, as well as that which is unadulterated and incorrupt in speech. For these also preserve this faith of ours in one God who created all things; and they increase that love which we have for the Son of God, who accomplished such marvelous dispensations for our sake: and they expound the Scriptures to us without danger, neither blaspheming God, nor dishonouring the patriarchs, nor despising the prophets."[10]

Theophilus of Antioch (c. 180)

"As in the sea there are islands, some of them habitable, and well-watered, and fruitful, with havens and harbors in which the storm-tossed may find refuge, so God has given to the world which is driven and tempest-tossed by sins, assemblies—we mean holy churches—in which survive the doctrines of the truth, as in the island-harbors of good anchorage; and into these run those who desire to be saved, being lovers of the truth, and wishing to escape the wrath and judgment of God."[11]

Tertullian of Carthage (c. 208)

"The flesh, indeed, is washed, in order that the soul may be cleansed; the flesh is anointed, that the soul may be consecrated; the flesh is signed (with the cross), that the soul too may be fortified; the flesh is shadowed with the imposition of hands, that the soul may be illuminated by the Spirit."[12]

"Then, having taken the bread and given it to His disciples, He made it His own body, by saying, 'This is my body,' that is, the figure of my body. A figure, however, there could not have been, unless there were first a veritable body."[13]

"The churches, although they are so many and so great, comprise but the one primitive church, founded by the apostles, from which they all spring. In this way all are primitive and all are apostolic, whilst they are all proved to be one, in unbroken unity, by their peaceful communion, and title of brotherhood, and bond of hospitality."[14]

Clement of Alexandria (c. 215)

"The Lord, in the Gospel according to John, brought this out by symbols, when He said: 'Eat ye my flesh, and drink my blood'; describing distinctly by metaphor the drinkable properties of faith and the promise, by means of which the Church, like a human being consisting of many members, is refreshed and grows, is welded together and compacted of both—of faith, which is the body, and of hope, which is the soul; as also the Lord of flesh and blood."[15]

Cyprian of Carthage (c. 250)

"The spouse of Christ cannot be adulterous; she is uncorrupted and pure. She knows one home; she guards with chaste modesty the sanctity of one couch. She keeps us for God. She appoints the sons whom she has borne for the kingdom. Whoever is separated from the Church and is joined to an adulteress is separated from the promises of the Church; nor can he who forsakes the Church of Christ attain to the rewards of Christ. He is a stranger; he is profane; he is an enemy. He can no longer have God for his Father, who has not the Church for his mother. If anyone could escape who was outside the ark of Noah, then he also may escape who shall be outside of the Church."[16]

"If even to the greatest sinners, and to those who had sinned much against God, when they subsequently believed, remission of sins is granted—and nobody is hindered from baptism and from grace—how much rather ought we to shrink from hindering an infant, who, being lately born, has not sinned, except in that, being born after the flesh according to Adam, he has contracted the contagion of the ancient death at its earliest birth, who approaches the more easily on this very account to the reception of the forgiveness of sins—that to him are remitted, not his own sins, but the sins of another."[17]

Apostolic Constitutions (c. 275)

"The Catholic Church is the plantation of God and His beloved vineyard; containing those who have believed in His unerring divine religion; who are the heirs by faith of His everlasting kingdom; who are partakers of His divine influence, and of the communication of the Holy Spirit; who are armed through Jesus, and have received His fear into their hearts; who enjoy the benefit of the sprinkling of the precious and innocent blood of Christ; who have free liberty to call Almighty God, Father; being fellow-heirs and joint-partakers of His beloved Son: hearken to this holy doctrine, you who enjoy His promises, as being delivered by the command of your Saviour, and agreeable to His glorious words."[18]

Basil of Caesarea (c. 364)

"Faith is perfected through baptism, baptism is established through faith, and both are completed by the same names. For as we believe in the Father and the Son and the Holy Ghost, so are we also baptized in the name of the Father and of the Son and of the Holy Ghost; first comes the confession, introducing us to salvation, and baptism follows, setting the seal upon our assent."[19]

Council of Constantinople (381)

"[We believe] in one, holy, catholic, and apostolic church. We confess one baptism for the remission of sins."[20]

Augustine of Hippo (c. 425)

"This is the meaning of the great sacrament of baptism which is solemnized among us, that all who attain to this grace should die to sin, as He is said to have died to sin, because He died in the flesh, which is the likeness of sin; and rising from the [baptismal] font regenerate, as He arose alive from the grave, should begin a new life in the Spirit.

"For from the infant newly born to the old man bent with age, as there is none shut out from baptism, so there is none who in baptism does not die to sin. But infants die only to original sin; those who are older die also to all the sins which their evil lives have added to the sin which they brought with them."[21]

"If the sentence [to be interpreted either literally or figuratively] is one of command, either forbidding a crime or vice, or enjoining an act of prudence or benevolence, it is not figurative. If, however, it seems to enjoin a crime or vice, or to forbid an act of prudence or benevolence, it is figurative. 'Except ye eat the flesh of the Son of man,' says Christ, 'and drink His blood, ye have no life in you.' This seems to enjoin a crime or a vice; it is therefore a figure, enjoining that we should have a share in the sufferings of our Lord, and that we should retain a sweet and profitable memory of the fact that His flesh was wounded and crucified for us."[22]

"This is the sacrifice of Christians: we, being many, are one body in Christ. And this also is the sacrifice which the Church continually celebrates in the sacrament of the altar, known to the faithful, in which she teaches that she herself is offered in the offering she makes to God."[23]

The Medieval Period (500–1500)

Boethius (c. 520)

"Therefore is that heavenly instruction spread throughout the world, the peoples are knit together, churches are founded, and, filling the broad earth, one body formed, whose Head, even Christ, ascended into heaven in order that the members might of necessity follow where the Head was gone. . . . This Catholic Church, then, spread throughout the world, is known by three particular marks: whatever is believed and taught in it has the authority of the Scriptures, or of universal tradition, or at least of its own and proper usage. And this authority is binding on the whole Church as is also the universal tradition of the Fathers, while each separate church exists and is governed by its private constitution and its proper rites according to difference of locality and the good judgment of each."[24]

John of Damascus (c. 740)

"We confess one baptism for the remission of sins and for life eternal. For baptism declares the Lord's death. We are indeed 'buried with the Lord through baptism,' as saith the divine Apostle. So then, as our Lord died once for all, we also must be baptized once for all, and baptized according to the Word of the Lord, *in the Name of the Father, and of the Son, and of the Holy Spirit*, being taught the confession in Father, Son, and Holy Spirit. . . . For although the divine Apostle says: *Into Christ and into His death were we baptized*, he does not mean that the invocation of baptism must be in these words, but that baptism is an image of the death of Christ. For by the three immersions, baptism signifies the three days of our Lord's entombment. The baptism then into Christ means that believers are baptized into Him. . . . And He laid on us the command to be born again of water and of the Spirit, through prayer and invocation, the Holy Spirit drawing nigh unto the water. For since man's nature is twofold, consisting of soul and body, He bestowed on us a twofold purification, of water and of the Spirit: the Spirit renewing that part in us which is after His image and likeness, and the water by the grace of the Spirit cleansing the body from sin and delivering it from corruption, the water indeed expressing the image of death, but the Spirit affording the earnest of life."[25]

"Seeing that this Adam is spiritual, it was meet that both the birth and likewise the food should be spiritual too, but since we are of a double and compound nature, it is meet that both the birth should be double and likewise the food compound. We were therefore given a birth by water and Spirit: I mean, by the holy baptism: and the food is the very bread of life, our Lord Jesus Christ, Who came down from heaven. . . . But one can put it well thus, that just as in nature the bread by the eating and the wine and the water by the drinking are changed into the body and blood of the eater and drinker, and do not become a different body from the former one, so the bread of the table and the wine and water are supernaturally changed by the invocation and presence of the Holy Spirit into the body and blood of Christ, and are not two but one and the same. Wherefore to those who partake worthily with faith, it is for the remission of sins and for life everlasting and for the safeguarding of soul and body; but to those who partake unworthily without faith, it is for chastisement and punishment, just as also the death of the Lord became to those who believe life and incorruption for the enjoyment of eternal blessedness, while to those who do not believe and to the murderers of the Lord it is for everlasting chastisement and punishment. The bread and the wine are not merely figures of the body and blood of Christ (God forbid!) but the deified body of the Lord itself: for the Lord has said, 'This is My body,' not, this is a figure of My body: and 'My blood,' not, a figure of My blood. And on a previous occasion He had said to the Jews, *Except ye eat the flesh of the Son of Man and drink His blood, ye have no life in you. For My flesh is meat indeed and My blood is drink indeed.* And again, *He that eateth Me, shall live.*"[26]

Ratramnus of Corbey (c. 830)

"Outwardly, the form of bread, which it was before, is presented, its colour is exhibited, its taste is perceived; but inwardly, a far different thing is signified, that much more precious, much more excellent, for it is heavenly, it is divine; that is, Christ's Body is shewn forth, which is beheld, is taken, is eaten, not by the bodily senses but by the gaze of the believing soul. . . .

"Do not then apply your bodily senses; they can discern nought here. Of a truth it is the Body of Christ, yet not His corporeal, but His spiritual Body; it is the Blood of Christ, yet not His corporeal, but His spiritual Blood. Nought then is to be understood here corporally, but all spiritually. It is the Body of Christ, yet not corporally; it is the Blood of Christ, yet not corporally. . . .

"In the bread which is placed on the altar, the Body of Christ is signified, as well as the body of the people who receive, to the intent he might plainly shew Christ's proper Body to be that in which He was born of the Virgin, in which He was suckled, in which He suffered, in which He died, in which He was buried, in which He rose again, in which He ascended into heaven, in which He sitteth at the right hand of the Father, and in which He shall come to judgment. But that which is placed on the Lord's Table containeth the mystery of that Body, as also again it containeth the mystery of the body of believing people, as the Apostle testifieth, 'We being many are one bread and one body in Christ.'"[27]

Gottschalk of Orbais (c. 840)

"Prudent reader, pay attention to what you are reading. Distinguish the one who has been redeemed through baptismal grace, who remains in sins by his own will, and who deservedly perishes, from the other one who was not only already redeemed by the grace of baptism, but was also in the past redeemed by the passion, death, and blood of Christ the Lord and who for this reason cannot perish, because his redeemer, by dying, deigned to find this lost one. By the redemption of baptism the infants are also absolved only from original sin. In the same way any adults are redeemed by baptism only from past sins. But the elect are justified gratuitously by the grace of the mediator in the blood of the second Adam.

"Blessed reader, pay special attention to what is said: *One Lord, one faith, one baptism, one God* (Eph. 4:5–6). For just as baptism is one, although each Christian is baptized three times, that is, dipped by a threefold immersion, so also the Father and Son and the Holy Spirit are one with respect to the nature and three with respect to the persons—God, the Lord, and the Spirit—and yet each person is undoubtedly in himself perfect God, Lord, and Spirit. Likewise, just as the Lord first baptized the apostles with water and then with the Holy Spirit and fire, as he himself had promised, still let them not be known and believed to have received three baptisms—God forbid!—but rather one, that is, on account of the Holy Spirit, whose baptism is wholly perfect and also complete in power."[28]

Peter Abelard (c. 1140)

"If someone already believes and loves before he is baptized . . . and truly repents of his previous sins . . . I do not hesitate to say that he is righteous or has righteousness, which renders to each person what is his. Therefore, we say that Jeremiah and John were sanctified from the womb, where, having been spiritually illuminated, they already knew and loved God, although it was still necessary for them to receive the sacrament of circumcision which then held the place of baptism.

"Why therefore, will you say, was it necessary that they be circumcised or baptized later who before were already righteous by the faith and charity they had and who, if they then died, would have had to be saved? . . . But we believe that everyone who loves God sincerely and purely for [God] himself is already predestined to life."[29]

Peter Lombard (c. 1160)

"Let us now proceed to the sacraments of the New Law, which are: baptism, confirmation, the bread of blessing (that is, the Eucharist), penance, extreme unction, orders, marriage. Of these, some offer a remedy against sin and confer helping grace, like baptism; others are only a remedy, like marriage; others fortify us with grace and virtue, like the Eucharist and orders.[30]

"Now let us proceed to the consideration of sacred ordination. . . .

"And in the sacrament of the sevenfold Spirit, there are seven ecclesiastical degrees, namely of door-keeper, lector, exorcist, acolyte, subdeacon, deacon, priest. And yet all are called clerics, that is 'chosen by lot.' . . .

"Although all [orders] are spiritual and sacred, yet the canons rate only two as excellently to be called sacred orders, namely the diaconate and presbyterate, because we read that these were the only two which the primitive Church had, and only concerning these do we have the Apostle's precept. For the Apostles ordained bishops and priests in each city. . . . But as for subdeacons and acolytes, the Church established them for herself in the course of time."[31]

Stephen Langton (c. 1200)

"The will to be baptized avails as much for the man who does not have the opportunity as the will plus the fact of baptism for the other, if you add, 'In the same state of charity.' For all works done in the same state of charity are equally meritorious, and yet to be baptized is nonetheless effectual for him who is baptized, because on the occasion of baptism charity grows in him."[32]

Thomas Aquinas (c. 1265)

"There are places called churches in which the Christian people gather together for the divine worship. Thus our church takes the place of both temple and synagogue: since the very sacrifice of the Church is spiritual; wherefore with us the place of sacrifice is not distinct from the place of teaching. The figurative reason may be that hereby is signified the unity of the Church, whether militant or triumphant."[33]

Meister Eckhart (c. 1300)

"Those who would like to partake of the body of our Lord should not wait until they feel an upsurge of emotion or devotion, but let them rather consider their attitude or disposition [toward it]. Attach significance, not to what you feel like, but rather to what you are to receive and to your thoughts about it. . . .

"But perhaps you say: 'Yes, sir, but I feel so bare and cold and dull that I dare not go to the Lord!' To which I reply:

"So much the more your need to go to God! Being joined to him, made one with him, you will be justified: for the grace you shall find in the sacrament will nowhere else be so evident. There, your physical powers will be assembled and focused by the superlative power of the presence of our Lord's body, the scattered senses brought together into union, and several of them, being aimed too low, will be lifted up so that they, too, point, like true offerings, to God."[34]

Pope Boniface VIII (1302)

"That there is one Holy Catholic and Apostolic church we are impelled by our faith to believe and to hold—this we do firmly believe and openly confess—and outside of this there is neither salvation or remission of sins. . . . The church represents one mystic body and of this body Christ is the head; of Christ, indeed, God is the head. In it is one Lord, and one faith and one baptism. . . .

"In this church and in its power are two swords, to wit, a spiritual and a temporal, and this we are taught by the words of the Gospel, for when the Apostle said, 'Behold, here are two swords' (in the church, namely, since the apostles were speaking), the Lord did not reply that it was too many, but enough. . . . Both, therefore, the spiritual and the material swords, are in the power of the church, the latter indeed to be used for the church, the former by the church, the one by the priest, the other by the hand of kings and soldiers, but by the will and sufferance of the priest. It is fitting, moreover, that one sword should be under the other, and the temporal authority subject to the spiritual power. . . . Hence this power, although given to man and exercised by man, is not human, but rather a divine power, given by the divine lips to Peter, and founded on a rock for Him and his successors in Him [Christ] whom he confessed; the Lord saying to Peter himself, 'Whatsoever thou shalt bind' etc. Whoever, therefore, shall resist this power, ordained by God, resists the ordination of God. . . . We, moreover, proclaim, declare, and pronounce that it is altogether necessary to salvation for every human being to be subject to the Roman Pontiff."[35]

John Wycliffe (c. 1380)

"If you say that Christ's Church must have a head here on earth, so it is, for Christ is Head, who must be here with His Church until the day of doom, and everywhere by his Godhead."[36]

John Hus (c. 1419)

"The holy catholic church is the number of all the predestinate and Christ's mystical body—Christ being himself the head—and the bride of Christ, whom he of his great love redeemed with his blood that he might at last possess her as glorious, not having wrinkle of mortal sin or spot of venial sin, or anything else defiling her, but that she might be holy and without spot, perpetually embracing Christ, the bridegroom."[37]

"The holy catholic—that is, universal—church is the totality of the predestinate—*omnium predestinatorum universitas*—or all the predestinate, present, past, and future."[38]

"[The] holy universal church is one and consists of all the predestinate that are to be saved and . . . Christ alone is the head of the church, just as he alone is the most exalted person in the church, imparting to it and to its members motion and understanding unto the life of grace."[39]

"No place, or human election, makes a person a member of the holy universal church, but divine predestination does in the case of every one who persists in following Christ in love. And, according to Augustine . . . predestination is the election of the divine will through grace; or, as it is commonly said, predestination is the preparation of grace—making ready—in the present time, and of glory in the future."[40]

The Protestant Period (1500–1700)

Martin Luther (c. 1525)

"I believe that there is upon earth a little holy group and congregation of pure saints, under one head, even Christ, called together by the Holy Ghost in one faith, one mind, and understanding, with manifold gifts, yet agreeing in love, without sects or schisms. I am also a part and member of the same, a sharer and joint owner of all the goods it possesses, brought to it and incorporated into it by the Holy Ghost by having heard and continuing to hear the Word of God, which is the beginning of entering it."[41]

The Augsburg Confession (1530)

"They [Lutheran Churches] teach that one holy Church is to continue forever. The Church is the congregation of saints, in which the Gospel is rightly taught and the Sacraments are rightly administered.

"And to the true unity of the Church it is enough to agree concerning the doctrine of the Gospel and the administration of the Sacraments. Nor is it necessary that human traditions, that is, rites or ceremonies, instituted by men, should be everywhere alike. As Paul says: One faith, one Baptism, one God and Father of all, etc."[42]

John Calvin (1559)

"The Church is called Catholic or Universal, for two or three cannot be invented without dividing Christ; and this is impossible. All the elect of God are so joined together in Christ, that as they depend on one head, so they are as it were compacted together into one body, being knit together like its different members; made truly one by living together under the same Spirit of God in one faith, hope, and charity, called not only to the same inheritance of eternal life, but to participation in one God and Christ."[43]

"Wherever we see the Word of God purely preached and heard, and the sacraments administered according to Christ's institution, there, it is not to be doubted, a church of God exists."[44]

The Church of England (1563)

"The visible Church of Christ is a congregation of faithful men, in which the pure Word of God is preached, and the Sacraments be duly ministered according to Christ's ordinance, in all those things that of necessity are requisite to the same.

"As the Churches of Jerusalem, Alexandria, and Antioch have erred, so also the Church of Rome hath erred, not only in their living and manner of Ceremonies, but also in matters of Faith."[45]

"Sacraments ordained of Christ be not only badges or tokens of Christian men's profession, but rather they be certain sure witnesses, and effectual signs of grace, and God's good will towards us, by the which he doth work invisibly in us, and doth not only quicken, but also strengthen and confirm our Faith in him.

"There are two Sacraments ordained of Christ our Lord in the Gospel, that is to say, Baptism, and the Supper of the Lord."[46]

"Baptism is not only a sign of profession, and mark of difference, whereby Christian men are discerned from others that be not christened, but it is also a sign of Regeneration or New-Birth, whereby, as by an instrument, they that receive Baptism rightly are grafted into the Church; the promises of the forgiveness of sin, and of our adoption to be the sons of God by the Holy Ghost, are visibly signed and sealed; Faith is confirmed, and Grace increased by virtue of prayer unto God.

"The Baptism of young Children is in any wise to be retained in the Church, as most agreeable with the institution of Christ."[47]

"The Supper of the Lord is not only a sign of the love that Christians ought to have among themselves one to another, but rather it is a Sacrament of our Redemption by Christ's death: insomuch that to such as rightly, worthily, and with faith, receive the same, the Bread which we break is a partaking of the Body of Christ; and likewise the Cup of Blessing is a partaking of the Blood of Christ.

"Transubstantiation (or the change of the substance of Bread and Wine) in the Supper of the Lord, cannot be proved by Holy Writ, but is repugnant to the plain words of Scripture, overthrows the nature of a Sacrament, and hath given occasion to many superstitions.

"The Body of Christ is given, taken, and eaten, in the Supper, only after a heavenly and spiritual manner. And the means whereby the Body of Christ is received and eaten in the Supper is Faith."[48]

Belgic Confession (1619)

"The marks by which the true Church is known are these: if the pure doctrine of the gospel is preached therein; if she maintains the pure administration of the sacraments as instituted by Christ; if church discipline is exercised in the punishing of sin: in short, if all things are managed according to the pure Word of God, all things contrary thereto rejected, and Jesus Christ acknowledged as the only Head of the Church. Hereby the true Church may certainly be known, from which no man has a right to separate himself."[49]

Westminster Confession (1646)

"The catholic or universal Church, which is invisible, consists of the whole number of the elect, which have been, are, or shall be gathered into one, under Christ the Head thereof; and is the spouse, the body, the fullness of Him that filleth all in all.

"The visible Church, which is also catholic or universal under the gospel (not confined to one nation, as before under the law), consists of all those throughout the world that profess the true religion; and of their children: and is the kingdom of the Lord Jesus Christ, the house and family of God, [apart from] which there is no ordinary possibility of salvation.

"Unto this catholic visible Church Christ hath given the ministry, oracles, and ordinances of God, for the gathering and perfecting of the saints, in this life to the end of the world: and doth, by His own presence and Spirit, according to His promise, make them effectual thereunto.

"This catholic Church hath been sometimes more, sometimes less visible. And particular churches, which are members thereof, are more or less pure, according as the doctrine of the gospel is taught and embraced, ordinances administered, and public worship performed more or less purely in them."[50]

"Baptism is a sacrament of the New Testament, ordained by Jesus Christ, not only for the solemn admission of the party baptized into the visible Church, but also to be unto him a sign and seal of the covenant of grace, of his ingrafting into Christ, of regeneration, or remission of sins, and of his giving up unto God, through Jesus Christ, to walk in newness of life: which sacrament is, by Christ's own appointment, to be continued in his Church until the end of the world. . . .

"Although it be a great sin to condemn or neglect this ordinance, yet grace and salvation are not so inseparably annexed unto it that no person can be regenerated or saved without it, or that all that are baptized are undoubtedly regenerated."[51]

"Our Lord Jesus, on the night wherein he was betrayed, instituted the sacrament of his body and blood, called the Lord's Supper, to be observed in his Church, unto the end of the world; for the perpetual remembrance of the sacrifice of himself in his death, the sealing of all benefits thereof unto true believers, their spiritual nourishment and growth in him, their further engagement in, and to all duties which they owe unto him; and to be a bond and pledge of their communion with him, and with each other, as members of his mystical body."[52]

"They who are effectually called and regenerated, having a new heart and a new spirit created in them, are further sanctified, really and personally, through the virtue of Christ's death and resurrection, by his Word and Spirit dwelling in them; the dominion of the whole body of sin is destroyed, and the several lusts thereof are more and more weakened and mortified, and they more and more quickened and strengthened, in all saving graces, to the practice of true holiness, without which no man shall see the Lord.

"This sanctification is throughout in the whole man, yet imperfect in this life; there abideth still some remnants of corruption in every part, whence ariseth a continual and irreconcilable war, the flesh lusting against the spirit, and the spirit against the flesh."[53]

Francis Turretin (c. 1680)

"[Sanctification] is used strictly for a real and internal renovation of man by which God delivers the man planted in Christ by faith and justified (by the ministry of the word and the efficacy of the Spirit) more and more from his native depravity and transforms him into his own image. Thus with separation from the world and sin and consecration to the service of God, it implies a renovation of his nature."[54]

Baptist Philadelphia Confession (1688)

"The Catholic or Universal Church which (with respect to the internal work of the Spirit and truth of grace) may be called invisible, consists of the whole number of the elect, that have been, are, or shall be gathered into one, under Christ, the head thereof: and is the spouse, the body, the fullness of him that filleth all in all."[55]

The Modern Period (1700–Present)

John Wesley (c. 1745)

"The catholic or universal Church is all the persons in the universe whom God hath so called out of the world as to entitle them to the preceding character; as to be 'one body,' united by 'one spirit;' having 'one faith, one hope, one baptism; one God and Father of all, who is above all, and through all, and in them all.'"[56]

Articles of the Reformed Episcopal Church (1876)

"The souls dispersed in all the world, who adhere to Christ by faith, who are partakers of the Holy Ghost, and worship the Father in spirit and in truth, are the body of Christ, the house of God, the flock of the Good Shepherd—the holy, universal Christian Church. A visible Church of Christ is a congregation of believers in which the pure Word of God is preached and Baptism and the Lord's Supper are duly ministered according to Christ's ordinance, in all those things that of necessity are requisite to the same. And those things are to be considered requisite which the Lord himself did, he himself commanded, and his apostles confirmed."[57]

Francis Pieper (1924)

"The doctrine of the Church is of such a nature that if a person erred earlier, all his doctrinal errors will reappear in his teaching concerning the Church. Since membership in the Christian Church is established solely by faith in Christ, the scriptural doctrine of the Church presupposes a correct understanding of justification by faith: the objective reconciliation of all sinful mankind by Christ's *satisfactio vicaria* [vicarious satisfaction], the bestowal of the forgiveness of sins by the means of grace, the appropriation of the remission of sins by faith, created and sustained solely by the Holy Ghost, without any cooperation of man. Without these prerequisites one's concept of the Church cannot be scriptural."[58]

"The Church is *universal* or catholic (*ecclesia universalis sive catholica*) because it embraces all believers in Christ, of all eras, among all nations, and at all places. The Christian faith has never changed its character in the course of the ages. It has always been faith in the remission of sins resulting from Christ's work of redemption. This teaching is not, as is frequently claimed, a dogma devised by Luther and the old Lutheran dogmaticians, but is the doctrine of the Apostles of Christ and of Christ Himself."[59]

Robert Saucy (1972)

"The presence of the Holy Spirit gives the church a supernatural dynamic and therefore makes it unique among all human bodies. The real church is manifest only where the holy presence and work of the Spirit are known. Failure of the church as a vital factor in the world is the result of failure to recognize the reality of the person of the Spirit living in the church as its dynamic force."[60]

Thomas Oden (1992)

"The church is one, finding its oneness in Christ. The church is holy, set apart from the world to mediate life to the world and bring forth the fruits of the Spirit amid the life of the world. The church is catholic in that it is whole, for all, and embracing all times and places. The church is apostolic in that it is grounded in the testimony of the first witnesses to Jesus' life and resurrection, and depends upon and continues their ministry."[61]

Evangelical Free Church of America (2008)

"We believe that the true church comprises all who have been justified by God's grace through faith alone in Christ alone. They are united by the Holy Spirit in the body of Christ, of which He is the Head. The true church is manifest in local churches, whose membership should be composed only of believers. The Lord Jesus mandated two ordinances, baptism and the Lord's Supper, which visibly and tangibly express the gospel. Though they are not the means of salvation, when celebrated by the church in genuine faith, these ordinances confirm and nourish the believer."[62]

Gregg Allison (2012)

"The church is the people of God who have been saved through repentance and faith in Jesus Christ and have been incorporated into his body through baptism with the Holy Spirit. It consists of two interrelated elements: the universal church is the fellowship of all Christians that extends from the day of Pentecost until the second coming, incorporating both the deceased believers who are presently in heaven and the living believers from all over the world. This universal church becomes manifested in local churches characterized by being doxological, logocentric, pneumadynamic, covenantal, confessional, missional, and spatio-temporal/eschatological."[63]

Shelf Space: *Recommendations for Your Library*

This book provides central themes, essential passages, and a basic orientation to major Christian doctrines from a broadly orthodox protestant evangelical perspective. One could spend several lifetimes exploring these topics in greater detail; for help with delving deeper into some of them, we've provided the following recommendations for your library. We've included brief notes describing the content and orientation of each book as well as a general rating (beginner, intermediate, or advanced). You should find representative voices from a variety of evangelical perspectives.

General Books on Ecclesiology

Allison, Gregg R. *Sojourners and Strangers: The Doctrine of the Church*. Wheaton, IL: Crossway, 2012. This well-rounded and comprehensive work on ecclesiology is written from an irenic dispensational perspective and is part of the respected *Foundations of Evangelical Theology* series. [INTERMEDIATE]

Bannerman, D. Douglas. *The Scripture Doctrine of the Church*. Reprint, Grand Rapids: Baker, 1976. This is perhaps the most famous work on the church from Bannerman, a Free Church of Scotland minister (a conservative Presbyterian). It presents a covenant view of the church from the time of Abraham to the present age. [INTERMEDIATE]

Berkouwer, G. C. *The Church*. Grand Rapids: Eerdmans, 1976. A magisterial presentation of ecclesiology from a Dutch Reformed perspective; it's unique enough to have earned its own label, "Middle Orthodoxy." This volume is esteemed by friend and foe alike. [ADVANCED]

Bonhoeffer, Dietrich. *The Communion of Saints: A Dogmatic Inquiry into the Sociology of the Church*. New York: Harper & Row, 1963. Bonhoeffer's famous wrestling with the concept of the *Sanctorum Communio*—the Communion of Saints. [ADVANCED]

Bonhoeffer, Dietrich. *Life Together*. Trans. John H. Doberstein. New York: Harper

& Row, 1954. Powerful and brief, this little gem alone would secure Bonhoeffer's place in history. [INTERMEDIATE]

Clowney, Edmund P. *The Church*. Downer's Grove, IL: InterVarsity, 1995. A current standard in ecclesiology and one of the best works on the church from the perspective of covenant theology. [INTERMEDIATE]

Dulles, Avery. *Models of the Church*. Expanded ed. New York: Doubleday, 1987. A probing and thoughtful analysis of various approaches to understanding the church from a modern Roman Catholic perspective. [ADVANCED]

Ferguson, Everett. *The Church of Christ: A Biblical Ecclesiology for Today*. Grand Rapids: Eerdmans, 1996. This highly regarded work of Ferguson, a renowned scholar, defends the doctrinal distinctives of the Churches of Christ. [INTERMEDIATE]

Horrell, J. Scott. *From the Ground Up: New Testament Foundations for the 21st Century Church*. Grand Rapids: Kregel, 2004. This booklet (ninety-four pages) introduces ecclesiology in a friendly format while staying in close contact with the New Testament text. [BEGINNER]

Littell, Franklin H. *The Anabaptist View of the Church*. Boston: Starr King, 1958. A respected investigation of the history of the Anabaptist movement and its more recent forms. [ADVANCED]

Radmacher, Earl D. *The Nature of the Church: A Biblical and Historical Study*. Hayesville, NC: Schoettle, 1996. Written from a dispensational perspective; respected for its thoroughness and clarity. [ADVANCED]

Saucy, Robert. *The Church in God's Program*. Chicago: Moody, 1972. Written from a dispensational perspective. [INTERMEDIATE]

Stackhouse, John G. Jr., ed. *Evangelical Ecclesiology: Reality or Illusion?* Grand Rapids: Baker, 2003. A collection of essays written by a variety of scholars, this volume is a mixed bag that offers challenging questions and stimulating discussion while depicting the breadth of evangelical thought on ecclesiology. [ADVANCED]

Stedman, Ray C. *Body Life*. 3rd ed. Glendale, CA: Gospel Light/Regal, 1979. Written in an easily accessible style, this book fueled widespread interest in biblical authenticity in thinking about the church. [INTERMEDIATE]

Svigel, Michael J. *RetroChristianity: Reclaiming the Forgotten Faith*. Wheaton, IL: Crossway, 2012. This easy-to-read and yet comprehensive book sorts through the nuggets of the ages and reclaims the best of the church's rich heritage. [INTERMEDIATE]

Volf, Miroslav. *After Our Likeness: The Church as the Image of the Trinity*. Grand Rapids: Eerdmans, 1997. Charting a most unique course, Volf's emphasis is on the Trinity as the basis for ecclesiology. [ADVANCED]

Walvoord, John F. *The Church in Prophecy*. Grand Rapids: Zondervan, 1964. A dispensational view, emphasizing the church's future. [ADVANCED]

Webber, Robert E. *Common Roots*. Grand Rapids: Zondervan, 1978. A thoughtful discussion of evangelicalism's historical roots with insightful suggestions on how it might stimulate further maturation in its ecclesiology. [ADVANCED]

Willimon, William H. *What's Right with the Church*. San Francisco: Harper & Row, 1985. Written from a broadly mainline church perspective, this volume celebrates the church's successes. [INTERMEDIATE]

Yancey, Philip. *Church: Why Bother?* Grand Rapids: Zondervan, 1998. Easy- to-read yet thought-provoking, this brief book encourages us to consider the church's strengths. [BEGINNER]

Books on Baptism and the Lord's Supper

Armstrong, John H., ed. *Understanding Four Views on Baptism*. Grand Rapids:

Zondervan, 2007. A presentation of the major views on baptism with responses from contributors. [INTERMEDIATE]

Armstrong, John H., ed. *Understanding Four Views on the Lord's Supper*. Grand Rapids: Zondervan, 2007. A presentation of the major views on the Lord's Supper with responses from contributors. [INTERMEDIATE]

Baillie, Donald. *The Theology of the Sacraments*. New York: Scribner's, 1957. A fairly broad-minded discussion of the sacraments' theological bases. [ADVANCED]

Barrett, C. K. *Church Ministry and Sacraments in the New Testament*. Grand Rapids: Eerdmans, 1985. A respected survey of the biblical bases of ministry in the church. [ADVANCED]

Beasley-Murray, George R. *Baptism in the New Testament*. Grand Rapids: Eerdmans, 1962. A towering work on baptism. [ADVANCED]

Berkouwer, G. C. *The Sacraments*. Grand Rapids: Eerdmans, 1969. An insightful and highly regarded discussion. Written from a moderate Dutch Reformed perspective. [ADVANCED]

Ferguson, Everett. *Baptism in the Early Church: History, Theology, and Liturgy in the First Five Centuries*. Grand Rapids: Eerdmans, 2009. The most respected and thorough investigation of the practice of baptism in the early church. Unequalled. [ADVANCED]

Jewett, Paul K. *Infant Baptism and the Covenant of Grace*. Grand Rapids: Eerdmans, 1978. A stunning defense of believer's baptism written from the perspective of covenant theology. [INTERMEDIATE]

Moore, Russell D. *Understanding Four Views on the Lord's Supper*. Grand Rapids: Zondervan, 2007. Essays defending and responses challenging Baptist, Reformed, Lutheran, and Roman Catholic views on the Lord's Supper. [INTERMEDIATE]

Witherington, Ben. *Making a Meal of It: Rethinking the Theology of the Lord's Supper*. Waco, TX: Baylor, 2007. An accessible treatment that emphasizes the practice's historical development. [INTERMEDIATE]

Witherington, Ben. *Troubled Waters: Rethinking the Theology of Baptism*. Waco, TX: Baylor, 2007. A middle-road approach, affirming aspects of believer's baptism and infant baptism. [INTERMEDIATE]

Books on Church Government and Polity

Cowan, Stephen B. *Who Runs the Church? Four Views on Church Government*. Grand Rapids: Zondervan, 2004. Essays defending and responses challenging Episcopal, Presbyterian, Single-Elder Congregational, and Plural-Elder Congregational views on the Lord's Supper. [INTERMEDIATE]

Strauch, Alexander. *Biblical Eldership*. Littleton, CO: Lewis and Roth, 1988. [INTERMEDIATE]

Warkentin, Marjorie. *Ordination: A Biblical-Historical View*. Grand Rapids: Eerdmans, 1982. An investigation into the biblical bases and historical practices of ordination in several different traditions. [INTERMEDIATE]

Books on Worship and Church Ministry

Peterson, David. *Engaging with God: A Biblical Theology of Worship*. Downers Grove, IL: InterVarsity, 2002. A comprehensive examination of biblical texts on worship in the church. [ADVANCED]

Wilson, Jonathan. *Why Church Matters: Worship, Ministry, and Mission*. Grand Rapids: Baker, 2006. A challenge to reconsider what worship in the church entails. [INTERMEDIATE]

Books on Distinct Denominational Ecclesiologies

Aarflot, Andreas. *Let the Church Be the Church: The Voice and Mission of the People of God*. Minneapolis: Augsburg, 1988. A Lutheran perspective from a bishop in the Church of Norway. [INTERMEDIATE]

Avis, Paul D. L. *The Church in the Theology of the Reformers*. Atlanta: John Knox, 1981. A well-written and well-respected work tracing the ecclesiological emphases of the Reformation. [INTERMEDIATE]

Avis, Paul D. L. *The Identity of Anglicanism: Essentials of Anglican Ecclesiology*. London: T. & T. Clark, 2007. An introduction to Anglicanism's unique protestant episcopal ecclesiology. [INTERMEDIATE]

Durnbaugh, Donald F. *The Believer's Church: The History and Character of Radical Protestantism*. New York: Macmillan, 1968. A defense of the unique ecclesiology of the Church of the Brethren. [INTERMEDIATE]

Harvey, H. *The Church: Its Polity and Ordinances*. Reprint ed. Rochester, NY: Backus, 1982. A classic defense of Baptist polity. [INTERMEDIATE]

Jackson, Paul R. *The Doctrine and Administration of the Church*. Des Plaines, IL.: Regular Baptist, 1968. A highly regarded exposition of Baptist polity from a conservative Baptist vantage. [INTERMEDIATE]

Kuiper, R. B. *The Glorious Body of Christ*. Grand Rapids: Eerdmans, 1967. Influential discussion from a Reformed perspective. [INTERMEDIATE]

MacGregor, Geddes. *Corpus Christi: The Nature of the Church According to the Reformed Tradition*. Philadelphia: Westminster, 1958. Classic defense of a Presbyterian ecclesiology from historical and dogmatic perspectives. [ADVANCED]

General Books on Sanctification and the Christian Life

Alexander, Donald L., ed. *Christian Spirituality: Five Views of Sanctification*. Downers Grove, IL: InterVarsity, 1988. This "five views" book follows the traditional format of essays and responses. Perhaps most compelling is its inclusion of a Lutheran view of sanctification. [INTERMEDIATE]

Bolsinger, Tod E. *It Takes a Church to Raise a Christian: How the Community of God Transforms Lives*. Grand Rapids: Brazos, 2004. A popularly written suggestion that church should be viewed as community life based on a Trinitarian spirituality. [BEGINNER]

Bonhoeffer, Dietrich. *The Cost of Discipleship*. New York: Macmillan, 1963. A classic work on the cost of commitment to Christ. [INTERMEDIATE]

Bridges, Jerry. *The Practice of Godliness*. Colorado Springs: NavPress, 1983. A collection of short devotionals pointing toward the value of living a godward life. [BEGINNER]

Bridges, Jerry. *The Pursuit of Holiness*. Colorado Springs: NavPress, 1996. Another such collection on the need for seeking godliness. [BEGINNER]

Dieter, Melvin, et al. *Five Views of Sanctification*. Grand Rapids: Zondervan, 1987. Another "five views" book (essays/responses format), including an essay on the "Augustinian-Dispensational" view. [INTERMEDIATE]

Elder, E. Rozanne, ed. *The Spirituality of Western Christendom*. Kalamazoo, MI: Cistercian, 1984. A respected treatment of various perspectives on spirituality throughout Christian history. [INTERMEDIATE]

Ferguson, Sinclair B. *Christian Spirituality*. Downers Grove, IL: InterVarsity, 1988. This "five views" book includes a controversial essay on Lutheran sanctification by Gerhard Forde. [INTERMEDIATE]

Foster, Richard J. *Celebration of Discipline: The Path to Spiritual Growth*. San Francisco: Harper & Row, 1978. Famous investigation of some traditional disciplines and their role in spirituality. [BEGINNER]

Foster, Richard J. *Streams of Living Water*. San Francisco: HarperSanFrancisco, 1998. An investigation of the major perspectives on Christian spirituality. [BEGINNER]

Land, Steven J. *Pentecostal Spirituality: A Passion for the Kingdom*. Journal of Pentecostal Theology Supplement Series 1. Sheffield, UK: Sheffield Academic, 1993. Defense of a Pentecostal view. [INTERMEDIATE]

Lawrence, Brother. *The Practice of the Presence of God with Spiritual Maxims*. Grand Rapids: Baker, 1967. Timeless classic; investigates an awareness of God's presence and its effect on spirituality. [BEGINNER]

Packer, J. I. *Keep in Step with the Spirit*. Old Tappan, NJ: Revell, 1984. Highly regarded work on the Christian life from a Reformed perspective. [INTERMEDIATE]

Piper, John. *Desiring God*. Portland, OR: Multnomah, 1986. The famous book that spawned a ministry; investigates a spirituality that emphasizes the believer's pleasure in God. [BEGINNER]

Schaeffer, Francis. *True Spirituality*. Wheaton, IL: Tyndale, 1971. A classic that wrestles with spirituality and the bonds of sin. [INTERMEDIATE]

Sproul, R. C. *Pleasing God*. Wheaton, IL: Tyndale, 1988. A discussion of sanctification from a Reformed perspective. [BEGINNER]

Toon, Peter. *Spiritual Companions: An Introduction to the Christian Classics*. Reprint, Grand Rapids: Baker, 1992. A collection of snippets taken from classic writings on Christian spirituality. [INTERMEDIATE]

Webber, Robert E. *The Divine Embrace: Recovering the Passionate Spiritual Life*. Grand Rapids: Baker, 2006. A look at how culture has influenced concepts of spirituality throughout church history. [INTERMEDIATE]

Books on Distinct Perspectives on Sanctification

Belew, Pascal P. *The Case for Entire Sanctification*. Kansas City, MO: Beacon Hill, 1974. Argues for the possibility of entire sanctification in this life from a Wesleyan/Holiness perspective. [INTERMEDIATE]

Berkouwer, G. C. *Faith and Sanctification*. Studies in Dogmatics Series. Trans. John Vriend. Grand Rapids: Eerdmans, 1952. A classic on sanctification from a Dutch Reformed vantage. [ADVANCED]

Chafer, Lewis Sperry. *He That Is Spiritual*. Grand Rapids: Zondervan, 1967. A short volume that expounds Chafer's unique approach to a life rightly related to the Holy Spirit. [INTERMEDIATE]

Grider, J. Kenneth. *Entire Sanctification: The Distinctive Doctrine of Wesleyanism*. Kansas City, MO: Beacon Hill, 1980. Highly respected book on entire sanctification and Spirit baptism in the Holiness movement. [INTERMEDIATE]

Pentecost, J. Dwight. *Designed to Be Like Him: Understanding God's Plan for Fellowship, Conduct, Conflict, and Maturity*. Chicago: Moody, 1966. A justly famous explication of a dispensational perspective on the Christian life. [INTERMEDIATE]

Pink, Arthur W. *The Doctrine of Sanctification*. Swengel, PA: Reiner, 1966. A time-honored presentation of sanctification from a Reformed perspective. [INTERMEDIATE]

Ryrie, Charles C. *Balancing the Christian Life*. Chicago: Moody, 1969. An approachable discussion of concepts and difficulties. [BEGINNER]

Wesley, John. *A Plain Account of Christian Perfection*. Reprint ed. London: Epworth Press. Probably the most influential work on sanctification in the entire Holiness movement. [INTERMEDIATE]

NOTES

Introduction: The Christian Story in Four Acts

1. See Steven A. Galipeau, *The Journey of Luke Skywalker: An Analysis of Modern Myth and Symbol* (Peru, IL: Carus, 2001); Mary Henderson, *Star Wars: The Magic of Myth* (New York: Spectra, 1997).

2. For a classic discussion of ancient hero myths, see Joseph Campbell, *The Hero with a Thousand Faces*, 3rd rev. ed., Joseph Campbell Foundation (Novato, CA: New World Library, 2008).

3. See James Bonnet, *Stealing Fire from the Gods: The Complete Guide for Writers and Filmmakers,* 2nd ed. (Studio City, CA: Michael Wiese, 2006); Christopher Vogler, *The Writer's Journey: Mythic Structures for Writers*, 3rd ed. (Studio City, CA: Michael Wiese, 2007); Stuart Voytilla, *Myth and the Movies: Discovering the Mythic Structure of 50 Unforgettable Films* (Studio City, CA: Michael Wiese, 1999).

4. Col. 1:15–16; see also Gen. 1:1–2, 26; John 1:1–3; Heb. 1:2.

5. Heb. 1:1–2

6. See, e.g., Eph. 2:10; Phil. 2:12–13; Matt. 28:19–20.

7. St. Augustine, *Confessions* [1.1.1], ed., trans. Henry Chadwick (Oxford: Oxford, 1998), 3.

Part One: "Created in Christ Jesus: Church, Churches, and the Christian Life" by Nathan D. Holsteen

High-Altitude Survey

1. Herman J. Selderhuis, ed., *The Calvin Handbook* (Grand Rapids: Eerdmans, 2009), 151.

Passages to Master

1. Michael J. Svigel, *RetroChristianity: Reclaiming the Forgotten Faith* (Wheaton, IL: Crossway, 2012), 25.

2. Augustine, *City of God,* 11.3, in *Post-Nicene Fathers of the Christian Church*, eds. Philip Schaff and Henry Wace. 1st series, 14 vols. (Grand Rapids: Eerdmans, 1956), 2:206.

3. Anselm, *Why God Became Man,* 1.18 (St. Anselm, *Proslogium; Monologium; An Appendix on Behalf of the Fool by Gaunilon;* and *Cur Deus Homo,* repr. ed., trans. Sidney North Deane [La Salle, IL: Open Court, 1926], 220).

4. Cited in William C. Placher, ed., *Readings in the History of Christian Theology,* vol. 2, *From the Reformation to the Present* (Philadelphia: Westminster, 1988), 11.

5. George Smeaton, *The Doctrine of the Holy Spirit* (Edinburgh: T&T Clark, 1882), 230.

6. R. B. Kuiper (1886–1966) was professor of theology at (and a founder of) Westminster Theological Seminary and also served as president of Calvin Theological Seminary.

7. Kuiper, *The Glorious Body of Christ* (Grand Rapids: Eerdmans, 1966), 21–22.

8. D. Douglas Bannerman, *The Scripture Doctrine of the Church* (Edinburgh: T&T Clark, 1887), 5.

9. Millard Erickson, *Christian Theology* (Grand Rapids: Baker, 1983), 1047–49.

10. Dan Piraro, *Bizarro*, syndicated cartoon distributed by King Features, December 21, 2009. Available at bizarrocomics.com.

11. Israel's relationship to these promises is affirmed, e.g., in Romans 9:4. Accordingly, Israel had inherited the promises God gave to Abraham (involving land, seed, and blessing—see Gen. 15 and Gen. 17), but her faithlessness has caused her to be cut off from the promises.

12. Edmund Clowney, *The Church* (Downer's Grove, IL: InterVarsity, 1995), 53–54.

13. For example, that unbelieving Israel is represented by the branches broken off the olive tree, and that believing Israel is represented by the natural branches of a cultivated olive tree, would seem to fly in the face of the assertion that the tree itself is Israel.

14. See George Eldon Ladd's essay, "Historic Premillennialism," in Robert G. Clouse, ed., *The Meaning of the Millennium: Four Views* (Downer's Grove, IL: InterVarsity, 1977), Kindle locations 208–209.

15. Scot McKnight, *1 Peter,* The NIV Application Commentary (Grand Rapids: Zondervan, 1996), Google Play edition, 99–100.

16. *Mrs. Doubtfire*. Dir. Chris Columbus (Los Angeles: Twentieth-Century Fox, 1993).

17. See, e.g., R. Scott Clark's well-written defense of this view at clark.wscal.edu/israel.php.

18. For a powerfully argued defense of this view, see S. Lewis Johnson Jr., "Paul and 'The Israel of God': An Exegetical and Eschatological Case-Study" in *The Masters Seminary Journal* 20/1 (Spring 2009): 41–55.

19. Dr. Seuss, *The Cat in the Hat* (New York: Random, 1957).

20. Anthony A. Hoekema, "The Reformed Perspective" in *Five Views on Sanctification,* ed. Melvin Dieter (Grand Rapids: Zondervan, 1987), 61.

21. For example, see C. E. B. Cranfield, *A Critical and Exegetical Commentary on the Epistle to the Romans,* vol. 1, *Introduction and Commentary on Romans I–VIII,* The International Critical Commentary on the Holy Scriptures of the Old and New Testaments, eds. J. A. Emerton, et al. (Edinburgh: T. & T. Clark, 1975), 347.

22. For a representative defense of this view, see C. K. Barrett, *A Commentary on the Epistle to the Romans*, Black's New Testament Commentaries (London: Black, 1957), 146–148.

23. For a more complete list of views, see Cranfield, *A Critical and Exegetical Commentary on the Epistle to the Romans,* 2:344.

24. See Dr. Seuss, *The Sneetches and Other Stories* (New York: Random, 1961).

25. See translators' note in the NET Bible for a clear and brief discussion of the challenges associated with translating the infinitives of indirect discourse in Eph. 4:22–23.

The Church and the Christian Life in Retrospect

1. The Constantinopolitan Creed, in John H. Leith, ed., *Creeds of the Churches: A Reader in Christian Doctrine from the Bible to the Present*, 3rd ed. (Louisville, KY: John Knox, 1982), 33.

2. Don't take my word for this. Read analyses from any major sporting news outlet to find abundant examples of those who know the game pleading with Jones to step aside and hire a qualified candidate for the team's management. Many are convinced that Dallas will never again taste success until Jones removes himself as GM; he has vowed that he never will.

3. Ignatius of Antioch, *Letter to the Trallians* 3.1 in Holmes, *The Apostolic Fathers*, 217.

4. Ignatius of Antioch, *Letter to the Smyrnaeans* 8.1–2 in Holmes, 255.

5. Earle E. Cairns, *Christianity through the Centuries: A History of the Christian Church*, 3rd rev. ed. (Grand Rapids: Zondervan, 1996), 76. Recently, scholars have read Ignatius more charitably, seeing a far more nuanced view of the early church's leadership structure. For example, Burtchaell has argued that what "the episcopate Ignatius portrays is not as monarchical as some have seen it to be. Throughout his letters he calls on the people to obey, not only the *episkopos*, but also the *presbyteroi* [*Magn.* 6; *Tral.* 12.2, 13.1, *Smryn.* 8.1]. The elders are to be in harmony with him; they are to honor him; they are to sustain him; but never does Ignatius say that they lie under his command (by contrast with the *diakonoi*, who are to obey the *episkopos*) [Eph. 4.1–2, 20.3; Tral. 12.2]" (James Tunstead Burtchaell, *From Synagogue to Church: Public Services and Offices in the Earliest Christian Communities* [Cambridge, UK: Cambridge, 1992], 308–309).

6. Irenaeus, *Against Heresies,* 3.3.1 (ANF 1:415).

7. Ibid., 3.3.2 (ANF 1:415–416).

8. As persecution came and went, some who had denied the faith under duress eventually decided they wanted to return to the church. Its leaders differed strongly, sometimes violently, on whether or not to allow *the lapsed* back into the church. Cyprian's recommended policy, more on the lenient side, came to be the church's selected response—and his fame was sealed.

9. J. N. D. Kelly, *Early Christian Doctrines*, rev. ed. (New York: HarperCollins, 1978), 206.

10. See, for example, Cyprian, *On the Unity of the Church,* 5. The attitude that the church is wholly represented by the bishop is also reemphasized by what has been called "Cyprian's maxim," *Ecclesia in Episcopo* ("the church is in the bishop").

11. See Michael J. Svigel, *RetroChristianity: Reclaiming the Forgotten Faith* (Wheaton, IL: Crossway, 2012), 188–190.

12. See Kelly, *Early Christian Doctrines,* 406–407.

13. Cyprian of Carthage, *On the Unity of the Church,* 7 (ANF 5:388).

14. Cyprian of Carthage, *Epistle,* 72.21 (ANF 5:384).

15. Augustine of Hippo, *On Baptism, Against the Donatists,* 1.10.14. (NPNF 1.4:417–18), emphases mine.

16. Millard Erickson notes that "at no point in the history of Christian thought has the doctrine of the church received the direct and complete attention that other doctrines have received. . . . By contrast, Christology and the doctrine of the Trinity had been given special attention in the fourth and fifth centuries, as had the atoning work of Christ in the Middle Ages, and the doctrine of salvation in the sixteenth century" (Erickson, *Christian Theology*, 1037).

17. R. E. O. White, "Sanctification" in *Evangelical Dictionary of Theology*, 2nd ed., Walter A. Elwell, ed. (Grand Rapids: Baker Academic, 2001), s.v. "Sanctification."

18. Margaret Deanesly, *A History of the Medieval Church, 590–1500*, 9th ed. (London: Routledge, 1969), 62.

19. On the Fourth Lateran Council, see Deanesly, ibid., 147–149.

20. Cited in ibid., 175.

21. See Victor Genke and Frances X. Gumerlock, *Gottschalk and a Medieval Predestination Controversy: Text Translated from the Latin,* Mediaeval Philosophical Texts in Translation, no. 47, ed. Roland J. Teske (Milwaukee: Marquette U., 2010), 58.

22. Deanesly, *A History of the Medieval Church,* 238.

23. The Constantinopolitan Creed (381).

24. Euan Cameron, *The European Reformation* (Oxford: Oxford, 1991), 88.

25. Jaroslav Pelikan, *The Christian Tradition: A History of the Development of Doctrine*, vol. 4, *Reformation of Church and Dogma (1300–1700)* (Chicago: U. of Chicago), 173.

26. Timothy George, *Theology of the Reformers* (Nashville: Broadman & Holman, 1988), 316.

27. Louis Berkhof, *The History of Christian Doctrines,* 237–238.

28. See Berkhof, ibid., 239.

29. This description is much indebted to Alister McGrath, who writes: "Evangelicalism is often held to center on a cluster of four assumptions: 1. The authority and sufficiency of Scripture; 2. The uniqueness of redemption through the death of Christ on the cross; 3. The need for personal conversion; 4. The necessity, propriety, and urgency of evangelism" (McGrath, *Christian Theology: An Introduction,* 5th ed. [West Sussex: John Wiley & Sons, 2011], 80).

30. Many evangelicals trace their theological pedigree through Wesleyans, Pentecostals, and Baptists of several varieties. Others from one of those traditions are distinguished by virtue of unique emphases in their understanding of sanctification—for instance, Keswick thought, or what's called in one book "Augustinian-Dispensational[ism]." See Stanley N. Gundry, et al., *Five Views on Sanctification* (Grand Rapids: Zondervan, 1987), 197.

31. If this structure occasions significant disagreement for some, my response to complaints will take this form: "View *x* may be legitimately categorized as a variety of tradition *y* for reasons both theological and historical." One example is the view of sanctification most often defended today in the Assemblies of God, which, after serious consideration, I suggest can be placed within the broader rubric of Wesleyan/Holiness sanctification views. This perspective is well defended by Bruce Rosdahl, an AOG member and professor at Southwestern Assemblies of God University, in his doctoral dissertation entitled "The Doctrine of Sanctification in the Assemblies of God" (Dallas Theological Seminary, 2008).

32. David P. Scaer says, "Luther's concept of *simul iustus et peccator* is fundamental for a Lutheran understanding not only of justification but also of sanctification" ("Sanctification in Lutheran Theology," *Concordia Theological Quarterly* 49:2 [April–July 1985]: 187).

33. Scaer, ibid., 188.

34. Francis Pieper, *Christian Dogmatics*, 3 vols. (St. Louis, MO: Concordia, 1953), 3:8.

35. Ibid., 3:29.

36. Johannes Wollebius, *Christianae Theologiae Compendium*, I.31.xiii. Cited by Heinrich Heppe, *Reformed Dogmatics Set Out and Illustrated from the Sources,* trans. G. T. Thomson (Grand Rapids: Baker, 1978), 566.

37. Herman Witsius, *The Economy of the Covenants Between God and Man,* vol. 3, 2nd American ed. (New York: Thomas Kirk, 1804), 221.

38. Louis Berkhof, *Systematic Theology,* new comb. ed. (Grand Rapids: Eerdmans, 1996), 532.

39. Melvin E. Dieter, "The Wesleyan Perspective" in *Five Views on Sanctification,* eds. Stanley N. Gundry, et al. (Grand Rapids: Zondervan, 1987), 25.

40. Kenneth J. Grider, *Entire Sanctification: The Distinctive Doctrine of Wesleyanism* (Kansas City, MO: Beacon Hill, 1980), Kindle location 479. Grider (later in the same chapter) also affirms that the experience of entire sanctification can be termed a *Second Work of Grace.*

41. See Grider, ibid., Kindle locations 511–516.

42. For example, the 1961 revision of *The Statement of Fundamental Truths* (the AOG doctrinal statement) removed all explicit reference to entire sanctification in the article on sanctification. See Bruce Rosdahl, "Sanctification in the Assemblies of God" (PhD. Dissertation, Dallas Theological Seminary, 2008), 198.

Facts to Never Forget

1. Anthony Hoekema, "The Reformed Perspective" in *Five Views on Sanctification,* 70.

Dangers to Avoid

1. Do you like how I deftly obscure the offender's gender? I fear that the statute of limitations on schoolyard infractions may not yet have expired. Hey, it happened only forty years ago.

2. From the Vincentian Canon (AD 434).

3. Thanks to Anthony Hoekema for this very helpful phrase. See Hoekema, "The Reformed Perspective" in *Five Views on Sanctification,* 70.

Principles to Put Into Practice

1. Alfred, Lord Tennyson, "The Charge of the Light Brigade." wikipedia.org/wiki/The_Charge_of_the_Light_Brigade_(poem) (accessed 01/20/13).

2. Dallas Theological Seminary, *Doctrinal Statement,* Article XIII. dts.edu/about/doctrinalstatement/ (accessed 12/20/12).

Voices From the Past and Present

1. Unless otherwise noted, patristic quotations come from the *Ante-Nicene Fathers* (ANF) or the *Nicene and Post-Nicene Fathers* (NPNF); the parenthetical citation after the early Christian writing points to these sources. For example, "(ANF 3:34)" refers to volume 3, page 34 of the Roberts and Donaldson edition of *The Ante-Nicene Fathers*. The NPNF span two separate series, so for these I indicate the series in the first number (1 or 2), then the volume within that series, followed by the page within that volume. For instance, "(NPNF 1.3:34)" would be for first series, volume 3, page 34. Though there are more contemporary translations of some of these writings, I've chosen to use these because they're in the public domain and are easily accessible online (at www.ccel.org).

2. *Didache* 7.1–4; from Michael W. Holmes, ed., *The Apostolic Fathers: Greek Texts and English Translations of Their Writings*, 3rd ed. (Grand Rapids: Baker, 2007), 355.

3. Clement of Rome, *First Epistle of Clement to the Corinthians,* 42.

4. Ignatius of Antioch, *To the Smyrnaeans* 8.1–2 in Holmes, *The Apostolic Fathers*, 255.

5. Ignatius of Antioch, *To the Trallians* 3.1 in Holmes, ibid., 217.

6. Justin Martyr, *First Apology* 61 (ANF 1:183).

7. Ibid., 66 (ANF 1:185).

8. Ibid., 67 (ANF 1:185–186).

9. Irenaeus of Lyons, *Against Heresies* 1.10.2 (ANF 1:331).

10. Ibid., 4.26.2–5 (ANF 1:497–498).

11. Theophilus of Antioch, *To Autolocus* 2.14 (ANF 2:100).

12. Tertullian, *On the Resurrection of the Flesh* 8 (ANF 3:551).

13. Tertullian, *Against Marcion* 4.40 (ANF 3:281).

14. Tertullian, *Prescription against Heretics* 20 (ANF 3:252).

15. Clement of Alexandria, *The Instructor* 1.6 (ANF 2:219).

16. Cyprian, *On the Unity of the Church* 6 (ANF 5:423).

17. Cyprian, *Epistle* 58.2 (ANF 5:354).

18. *Apostolic Constitutions*, 1.1.pref. (ANF 7:391).

19. Basil of Caesarea, *On the Holy Spirit* 12.28 (NPNF 2.8:18).

20. The Constantinopolitan Creed, in Leith, *Creeds of the Churches,* 33.

21. Augustine, *The Enchiridion* 42–43 (NPNF 1.3:252).

22. Augustine, *On Christian Doctrine* 3.16 [24] (NPNF 1.2:563).

23. Augustine, *City of God* 10.6 (NPNF 1.2:184).

24. Boethius, "On the Catholic Faith" in *The Theological Tractates, The Consolation of Philosophy*, trans. H. F. Stewart and E. K. Rand, The Loeb Classical Library (London: Heinemann, 1918), 69, 71.

25. John of Damascus, *An Exact Exposition of the Orthodox Faith* 4.9 (NPNF 2.9:77–78).

26. John of Damascus, ibid., 4.13 (NPNF 2.9:82–83).

27. Ratramnus, *On the Body and Blood of the Lord*, 9, 60, 96, in *Book of Ratramnus the Monk of Corbey, Commonly Called Bertram, on the Body and Blood of the Lord* (Oxford: John Henry Parker, 1838), 5, 32, 52–53.

28. Gottschalk of Orbais, *On Different Ways of Speaking about Redemption* in Victor Genke and Francis X. Gumerlock, eds. and trans., *Gottschalk and a Medieval Predestination Controversy: Texts Translated from the Latin,* Mediaeval Philosophical Texts in Translation, vol. 47, ed. Roland J. Teske (Milwaukee: Marquette U., 2010), 157–158.

29. Peter Abelard, *Commentary on Romans* 2:4 (on Romans 3:27) in Stephen R. Cartwright, *Peter Abelard: Commentary on the Epistle to the Romans,* The Fathers

of the Church: Medieval Continuation (Washington, DC: The Catholic University of America Press, 2011), 169–170.

30. Peter Lombard, *The Sentences,* vol. 4 (4.2.1), trans. Giulio Silano (Toronto: Pontifical Institute of Mediaeval Studies, 2010), 9.

31. Ibid., 138–139, 147.

32. Stephen Langton, *Fragments on the Morality of Human Acts* 3, in Eugene R. Fairweather, ed., *A Scholastic Miscellany: Anselm to Ockham,* The Library of Christian Classics (Louisville, KY: Westminster John Knox, 1956), 358.

33. Thomas Aquinas, *Summa Theologica* (New York: Fathers of the English Dominican Province, 1911), 2(1).102.4.

34. Meister Eckhart, *About the Body of Our Lord, How Often One Should Partake of It, with What Devotion and in What Manner* in Raymond Bernard Blakney, *Meister Eckhart: A Modern Translation* (New York: Harper & Brothers, 1941), 27–30.

35. Pope Boniface VIII, *The Bull Unam Sanctum* in James Harvey Robinson, ed., *Translations and Reprints from the Original Sources of European History*, vol. 3.6, *The Pre-Reformation Period* (Philadelphia: U. of Pennsylvania, 1897), 19–21.

36. John Wycliffe, *The Church and Her Members*, 2.

37. John Hus, *The Church,* trans. David Schaff (New York: Charles Scribner's Sons, 1915), 10.

38. Ibid., 3.

39. Ibid., 83.

40. Ibid., 22–23.

41. Martin Luther, *The Large Catechism*.

42. The Augsburg Confession, Article VII.

43. John Calvin, *Institutes of the Christian Religion*, IV.i.2.

44. Ibid., IV.i.9.

45. *The Thirty-Nine Articles* 19 in Leith, *Creeds of the Churches*, 273.

46. *The Thirty-Nine Articles* 25 in ibid., 274.

47. Ibid., 275–276.

48. *The Thirty-Nine Articles* 28 in ibid., 276.

49. The Belgic Confession, Article 29.

50. *The Westminster Confession* 25:1–4 in Leith, *Creeds of the Churches*, 222.

51. *The Westminster Confession* 28:1, 5 in ibid., 224.

52. *The Westminster Confession* 29:1 in ibid., 225.

53. *The Westminster Confession* 13:1–2 in ibid., 225.

54. Francis Turretin, *Institutes of Elenctic Theology,* II.xvii.2.

55. The Philadelphia Confession 26.1 in Philip Schaff, *The Creeds of Christendom*, vol. 3, The Evangelical Protestant Creeds, 4th ed. (New York: Harper & Row, 1919), 738.

56. John Wesley, "Sermon 74: Of the Church," in *Sermons on Several Occasions*, Christian Classics Ethereal Library (ccel.org/ccel/wesley/sermons.vi.xxi.html).

57. Articles of Religion of the Reformed Episcopal Church in America 21 in Schaff, *The Creeds of Christendom,* 3:821.

58. Francis Pieper, *Christian Dogmatics*, 3 vols. (St. Louis: Concordia, 1953), 3:402.

59. Ibid., 3:410–11.

60. Robert L. Saucy, *The Church in God's Program* (Chicago: Moody, 1972), 22.

61. Thomas Oden, *Systematic Theology*, vol. 3, "Life in the Spirit" (San Francisco: HarperCollins, 1992), 303.

62. *The Statement of Faith of the Evangelical Free Church of America,* Article 7, in EFCA, *Evangelical Convictions* (Minneapolis: Free Church Pub., 2011), Kindle Locations 50–54.

63. Gregg Allison, *Sojourners and Strangers: The Doctrine of the Church* (Wheaton, IL: Crossway, 2012), 29.

PART TWO

When He Returns

Resurrection, Judgment, and the Restoration

BY MICHAEL J. SVIGEL

High-Altitude Survey

If you were to ask various Christians to rank theological doctrines from most vital to the faith to least vital, chances are you'd end up with something like this: the Trinity, the person and work of Christ, and salvation. . . followed by the authority of Scripture, then the creation and fall of humankind. Press a little harder and they might include something about the church and the Christian life; some might even mention angels and demons. But chances are good that nowadays the doctrine of the end times ("eschatology") would fast settle to the bottom of the list like a lump of lead dropped into a pool of water.

Certainly there will be someone who lists eschatology first and believes that the second coming of Jesus deserves central attention. However, such people are few and far between. You might get a handful of folks who put it somewhere in the middle, maybe above angels and demons, or above the church. But most place it somewhere near the bottom.

Overall, many Christians aren't all that concerned about the end times. Yes, they believe Jesus will return. All our churches proclaim this truth from the pulpit, write it in their doctrinal statements, and confess it in their songs, hymns, or liturgies. But beyond these affirmations, most aren't sure how—or if—details of what will happen in the future actually affect how they think and act in regard to God, themselves, salvation, and the world around them. Many make little or no connection between coming events and their own lives.

Yet if we can climb out of eschatological nooks and crannies to a vantage point that allows us a bird's-eye view, we'll get a different perspective. Instead of being tangled in the twisted underbrush of confusing controversies and tripping over the strewn debris of deep-seated doctrinal battles, we'll find a beautiful panoramic vista. This overlook will reveal one major theme that puts all the details in their proper place: *HOPE.*

Eschatology: It's All About Hope

Shakespeare once wrote, "The miserable have no other medicine. But only hope."[1] Had he lived in the twenty-first century he would not have penned these words. We have innumerable medicines and remedies and programs to treat misery. In many respects, "treatment" of human despair has been placed almost entirely in the realm of secular science. As Janet Soskice observes, "Lack of faith and charity can be treated by prayer, but lack of hope is treated with antidepressants."[2]

While Christians have neglected future hope as a major theme of their faith story, they have also lost the healing power of hope. Simply put, hope in the future has value for the present. Not some general notion that "things will be better in the sweet by-and-by" or a vague sense that "Jesus will come back and make it all right." A fuzzy hope in a brighter tomorrow might work for politicians trying to drum up support or poets hoping to tap sentimentality. Hope in Christ has therapeutic value because it's *concrete*. Specific promises. Particular expectations. Detailed descriptions. These facets present a painting that to our minds looks more like a Rembrandt than a Monet.

Knowledge of and trust in what God says is coming have healing and motivating power for us today because hope lifts our hearts and minds from our circumstances. It gives us glimpses of a glorious future. It inspires us to look upward and outward at an infinitely better life rather than drawing us downward and inward to obsess over our situations and scenarios. Awareness about what's still ahead takes our eyes and minds and hearts off things that seem important and turns them to what is vitally significant. The more we recognize here and now the brevity and uncertainty of this time compared to the "eternal weight of glory" (2 Cor. 4:17), the more our attitudes and actions will be permanently affected for the better—in fact, for the best.

John Polkinghorne puts it this way:

> This human attitude [of hope] is of religious significance because it points beyond the limits of the present and it must seek its ground beyond human individuals. Hope involves holding fast to promise in the context of apparent contradiction. The opposite of hope is despair, a nihilistic rejection of trust in the meaningfulness of life.[3]

Think back to your brief days in grade school. Think about the things you worried about and obsessed over—the petty squabbles with fickle friends, the troubles that somehow seemed so insurmountable, the fears that would prove shortsighted. If you'd known then what you know now—that most of the "problems" that took up so much emotional energy were child's play—how would your thoughts, feelings, and actions have been impacted? The same is true when we compare our present earthly lives with the reality of what's to come. The great thing is, God *does* inform us of the future happenings in a way that can transform our minds, lifting our heads from temporal darkness and letting us catch energizing glimpses of eternity's never-ending light.

False Sources of Hope

1. Human Means of Success (Ps. 33:17)
2. Personal Strength (Prov. 11:7)
3. The Uncertainty of Riches (1 Tim. 6:17)
4. False Revelations (Ezek. 13:6)
5. Wrong Interpretations (John 5:45)

True Sources of Hope

1. God the Father (Ps. 62:5)
2. God the Son (1 Tim. 1:1)
3. God the Spirit (Rom. 5:5)
4. Remembrance of God's Faithfulness (Lam. 3:21–23)
5. Perseverance in Suffering (Rom. 5:3–4)
6. The Encouragement of Scripture (Rom. 15:4)

When we speak of the transforming power that comes from embracing details about the coming future, we're not speculating about the Antichrist's origins, or the seat of his reign, or how to calculate his "number." We aren't referring to obsessing over what happens when and to whom during the days leading up to Christ's return. And we aren't fixated on the exact meaning of certain prophetic symbols from Daniel, Zechariah, or John the apostle. We mean the straightforward, unambiguous, central content of Christian hope. Scripture contains divine promises to which believers have looked forward from the earliest generations.

The Promise of Christ's Return

Peter, fisherman-turned-fisher-of-men, stood among the disciples, staring into the clouds, when Christ ascended to the Father's right hand after giving them a forty-day crash course on God's kingdom. After He was hidden from their sight in the clouds, two angels appeared and said, "Men of Galilee, why do you stand looking into the sky? This Jesus, who has been taken up from you into heaven, will come in just the same way as you have watched Him go into heaven" (Acts 1:11 NASB). From then on, I can imagine, not a day went by when Peter didn't at least glance upward, wondering if his Lord, Savior, God, and Friend was about to step back into this world.

Nearing his end over thirty years later, Peter still clung to that pledge of Messiah's return, noting that ignorant, arrogant mockers frequently and sarcastically taunted this faith (2 Peter 3:4). Yet his mind remained steadfast, his focus sure, his senses alert as he urged his own followers, "Fix your hope completely on the grace to be brought to you at the revelation of Jesus Christ" (1 Peter 1:13 NASB). Paul likewise exhorted Titus, his understudy, to spend his life "looking for the blessed hope and the appearing of the glory of our great God and Savior, Christ Jesus" (Titus 2:13 NASB).

Jesus' future bodily return is the focal point of several interconnected promises woven into the King's coming. Though these relate to earth-shaking events and revolutionary experiences for God's people, we must never forget that without the central certainty of Christ's return, *none* would be possible. Just as fresh water nourishes parched land when a dam's floodgates are opened, the second coming will unleash a deluge of guaranteed blessings that will transform this world and everything in it.

Let's look at this river of sureties more closely: resurrection, kingdom, righteousness, glory, and eternal life.

The Promise of Resurrection

Yearning for the body's resurrection flies like a banner over the opulent realm of Christian hope. Because we will be raised when Christ returns, believers, when mourning the deaths of those we love, need not mourn in the way that nonbelievers do (1 Thess. 4:13). We do mourn, but it is a mourning informed by assured hope. Just as Jesus himself was raised from death, one day He will raise all His children to eternal life in a new, glorified body. We'll see our loved ones again if they belong to the One who has conquered death!

Hope in and focus on the coming bodily resurrection has waned over the ages, often replaced by a notion of arriving in an ethereal place of white light and bright clouds, strumming harps while humming along with a heavenly choir or wandering endless golden streets lined with buildings made of gems. *The biblical hope entails physical resurrection, not just spiritual release to heaven.* So crucial is this to our faith that Paul gave it as the reason he suffered persecution by his opponents (Acts 26:6–8). Even creation itself longs for the saints to be raised, for this will usher in creation's "resurrection" from bondage to corruption (Rom. 8:20–25). Just as our present mortal bodies are chained to this physical world's deterioration and degeneration, so the fallen world's restoration is linked to the transformation of our bodies into their immortal, incorruptible state of glory (1 Cor. 15:53–54).

The Promise of the Kingdom

Christ's return, the body's resurrection, and creation's transformation will coincide with the advent of the fullness of God's eternal kingdom. The kingdom of God has always been a subject of believers' prayers (Matt. 6:10). Though this world's sin, injustice, and suffering can be eased somewhat when believers live out the kingdom's values and virtues, the ultimate triumph of good over evil, peace over calamity, and righteousness over wickedness awaits the coming of the promised Messiah and King (Isa. 9:7; Dan. 6:26). By preaching God's kingdom, the church preaches not only its own testimony of lives worthy of our King in the present age but also our hope in the certain fact of God's universal and eternal reign through Jesus (Acts 28:20–31).

What a bold hope amid atrophy, entropy, tyranny, and instability! A kingdom not of this world transforms this world. Not by human might or reason, or scientific advances, or military or economic prowess. No such instrument could ever satisfy the deepest longings of all nations and peoples: peace, justice, security, and prosperity. Only God's kingdom breaking into this world can usher in the establishment of heaven's virtues and values in it:

> Then the sovereignty, the dominion and the greatness of all the kingdoms under the whole heaven will be given to the people of the saints of the Highest One; His kingdom will be an everlasting kingdom, and all the dominions will serve and obey Him. (Dan. 7:27 NASB)

The Promise of Ultimate Righteousness

The godliest Christian falls miserably short of God's holiness. When we dwell on what we dread is our wretched standing before an immaculate Judge, we sink into desperate misery. Even for a seasoned saint, "sin conquered" can suddenly seem to become "sin empowered." Our fortunes in the spiritual battle against temptation can turn in a moment of weakness. Like Paul himself, many of us have cried out in agony, in conflict with sin: "Wretched man that I am! Who will deliver me from this body of death?" (Rom. 7:24).

At the end, God will finally grant to us eternal triumph over temptation and sin: "Through the Spirit, by faith, we ourselves eagerly wait for the hope of righteousness" (Gal. 5:5). The glorious coming future will not contain even a smudge or speck of unrighteousness, for we ourselves will be conformed to the righteousness of Christ (Phil. 3:21). In our moment-by-moment battle against wickedness in our lives, we must continue to persevere as we look up in hope for the heavenly "air support" that will provide decisive victory on behalf of justice and righteousness.

The Promise of Glory

By the Creator's original plan and purpose, men and women were to share jointly in reflecting His glory. King David once meditated on this truth:

> What is man that You take thought of him,
> And the son of man that You care for him?
> Yet You have made him a little lower than God,
> And You crown him with glory and majesty!
> You make him to rule over the works of Your hands;
> You have put all things under his feet. (Ps. 8:4–6 NASB)

Adam and Eve were to be crowned with glory and majesty, equipped to subdue and rule over the earth, and reflect God's splendor into this created realm. But they fell infinitely short of this magnificent ideal (Gen. 3). They chose sin, dishonoring their good and holy God instead of honoring Him with goodness and holiness. Now on the other side of Eden's gate and apart from the Lord's personal presence, His glory reflected in humanity has withered like a flower without sunlight. Like our original parents long ago, all of us without exception "fall short of the glory of God" (Rom. 3:23). *Any* glory we strive to achieve for ourselves in this life is destined for the grave (Ps. 7:5).

Yet, in Jesus, God will completely restore and even surpass the glory originally intended for us. Believers have Christ within them—He who is "the hope of glory" (Col. 1:27). When He returns, He will "transform the body of our humble state into conformity with the body of His glory" (Phil. 3:21 NASB). And God's Spirit, through His empowering presence, has already begun His work of revolution in our lives: "We all, with unveiled face, beholding as in a mirror the glory of the Lord, are being transformed into the same image from glory to glory, just as from the Lord, the Spirit" (2 Cor. 3:18 NASB).

The Promise of Eternal Life

In a real sense, eternal life began the moment we believed in Christ: "God has given us eternal life, and this life is in His Son" (1 John 5:11 NASB). Thus, eternal life is something we presently *have* (v. 13). However, when Jesus returns, establishing His righteous kingdom and resurrecting believers in their glorious bodies, He will bestow upon us that for which we've been eagerly hoping: *eternal life.* This is "the hope of eternal life, which God, who cannot lie, promised long ages ago" (Titus 1:2 NASB). Having been justified already when we believed, we now look forward to eternal life with unwavering hope (3:7). Though we'll fully experience eternal life "in the age to come" (Luke 18:30), we can live "abundantly" *now* through the Spirit's power (John 10:10).

Eschatology: It's All About Him

All these promises of hope center on the Lord, specifically in relation to His return. In fact, "Christ Jesus . . . *is* our hope" (1 Tim. 1:1 NASB); *He* is hope incarnate. When we despair, we look to Him. When we grieve, we find strength in Him. When we lose heart, we long for His coming. In the final analysis, at the center of Christian hope stands not a promise, not a principle, not even a prophecy but a *Person*—the Lord Jesus Christ.

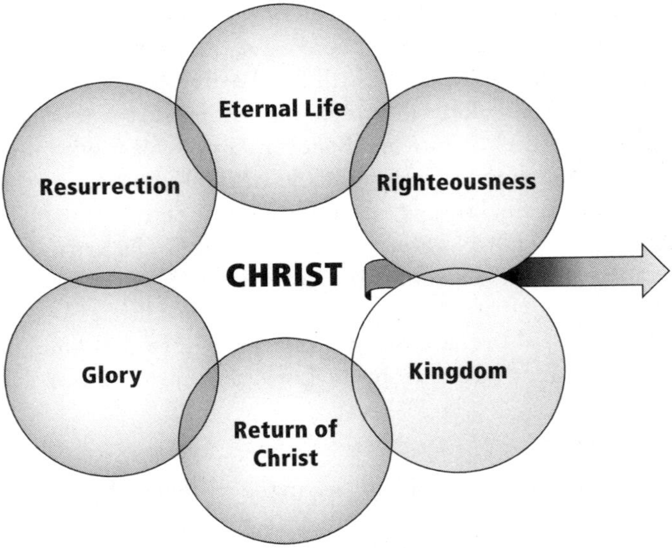

Christ Jesus our hope.

1 Timothy 1:1

The book of Revelation, written explicitly to reveal to God's people "the things that must soon take place" (1:1) confirms that Christ himself is the theme of the Bible's prophecies and therefore of eschatology itself. The angel who showed the prophetic visions to John said, "The testimony of Jesus is the spirit of prophecy" (19:10). Like a master key that can unlock any door of a building, the teaching about the person and work of Jesus Christ in His first and second comings unlocks the deepest mysteries of God's Word.

When Jesus confronted astute Bible scholars who spent their whole lives conducting microsurgery on every jot and tittle of Holy Writ, He said, "You search the Scriptures because you think that in them you have eternal life; it is these that testify about Me" (John 5:39

NASB). His words apply equally to today's students who are fervent in their study of all biblical details. This is especially true of those who take it upon themselves to study biblical prophecy. How easy it is to get tangled in minutiae, obsessing over unanswered questions or dogmatizing over personal opinions. By staying focused on Jesus Christ, the Star of the scriptural drama, we can avoid any tendency to overemphasize a minor plot point or ancillary character.

Scripture not only points to Christ as the Suffering Servant (the first coming),[4] it also points beyond our own age to the endless era of righteousness that will accompany His restoration of all things (the second coming). In a sermon to his unbelieving Israelite kinsmen, Peter drew together Christ's first coming and return as subjects of the same prophecies:

> The things which God announced beforehand by the mouth of all the prophets, that His Christ would suffer, He has thus fulfilled. Therefore repent and return, so that your sins may be wiped away, in order that times of refreshing may come from the presence of the Lord; and that He may send Jesus, the Christ appointed for you, whom heaven must receive until the period of restoration of all things about which God spoke by the mouth of His holy prophets from ancient time. (Acts 3:18–21 NASB)

Did you notice that? In *the past* Christ fulfilled the sufferings declared beforehand by the Old Testament prophets (e.g., Ps. 22; Isa. 53; Zech. 12:10). The same holy prophets had spoken about *the future* restoration of all things that will come when He returns. In light of both the predicted past and future, during the *present* we're to continue proclaiming God's call to salvation by grace through faith in the person and work of Jesus (Eph. 2:8–9). Once again: *past, present, and future all center on the person and work of the Lord Jesus Christ in His first and second comings.*

We said earlier that eschatology is all about hope. It's also all about *Him*. The attitude-altering, life-changing hope of our faith finds its epicenter and source only in Christ, "who is our hope" (1 Tim. 1:1). As we prepare to delve into specific passages important for understanding eschatology, let's keep Jesus, our hope, close to our hearts and at the forefront of our minds.

Passages to Master

> I am God, and there is no other;
>   I am God, and there is none like me,
> declaring the end from the beginning
>   and from ancient times things not yet done,
> saying, "My counsel shall stand,
> and I will accomplish all my purpose." (Isa. 46:9–10)

The God-inspired Scriptures have a lot to say about the future. Furthermore, many biblical prophecies about coming events already have been fulfilled in what's now the past, leaving us a permanent record not only of God's ability to *foresee* the future but also of His willingness to *foretell* it.

The following Old and New Testament texts represent some of the most central passages on eschatological issues. We could include many other verses, chapters, and books also, but become familiar with these and you'll find you're equipped to navigate some oft-turbulent waters of end-times dialogues and debates. Along with basic discussion on points of agreement and disagreement among Bible-believing Christians regarding the meaning of these passages, you'll also find suggested verses for committing to memory.

(1) *Isaiah 65–66:* The New Heavens and New Earth

Already in Isaiah 2, written centuries before the earthly life of Jesus Christ, the great prophet was looking past Israel's stubborn wickedness to an era of universal peace among the world's peoples, when "they will hammer their swords into plowshares and their spears into pruning hooks. Nation will not lift up sword against nation, and never again will they learn war" (v. 4 NASB). Throughout the book he continues pointing to a coming king—an heir to the Davidic throne—who will usher in an everlasting reign of peace, justice, righteousness, and prosperity for all, and restore to harmony all enmity in the fallen order.[1] In one strikingly vivid image of this reversal and renewal:

> The wolf will dwell with the lamb, and the leopard will lie down with the young goat, and the calf and the young lion and the fatling together; and a little boy will lead them. Also the cow and the bear will graze, their young will lie down together, and the lion will eat straw like the ox. (11:6–7 NASB)

In the last two chapters of Isaiah, God promises "new heavens and a new earth," swearing that "the former things shall not be remembered or come into mind" (65:17). No more weeping, distress, untimely death, famine, injustice, futility, calamity, evil, or harm (65:18–25). Instead "the wolf and the lamb shall graze together; the lion shall eat straw like the ox" (65:25). Following a time of fiery judgment (66:15–16), the Lord God will reveal himself as King over all the earth, ushering in "the new heavens and the new earth" (66:22).

Scripture Memory 1

Isaiah 65:17

Behold, I create new heavens and a new earth, and the former things shall not be remembered or come into mind.

The new heavens/new earth theme, first mentioned here, echoes forward through the canon of Scripture. Christ also may be referring to this renewal of creation in speaking of the "regeneration when the Son of Man will sit on His glorious throne" (Matt. 19:28 NASB). The Greek word describing this, *paliggenesia*, literally means "re-creation." The terms themselves appear in 2 Peter 3:13 as the specific object of Christian expectation: "According to his promise we are waiting for new heavens and a new earth in which righteousness dwells." And John's grand apocalyptic drama culminates in a vision of "a new heaven and a new earth" (Rev. 21:1).

(2) *Jeremiah 31:* The New Covenant

When the author of Hebrews wanted to demonstrate the superiority of Christ's priesthood over that established by Moses, he quoted at length from Jeremiah 31, a key passage on the new covenant.[2] The term *new covenant* occurs only here in the Old Testament, though the themes of restoration, relationship, and forgiveness are found throughout the prophetic writings from centuries before the New Testament period.[3]

Key New Covenant Passages

1. Isaiah 42:6–7
2. Isaiah 59:20–21
3. Jeremiah 32:37–40
4. Ezekiel 16:60–63
5. Ezekiel 37:21–28
6. Luke 22:20
7. 1 Corinthians 11:25
8. 2 Corinthians 3:6
9. Hebrews 8:6–13
10. Hebrews 9:15
11. Hebrews 12:24

Christians understand this covenant to be mediated by Jesus Christ, through whom all promises and blessings will be fulfilled. Jesus himself associated the new covenant with His shed blood for the forgiveness of sins.[4] The apostles viewed themselves as "servants of a new covenant" (2 Cor. 3:6 NASB), pointing to Christ as its guarantee and mediator (Heb. 7:22; 8:6). In some sense, then, the new covenant relates to Christ's person and work. The Old Testament foresaw that the new covenant would be fulfilled through the Messiah,[5] and the New Testament sees Jesus Christ as its mediator.[6]

Believers discuss and debate exactly *how* the new covenant blessings relate to Christ, the church, and Israel. Are they for the present age . . . or the future . . . or both? Does the phrase describing its original recipients—"the house of Israel and the house of Judah"—refer to literal ethnic Hebrews, to Jesus Christ as the sole Jewish recipient of the covenant blessings (the true "Israel"), or to the church of both Jews and Gentiles as the spiritual "Israel"? If the church today is fulfilling or at least partly fulfilling new covenant promises, then *which* promises? Will others be fulfilled later?

Scripture Memory 2

Jeremiah 31:33–34

33 For this is the covenant that I will make with the house of Israel after those days, declares the LORD: I will put my law within them, and I will write it on their hearts. And I will be their God, and they shall be my people.
34 And no longer shall each one teach his neighbor and each his brother, saying, "Know the LORD," for they shall all know me, from the least of them to the greatest, declares the LORD. For I will forgive their iniquity, and I will remember their sin no more.

Such questions haven't been easy to answer. Sincere Christians have advanced numerous views to explain the relationship of Israel and the church to the promised blessings. The following chart provides just a sampling:

View	Representative	Description
Classic Amillennial	Oswald T. Allis	Israel, the true heir of the new covenant promises, has rejected Christ and thus given way to the church as recipient.[7]
Postmillennial Variations	Charles Hodge	While the church receives new covenant blessings by being grafted in, literal Israel still will be restored and will receive the blessings during the (pre-second coming) millennial golden age.[8]
	Keith A. Mathison	Christ inaugurated the new covenant at His advent; it is being fulfilled currently in and through the church. It awaits no future fulfillment for Israel or after Christ's return.[9]
Classic Premillennial	George Eldon Ladd	Christ, by His death, has procured the new covenant promises. As Israel has rejected Him (through whom they might receive the blessings) as Messiah, these now have a spiritual fulfillment in the church, though they also point to the future millennial period.[10]
Dispensational Premillennial Variations	John Nelson Darby	The new covenant is promised to Israel only, and so only national Israel will receive the blessings. The church receives benefits of Christ's death apart from new covenant participation.[11]
	C. I. Scofield	The (one) new covenant will be fulfilled literally with Israel; until then, the church participates in its saving blessings.[12]
	Lewis Sperry Chafer	There are actually two "new" covenants—one promised (in OT) to Israel, to be fulfilled in the millennium, and one with the church, experienced in the present age and in the age to come.[13]
	Craig Blaising	The new covenant has been inaugurated in the church and will be fulfilled fully in the coming kingdom; the church (present) and Israel (future) are intended beneficiaries of its blessings.[14]

(3) *Ezekiel 37–48:* Resurrection and Restoration

When I was a boy, my grandparents' massive family Bible was nearly my size. Besides its bulk and heft, I remember one (*only* one) thing: its full-page print of Gustave Dore's engraving *The Vision of the Valley of Dry Bones.*[15]

That mysterious Old Testament vision begins one of the most powerful and puzzling sections of Scripture. Ezekiel 37–48 contains foundational ideas and images developed by further revelation in both Testaments.

Chapter 37: The Valley of Dry Bones and the Restoration of God's People

Ezekiel saw a valley full of bones become miraculously restored to life, representing "the whole house of Israel" (v. 11). Based on verses 11–14, many consider this vision to have a dual fulfillment: the literal resurrection of the bodies from their graves as well as a restoration of God's people from exile to their own land. The Lord emphasizes the hope of ultimate restoration in verses 15–28 with promises of the divided monarchy's reunification, the forgiveness of sins, the establishment of a kingdom, and an eternal covenant of peace. All of these aspects point forward to the new covenant blessings that will come through the Messiah, Jesus Christ (see Jer. 31:31–34).

> **Scripture Memory 3**
>
> ***Ezekiel 37:26–27***
>
> 26 I will make a covenant of peace with them. It shall be an everlasting covenant with them. And I will set them in their land and multiply them, and will set my sanctuary in their midst forevermore.
> 27 My dwelling place shall be with them, and I will be their God, and they shall be my people.

Chapters 38–39: The Prophecy Against Gog of Magog

In contrast to resurrection from death and restoration from among the nations, chapter 38 presents the pagan peoples—allied around the enigmatic Gog of Magog—utterly defeated and ultimately destroyed when they try to attack God's people. Futurists tend to see these prophecies (together with Ezekiel 37) being fulfilled in some way during the tribulation period; some emphasize the restoration of ethnic Israel more than others. In that case, the judgment on Gog relates either to a battle at the beginning of the tribulation or to judgment against the Antichrist at the tribulation's end. Other interpreters tie this prophecy in to the battle of Gog and Magog (described in Revelation 20:7–10)—the last great conflict not only between Israel and the nations but also between Satan with his wicked hosts and Christ with His army of saints.

Chapters 40–48: The Restoration of the Temple and the People

Written when Israel was still in exile, the Babylonians having destroyed Jerusalem and the temple, this intricately detailed description of the new temple was intended to humble the people for their sin, motivate them to repent, and then, at the designated time, to rebuild. Ezekiel 43:10–11 says,

> As for you, son of man, describe to the house of Israel the temple, that they may be ashamed of their iniquities; and they shall measure the plan. And if they are ashamed of all that they have done, make known to them the design of the temple, its arrangement, its exits and its entrances, that is, its whole design.

In light of that conditional promise, some commentators have understood this vision to refer to an unrealized restoration, one that could have been, had the exiles of Israel repented with all their hearts. Instead, they received a partial restoration and a relatively puny temple, in keeping with their partial and halfhearted repentance. Others interpret Ezekiel 40–48 as "a typological vision of the present church age."[16] But some premillennialists, especially many dispensationalists, believe this temple oracle still will be fulfilled literally during the millennium, with Christ reigning from Jerusalem over a restored nation of Israel.[17] Only then will Israel repent fully, embracing Jesus as her Messiah and experiencing the fullness of the promised blessings.

(4) *Daniel 2, 7, 9–12:* The End of the Wicked Rulers

I've never seen a children's Bible storybook that didn't include "Daniel in the Lion's Den" . . . right beside "Jonah and the Big Fish." The book of Daniel also has supplied us with variations on the popular saying "He saw the handwriting on the wall," that is, a sign that warns of impending doom (see 5:5). And many churchgoers remember Daniel's three friends—Shadrach, Meshach, and Abednego—who survived their trial of faith in a fiery furnace (3:1–30).

Beyond these well-known stories, this book contains numerous pillars that support a biblical doctrine of the end times; it's virtually impossible to exaggerate the role of Daniel in the study of eschatology. The New Testament appeals to his dramatic apocalyptic visions as foundational to understanding the coming of Christ's kingdom.[18] And those who study end-times prophecy draw extensively on Daniel as a key to understanding the scriptural timetable for past history and future events. All of this is what we might expect when it comes to the interpretation of visions so stunning that they left even their original witness stunned and overwhelmed (8:15, 27).

Nebuchadnezzar's Statue (Daniel 2)

One night Babylon's King Nebuchadnezzar (c. 605–562 BC) dreamt of a giant statue with a head of gold, arms and torso of silver, midsection and thighs of bronze, legs of iron, and feet of iron mixed with clay (2:31–33). The entire statue was broken to pieces by a great stone that demolished it once and for all (vv. 34–35). Then the stone grew to fill the whole earth (v. 35).

Daniel interpreted the king's dream as indicating four successive Gentile kingdoms, beginning with Babylon—the head of gold (vv. 36–38). The rest of the dream was yet future in his day, yet the other four parts have been fulfilled throughout history: the empire of Media-Persia, succeeding Babylon (c. 539–331 BC); that of Greece under Alexander the Great (331–63 BC), and then the Roman, lasting from 63 BC to about AD 476, well into the Christian era.

Though this identification has been well established among Christian interpreters, the exact meaning of the great stone that destroys the statue has been variously understood. Daniel said, of this symbol:

> The God of heaven will set up a kingdom that shall never be destroyed, nor shall the kingdom be left to another people. It shall break in pieces all these kingdoms and bring them to an end, and it shall stand forever. (v. 44)

Certainly this refers to the establishment of God's kingdom, but does it refer to Christ's second coming, as Judge and King, to establish an earthly kingdom (premillennial)? Or does it refer to the establishment of Christ's eternal, spiritual kingdom, when He took His throne at the ascension and established His reign through His church (amillennial)? Or perhaps the stone's growth from small rock to earth-covering mountain (v. 35) indicates a postmillennial fulfillment, in which God slowly but surely establishes His kingdom on earth as the gospel is proclaimed and the nations are converted?[19]

That the heaven-born kingdom of God will one day conquer all man-made powers, nobody disputes. *How* and *when* this will happen has been disputed.

The Four Beasts (Daniel 7)

Several years after Nebuchadnezzar's dream, Daniel the prophet had his own night vision regarding a succession of world empires that would end with the establishment of God's kingdom. Those who have understood the statue's four metals (Dan. 2) as the aforementioned empires almost always understand this vision of four beasts (Dan. 7) in the same way.

Kingdom	Daniel 2	Daniel 7
Babylonian	Head of Gold	Lion
Medo-Persian	Torso/Arms of Silver	Bear
Greek	Midriff/Thighs of Bronze	Leopard
Roman	Legs of Iron	Monstrosity

However, Daniel's vision adds far more detail regarding the final demise of worldly rule and the divine kingdom's establishment. Two figures in the end play particularly prominent roles—the "little horn" (7:8) and the "son of man" (v. 13). The first, symbolically represented by a little horn on the head of the fourth beast, had "eyes like the eyes of a man, and a mouth speaking great things" (v. 8). Interpreted as a world ruler growing out of the final empire, this man will wage war against the saints for a short time; ultimately God's kingdom will destroy him (vv. 21–22). This kind of blaspheming, godless dictator and persecutor is known as the Antichrist, and his exploits are further echoed in Scripture—perhaps in the Old Testament (see Dan. 9:27; 11:36–45) and directly in the New (see 2 Thess. 2:3–12; Rev. 13:1–10).

The second figure, represented as coming "with the clouds of heaven" to be presented before God's throne, is called "one like a son of man" (Dan. 7:13). His destiny reveals that this is an Old Testament prophecy of Messiah's coming (v. 14):

> To him was given dominion and glory and a kingdom, that all peoples, nations, and languages should serve him; his dominion is an everlasting dominion, which shall not pass away, and his kingdom one that shall not be destroyed.

In Jesus' earthly ministry, He frequently identified himself as the Son of Man who would come and receive God's kingdom in the end times.[20] This same title and image appears again in Revelation 1:13 and 14:14.

So in Daniel 7, not only do we watch the unfolding drama of the nations in their futile attempt at global domination without God, but we also see the final outcome of this conflict: the defeat of Antichrist by the Son of Man's power.

The End of the Days (Daniel 9–12)

You could likely spend the rest of your life studying Daniel 9–12 and still have countless questions unanswered. These chapters combine startling visions, meticulous prophecies, cryptic interpretations, and confounding details regarding things that apparently will come to full fruition "at the end of the days" (12:13). Some commentators simply interpret the prophecies in light of the statue in chapter 2 and the beasts in chapter 7. Others see most of the elements in chapter 11 as a blow-by-blow account of Israel's history—yet future at the time of the prophecies, written centuries before Christ—under the successors of Alexander the Great, especially Antiochus IV Epiphanes (r. 175–164 BC), who mercilessly wore down the Jewish people in Palestine.

The designations for periods such as "a time, times, and half a time" are picked up in New Testament discussions of the end times (Rev. 11:2; 12:14; 13:5). Also, there's a very early and clear indication of an end-times bodily resurrection of both the righteous and the wicked in Daniel 12:2.

No matter how—or even *if*—we understand these visions, the prophetic portions of Daniel point us to more central truths. As mortals tossed to and fro by the epochal events of history, we can rest in the fact that all events—past, present, and future—are in God's hands. Perhaps instead of obsessing about when these things will be and how they'll be accomplished, wise people should live hopeful lives because of the promise of Christ's coming and our own future resurrection. We must trust that God will take care of the details leading up to these climactic events according to His all-encompassing plan.

Scripture Memory 4

Daniel 12:2–3

2 And many of those who sleep in the dust of the earth shall awake, some to everlasting life, and some to shame and everlasting contempt.
3 And those who are wise shall shine like the brightness of the sky above; and those who turn many to righteousness, like the stars forever and ever.

(5) *Joel 1–3:* The Day of the Lord

The stipulations of the covenant God had made with Israel at Mount Sinai were straightforward. If they'd love Him and obey His commands, He'd bless them with security, hope, and prosperity in the Promised Land. Yet if they rejected and disobeyed God, He would send judgments in the form of warfare, sickness, and calamities (Deut. 30:15–20). God didn't leave His people with a fuzzy picture of general possibilities, but a full catalogue of benefits they'd experience if they lived in heartfelt devotion and obedience to Him (28:1–14).

God also didn't leave the Israelites with a vague warning of abstract judgment for unfaithfulness to the covenant. Rather, He spelled out curses that would come as a price for disobedience (28:15–68). Among these details, He warned of an invading army that would conquer and haul them into exile:

> The LORD will bring a nation against you from far away, from the end of the earth, swooping down like the eagle, a nation whose language you do not understand, a hard-faced nation who shall not respect the old or show mercy to the young. It shall eat the offspring of your cattle and the fruit of your ground, until you are destroyed; it also shall not leave you grain, wine, or oil, the increase of your herds or the young of your flock, until they have caused you to perish. (28:49–51)

These two-way promises set the stage for the apocalyptic drama of the book of Joel, written perhaps five centuries before Christ's birth. In the seventy-five verses packed into this prophecy of imminent judgment, God calls the people of Judah to repent because the day of the Lord is near (Joel 1:15). He begins the invective by noting a devastating plague of locusts—a sure sign the nation was beginning to experience the curses for covenant unfaithfulness. Without repentance, even greater judgments would come: a massive foreign invasion and the dreaded day of the Lord (2:1–11).

Scripture Memory 5

Joel 2:30–32

30 And I will show wonders in the heavens and on the earth, blood and fire and columns of smoke.
31 The sun shall be turned to darkness, and the moon to blood, before the great and awesome day of the LORD comes.
32 And it shall come to pass that everyone who calls on the name of the LORD shall be saved.

Yet amid this harsh foretelling of literal doom and gloom, the Lord reminds the people of His love, mercy, and grace: "'Even now,' declares the LORD, 'return to me with all your heart, with fasting, with weeping, and with mourning; and rend your hearts and not your garments'" (2:12–13). If they would return to Him, He would instantly turn away the judgment poised against His people and judge their enemies instead (2:20).

With this promise of restoration in response to their repentance, the Lord also promises to send His Spirit in a new way, ushering in an era of blessing unparalleled in their history:

> It shall come to pass afterward, that I will pour out my Spirit on all flesh; your sons and your daughters shall prophesy, your old men shall dream dreams, and your young men shall see visions. Even on the male and female servants in those days I will pour out my Spirit. (2:28–29)

This time of final judgment and final restoration will be accompanied by astounding signs and wonders *and* miraculous salvation by the name of the Lord (2:30–32). During this time the nations will be gathered for judgment; Israel will be saved and restored (3:1–8). Though deadly warfare dominates the scene in Joel 3, the dark hues of judgment give way to a brilliant spectrum of vibrant blessings that stir faith and hope in the believer (3:9–21).

Joel's basic message is simple: with repentance, judgment gives way to blessing . . . and, in the future, *ultimate* judgment will usher in *ultimate* blessing. But when was, or is, this prophecy to be fulfilled? Does it refer to events now past? To repeated events throughout history? Have some parts been fulfilled (or partly fulfilled) while other parts await future fulfillment? Or is the entire prophecy reserved for the tribulation and the second coming?

Much debate centers on when the pouring out of the Spirit described in Joel 2:28–32 did or will occur. Many see this outpouring at Pentecost (Acts 2) as a direct fulfillment, while others see it as a partial fulfillment or at least a foreshadowing of a future end-times fulfillment.[21] Peter's quotation of the Joel 2 passage in his first evangelistic message at Pentecost demonstrates some kind of connection between the two. And most commentators—amillennial, premillennial, or postmillennial—would agree that since the outpouring of the Spirit at Pentecost, we have been living in what the Bible considers to be "the last days."[22] The final judgments associated with the return of Christ and the ultimate day of the Lord could begin to unfold in our generation.

(6) *Zechariah 12–14:* Judgment and Restoration

The rhythmic beat of judgment and restoration for God's people that had been drumming throughout the Old Testament prophets reaches a reverberating climax in Zechariah. The immediate historical context relates primarily to the post-exilic rebuilding of the temple in Jerusalem, five hundred years before Christ. But several of Zechariah's visions and oracles echo forward into the New Testament, finding corresponding images and themes in its prophetic material. This suggests that the Holy Spirit intended Zechariah's book to speak both to its immediate generation of Jews, returning from exile, *and* to the ultimate judgment and restoration of all things in the end times.

The following chart proposes some similarities between Zechariah's visions and prophecies and those that appear in the New Testament:

Zechariah	New Testament
Vision of Horses and Riders (1:7–17) Vision of the Four Chariots (6:1–8)	Vision of the Four Horsemen (Rev. 6:1–7)
Vision of the Measuring Line (2:1–5)	Vision of Measuring the Temple (Rev. 11:1–2)

Vision of the Lampstand and Olive Trees (4:1–14)	Vision of the Two Olive Trees and Lampstands (Rev. 11:3–4)
Prophecy of the King Riding on a Donkey (9:9)	Fulfillment: Christ Entering Jerusalem on a Donkey (Matt. 21:5; John 12:15)
Prophecy of Thirty Pieces of Silver (11:12–13)	Fulfillment: Judas's Wage, Thirty Pieces of Silver (Matt. 27:9)
Prophecy of Israel Looking on the One They Pierced (12:10–14)	Fulfillment: All People Look Upon Christ, Who Was Pierced (John 19:37; Rev. 1:7)
Prophecy of the Shepherd Struck and the Sheep Scattered (13:7–9)	Fulfillment: Christ Was Struck, Disciples Scattered (Matt. 26:31)
Prophecy of the Nations Gathered for the Final Battle and the Coming of the Lord as Judge and King (14:1–5)	Fulfillment: When Christ Returns to Judge the Nations and Reign (Rev. 17:14; 19:11–21)

Here, at the Old Testament apex, Zechariah's visions direct the hopes of God's people toward the future. Like the bittersweet visions of Revelation itself, his montage presents both terrifying scenes of judgments (e.g., Zech. 14:12) and inspirational visions of restoration (Zech. 14:6–11).

Scripture Memory 6

Zechariah 12:10

And I will pour out on the house of David and the inhabitants of Jerusalem a spirit of grace and pleas for mercy, so that, when they look on me, on him whom they have pierced, they shall mourn for him, as one mourns for an only child, and weep bitterly over him, as one weeps over a firstborn.

Despite uncertainties and disagreements over how, when, and where, believers can be certain of this all-important fact: God's purifying judgments will bring about a glorious restoration beyond our imagination.

(7) *Matthew 24–25 (Mark 13; Luke 21:5–38):* The Great Tribulation

In this speech—known as the Olivet Discourse because of the setting on the slope of the Mount of Olives—Jesus answers the disciples' questions about Jerusalem's destruction, the signs of the Messiah's coming in judgment, and the end of the age. The details of His words have intrigued and frustrated readers for centuries; D. A. Carson once wrote, "Few chapters of the Bible have called forth more disagreement among interpreters than Matthew 24 and its parallels in Mark 13 and Luke 21."[23] Let's briefly survey four perspectives.

Preterist Fulfillment

Preterist interpreters say most prophesied elements in Matthew 24 already took place when the Romans crushed the Jewish nation later in the first century. As one author writes, "The 'great tribulation' spoken of by Jesus is not something in *our* future. It occurred when Jerusalem and the temple were destroyed in AD 70."[24] Yet orthodox preterists who see Christ's prophecy here fulfilled historically, in this way, still expect His future literal return. Thus the prophecies of Matthew 24 "are to be distinguished from those that refer to Christ's visible coming at the consummation of all things."[25]

Futurist Fulfillment

Just as most preterists see some Olivet Discourse events as still awaiting fulfillment, most futurists believe a few of these prophecies[26] refer to Rome's first-century destruction of Jerusalem. For the most part, the dividing line between preterists and futurists is not whether these prophecies are *entirely future* or *entirely past* but whether they're *mostly future* or *mostly past*.

Partial Fulfillment

The view I'm calling "partial fulfillment" is more a mediating position between the futurist and preterist outlooks. Rather than *most* of these events being fulfilled *either* future *or* past, this view tends to see Jesus as having spoken equally about near and far fulfillments.[27] So as we read the different accounts of the Olivet Discourse, we must be ready to identify some things as having occurred already and others that await a future fulfillment.[28]

But why would Jesus provide information for both the first century and the end times? This view notes that the disciples asked three questions relating to events of their own lifetime (destruction of the temple), of the distant future (signs of Christ's coming), *and* of what could apply to both the near and the far (end of the age). In short, they were broaching several queries in aiming to ask only one, as, from their vantage, these events were to occur all at the same time. Further New Testament revelation would sort these out as distinct future happenings that would each occur on their own, and hence, those who adhere to this view seek to sort them out in retrospect in the Olivet Discourse.

Double Fulfillment

Rather than assigning fulfillment of some aspects to the past and others to the future, as in the previous approach, some interpreters understand Christ's words to blend the two perspectives. So even though much of the prophecy was fulfilled either literally or figuratively in the first century, this *near*-fulfillment becomes a type (or foreshadowing) of the final end-times fulfillment preceding the return of Jesus. C. E. B. Cranfield puts it this way: "We must allow for a double reference, for a mingling of historical and eschatological."[29] Thus, for example, the siege of Jerusalem, with its impending destruction (see Luke 21:20), was historically fulfilled with the first-century destruction of temple and city. Yet this *also* refers to the end-times siege and destruction of Jerusalem; the initial fulfillment guarantees the truthfulness of Jesus' promise, and it applied directly to His original hearers, but that fulfillment itself becomes prophetic, illustrating another, even greater fulfillment we can expect to take place in the days leading up to His return.

Scripture Memory 7

Matthew 24:36

But concerning that day and hour no one knows, not even the angels of heaven, nor the Son, but the Father only.

(8) *Acts 1:6–11:* The Manner of Christ's Return

"Are we there yet?!"

It doesn't matter if the journey is two hours or twenty (or, sometimes, twenty minutes)—nearly every parent of kids from toddlers to teens has heard these impatient words from the back seat during a road trip. And, regardless of how patient and reasoned their response, Mom and Dad can count on another whiny *"Are we there yet?"* far too soon. It's part of the family-journey "fun."

At the end of Jesus' forty-day sojourn with His disciples after He was resurrected, they asked their own version of "Are we there yet?" When He said they would be baptized by the Holy Spirit "not many days from now" (Acts 1:5), they inquired, "Lord, will you at this time restore the kingdom to Israel?" (1:6). Impatient zeal . . . eager anticipation . . . enthusiastic hope—all these likely fueled their curiosity about the timing of the promised restoration. Perhaps Jesus' mention of the

Spirit's coming directed their minds to Joel's words about the day of the Lord.[30] Like a parent trying to ready the children for a longer journey than they expected, Jesus said, "It is not for you to know times or seasons that the Father has fixed by his own authority" (v. 7). Instead of answering their *when* question, He turned them toward the matter at hand—preaching the gospel throughout the world by the coming Spirit's power (1:8).

However, those premillennial interpreters who believe national Israel will experience a future conversion and literal Promised Land restoration in fulfillment of Old Testament promises point out that Jesus never corrected the disciples' expectation (1:7), but rather appears to postpone or delay such a reestablishment to make room for the gospel's proclamation to all the nations:

> When the disciples wanted to know when the kingdom was going to be restored to Israel, they were not told that they were in error, that the kingdom would never be restored to Israel, but only that it was not for them to know the "times or seasons."[31]

On the other hand, many amillennialists (and postmillennialists) note that Jesus also didn't endorse their expectation but gently turned their misguided understanding toward the truth. By pointing to the Spirit's power coming upon them and the worldwide spread of the gospel of the kingdom, He redefined the scope and nature of the kingdom—global and spiritual. They were to take the gospel to all nations for their salvation and for the church's formation: "Jesus clearly intends the focus of the kingdom to be away from Jerusalem. . . . Israel is only a tiny country, and the gospel is to conquer *the world*."[32]

All agree, though, that Jesus intended that His disciples—and we—avoid date-setting and sign-seeking. Our focus should be on sharing the gospel, making disciples, and being ready for Christ's coming whenever it occurs.

Following His correction and words of commission, Jesus ascended into the clouds. Clouds often symbolized God's presence—on Sinai, in the wilderness, in the temple, and at the transfiguration.[33] The Son has been exalted ("lifted up") in glory to the Father's right hand and, as the angels were sent to promise (Acts 1:11), He will return one day in glory. Their words refute any belief that Jesus' return would be invisible, spiritual, or merely heavenly, as some cults and false teachers have alleged. Rather, just as He ascended to heaven *visibly* and *physically* in the presence of many witnesses, He will "come in the same way" as He went (1:11). Perhaps the disciples would have remembered His very words in the Olivet Discourse, where He said He would come "on the clouds of heaven with power and great glory" (Matt. 24:30).

> **Scripture Memory 8**
>
> ***Acts 1:7–9***
>
> 7 He said to them, "It is not for you to know times or seasons that the Father has fixed by his own authority.
> 8 But you will receive power when the Holy Spirit has come upon you, and you will be my witnesses in Jerusalem and in all Judea and Samaria, and to the end of the earth."
> 9 And when he had said these things, as they were looking on, he was lifted up, and a cloud took him out of their sight.

When Christ returns as Judge and King, there will be no confusion, no uncertainty, no wondering whether the kingdom has come or what it will be like. *All* will be made clear in the light of His power and glory.

(9) *Romans 8:18–25:* The Restoration of All Creation

Chances are Romans 8 wouldn't appear on most Christians' Top Ten List of Important End-Times Passages. However, one could argue that verses 18–25 present the crux of the Bible's teaching on creation, fall, redemption, and ultimate personal and cosmic restoration. It's one of my favorite "go-to" texts for teaching on eschatology.

Here Paul turns our attention from present sufferings to the certain hope of the coming renewal (v. 18). This hope, stretching beyond individual salvation, is infinitely larger than escaping an awful world for a wondrous heaven; it also involves the entire restoration of all creation (v. 19). The whole created realm—things visible and invisible, physical and spiritual—has been subject to the bondage of corruption since the fall of Adam and Eve (Gen. 3). But then, just as our physical bodies will be resurrected and glorified, so the whole cosmos will be restored and renewed (Rom. 8:21–23). Peter called this long-awaited reinstatement the "times of refreshing" that will accompany Christ's return (Acts 3:20); Jesus himself called it "the new world, when the Son of Man will sit on his glorious throne" (Matt. 19:28).

Cranfield notes:

> Paul's meaning [is] that the subhuman creation has been subjected to the frustration of not being able properly to fulfill the purpose of its existence, God having appointed that without man it should not be made perfect. We may think of the whole magnificent theatre of the universe together with all its splendid properties and all the chorus of subhuman life, created to glorify God but unable to do so fully, so long as man the chief actor in the drama of God's praise fails to contribute his rational part.[34]

This is eschatologically vital because it conjoins the physical resurrection of believers and the renewal of all else God has made. Simultaneously it conveys the crucial fact that we're stuck between His promise of a perfect world and His fulfillment of the promise. Accordingly, the ongoing frustration we feel with this fallen world's "thorns and thistles" (Gen. 3:17–19) is normal. Deep down we feel, we *know*, that things aren't supposed to be like this. God didn't intend that perfection be marred; He didn't want love and beauty to see decay or suffer distortion; He did not create us to die.

We long for a time when the weeds will be pulled, the thorns crushed, and the thistles clipped. We ache for wrongs to be made right, for truth and goodness to win out, for light to vanquish all darkness. We groan inwardly for our redemption, for our resurrection, and for creation's renewal (Rom. 8).

While here and now we try to keep our balance and manage the tension between the original fall and the everlasting redemption, sometimes mediocre to poor is all we can expect. But don't get cynical or become jaded. Through His death and resurrection, Jesus Christ *has* overcome the world. He came first as the Lamb, to take away the world's sin, but He is coming back as the Lion, to reign forever, and when He does return, His blessings will drive out the curse; the thorns and thistles, the sin and suffering, will be no more.

(10) *1 Corinthians 15:12–58:* The Resurrection of the Body

The resurrection of our physical bodies is not an optional article of the faith but is—and always has been—a central tenet of Christianity. In one of the earliest confessions of faith for baptism, the new convert declared, "I believe in . . . the resurrection of the body and life everlasting."[35]

Contrary to common misconception, this affirmation in the creed refers not to Christ's resurrection body but to the resurrection of believers unto eternal life in their restored (and glorified) *physical* state. Though resurrection language runs throughout the New Testament, the central passage for Christian doctrine on our future bodily restoration is found in 1 Corinthians 15, specifically verses 12–58.

Scripture Memory 9

Romans 8:18–23

18 For I consider that the sufferings of this present time are not worth comparing with the glory that is to be revealed to us.
19 For the creation waits with eager longing for the revealing of the sons of God.
20 For the creation was subjected to futility, not willingly, but because of him who subjected it, in hope
21 that the creation itself will be set free from its bondage to corruption and obtain the freedom of the glory of the children of God.
22 For we know that the whole creation has been groaning together in the pains of childbirth until now.
23 And not only the creation, but we ourselves, who have the firstfruits of the Spirit, groan inwardly as we wait eagerly for adoption as sons, the redemption of our bodies.

Paul laid the groundwork for his teaching on our someday resurrection by turning our attention back to the resurrection of Jesus (vv. 1–11). He reminds us that the gospel includes not only Christ's death for our sins but also His being physically raised (vv. 3–4). This truth is so essential to the faith that Paul calls it a doctrine "of first importance" (v. 3). No wonder, then, that he repeatedly ties Christ's past resurrection to ours in the future and to the faith itself. In other words, *hope in our future resurrection is not optional; it's essential.*

Beginning in verse 12, he challenges those who would deny, downplay, spiritualize, mythologize, marginalize, or neglect the fact of our bodily resurrection. His logic flows from the fount of Christ's resurrection: If He has been raised, how can anyone deny the resurrection of believers? Conversely, how can Christ have been resurrected if there's no such thing as bodily resurrection? If Christ himself were not to have been resurrected—if God having raised Him from death to life is not true but rather false—then the whole of Christianity is worthless, hopeless, and, in fact, a lie (vv. 12–19). Those who deny the fact of the resurrection deny the faith itself. Once again, *hope in our future resurrection is not optional; it's essential.*

Having permanently welded together the resurrection and the Christian faith, Paul next describes the order of resurrection, again drawing upon the gospel, showing how Christ's own resurrection constitutes the "firstfruits" of all who will be raised (v. 20). In agriculture, picking the firstfruits guaranteed that a larger harvest would follow. First, Christ was raised in His immortal, incorruptible, glorious body. Then, "at His [second] coming," those who belong to Him (believers) will be raised in bodies that match His own. Lastly, "the end" comes, when all things will be brought to a final consummation and death itself is utterly vanquished (vv. 22–24).

Some interpreters understand verses 20–25 to refer to two stages in God's plan of resurrection: (1) Christ's past resurrection and (2) then, at His return, the raising of all others—some to eternal life (emphasized in v. 23), and others to eternal condemnation (see Dan. 12:2; John 5:29).[36] This amillennial and postmillennial perspective sees no time elapsing between the resurrection of believers (v. 23) and "the end" described in verses 24–26.[37]

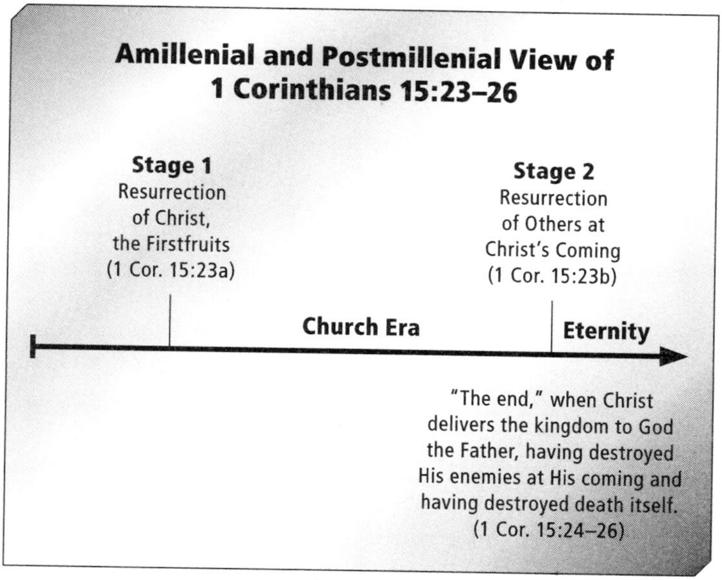

Premillennialists interpret the chronology of 1 Corinthians 15:23–26 differently. Instead of seeing one long period—the present church era—in verse 23, indicated by Paul's use of the word *then,* they see an additional long period of time (the millennial kingdom) indicated by the second use of *then* (verse 24). Millard Erickson notes, "It appears that just as the first coming and resurrection of Christ were distinct events separated by time, so will there be an interval between the second coming and the end."[38]

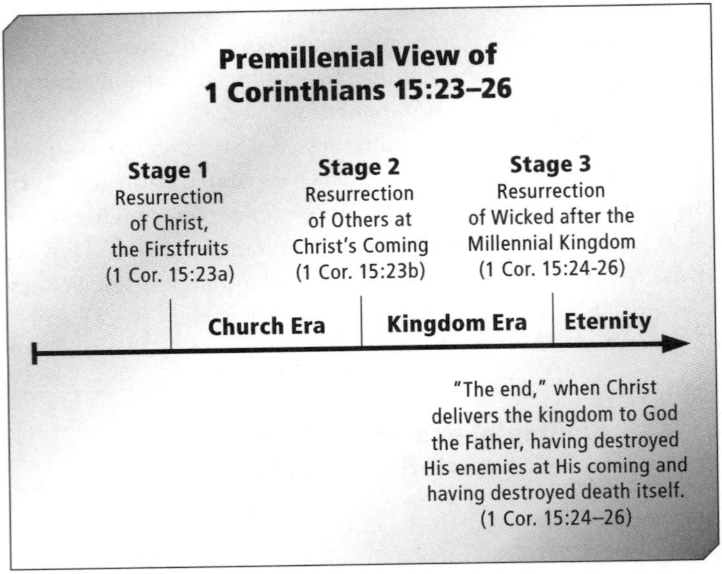

Regardless of which view one takes, the future bodily resurrection is a reality. By this miraculous restoration of life, God's kingdom purposes will be accomplished and death itself will be destroyed.

After giving additional practical support for our resurrection hope (vv. 29–34), Paul responds to objections (v. 35). People today have questions too:

- "What will my resurrection body be like?"
- "Will it be different from my current body? If so, how different?"
- "Will I be able to recognize other people in their new bodies?"
- "Will it be physical or spiritual—material or ghostly?"
- "Will I be able to walk through walls? fly? travel with just a thought?"

Paul doesn't answer all possible questions, yet he does lay out some key principles to give us a general image of the nature of our resurrection bodies (vv. 36–42); he also compares and contrasts the "natural" and "spiritual" bodies (vv. 42–49). Like a seed, the natural body is planted in the ground upon death, subject to weakness and dishonor. But the spiritual body is raised from the ground imperishable, characterized by power and glory. This language of "spiritual body" has led some to believe the resurrection body will be ghostly and immaterial, without any physical part. Actually, the contrasts between the natural and spiritual are used to describe the latter's superior *quality* and *power*, not the substance from which it's composed.

As believers share in the weak, mortal, and corruptible body inherited from Adam, so we'll share in the powerful, immortal, and incorruptible body inherited through Jesus (vv. 46–49). Christ's body came forth from the tomb in a glorified state, and believers, upon resurrection, will have material bodies designed for existence in the spiritual realm: "The present body is animated by 'soul' and is therefore mortal; the resurrection body is animated entirely by immortal and life-giving spirit, and is therefore called a spiritual body."[39]

Proceeding to the concluding argument, Paul again ties the resurrection to the gospel of Christ (e.g., v. 57) and explains that "flesh and blood cannot inherit the kingdom of God, nor does the perishable inherit the imperishable" (v. 50). For humans to receive eternal life and immortality, our fallen, mortal, corruptible bodies must be transformed from perishability to imperishability. So just as a visitor to a construction zone must wear a hard hat, a surgeon must wear sterile gear, and a man must wear a suit to a black-tie affair, to enter the realm of immortality, "this perishable body must put on the imperishable, and this mortal body must put on immortality" (v. 53).

Scripture Memory 10

1 Corinthians 15:51–53

51 Behold! I tell you a mystery. We shall not all sleep, but we shall all be changed,
52 in a moment, in the twinkling of an eye, at the last trumpet. For the trumpet will sound, and the dead will be raised imperishable, and we shall be changed.
53 For this perishable body must put on the imperishable, and this mortal body must put on immortality.

In connection with this glorious change, Paul bursts into an electrifying promise for all of us suffering from the physical deterioration of this fallen world. When Christ returns, all those who have died will be raised in new glorious bodies . . . and all those who are alive will be instantly transformed into their new bodies without having to taste death:

> Behold! I tell you a mystery. We shall not all sleep, but we shall all be changed, in a moment, in the twinkling of an eye, at the last trumpet. For the trumpet will sound, and the dead will be raised imperishable, and we shall be changed.[40]

With such great and glorious promises tied to our certain hope and the ultimate defeat of sin and death (vv. 54–58), no wonder Paul makes it clear: *the Christian's hope in our future resurrection is not optional; it's essential.*

(11) 2 *Corinthians 5:1–10:* Bodily Resurrection and the Intermediate State

"What will happen to us when we die?" is a frequent eschatological query. It's the basic question answered in the realm of personal eschatology—the destiny of saved and unsaved individuals, especially where their souls go between their physical death and their physical resurrection.

With language and imagery reminiscent of Romans 8, Paul answers this (5:1–5), turning our attention from this life's "light momentary affliction" toward an "eternal weight of glory" that awaits us in the next (4:17). The timing of this transition is unknown, yet its occurrence is a fact: "We know [*certainty*] that if the tent that is our earthly home is destroyed, we have [*certainty*] a building from God" (5:1).

Why does he use "we have"—present tense—in reference to our future glorified bodies that we'll receive at the resurrection when Christ returns? Is our resurrection body already sitting in some heavenly closet, waiting for us to step into it when we die? No. The seemingly best explanation is that he wanted to mark the *absolute certainty* of our glorious new body. Our resurrection is guaranteed by the indwelling Holy Spirit (v. 5), so he can speak of our resurrection body as something already in our possession.[41]

Surely, Paul hoped Christ would return in his own day, and he wouldn't experience physical death before putting on his new heavenly body (1 Cor. 15:51–53). However, whether or not he would die before the resurrection of believers, he knew that the promise of future resurrection is secure. During the intervening period between death and resurrection, he would be "away from the body" but "at home with the Lord" (2 Cor. 5:8). In fact, the moment he departed this world by physical death, his soul would "be with Christ" until his bodily resurrection (Phil. 1:23).

We should not, however, be misled about Paul's primary hope—he isn't teaching that the ultimate goal of Christian salvation is simply to die and go to heaven, that is, to escape the physical body and dwell as a disembodied spirit eternally with Christ in some ethereal realm. He clearly says we do not want to be "unclothed," that is, left without a body, but that we wish to be "further clothed" with our new resurrection body (2 Cor. 5:4). Even better would be to have our mortal bodies "swallowed up by life" without ever having to experience the temporary separation of physical death.

Believers who undergo physical death will be among those who enjoy an intermediate spiritual sojourn with Christ before their physical resurrection. Believers who are alive at the time of the resurrection will experience not physical death but instead a sudden transformation from their mortal bodies to their immortal bodies. Whichever group we're in, we make it our aim to please Jesus Christ, walking always by faith rather than by sight (vv. 7–9).[42]

To underscore our need to look forward and upward in faith and hope, Paul provides a series of contrasts between what we see (this life) and what we do not yet see (the life to come). *Hope* is his focus and agenda here; originally he was conveying his own confident hope to the Corinthian believers with the goal of kindling that hope in them as well.

Verse	Present Reality	Future Hope
5:1	Our earthly tent is being destroyed.	We are certain of our eternal building.
5:2	We groan in our present tent.	We long for our heavenly home.
5:3	We don't want to be naked.	We want to be clothed with our eternal dwelling.
5:4	We groan in our mortality.	We long to be, and will be, clothed with life.
5:6	We are at home in the body.	We want to be with the Lord.
5:7	We now walk by faith.	We will one day walk by sight.

During this in-between time, as we cope with this present reality's suffering and frustration, Paul's goal, in light of our certain future hope, is to motivate us to please the Lord in all we do (v. 9). Ultimately, "we must all appear before the judgment seat of Christ, so that each one may receive what is due for what he has done in the body, whether good or evil" (v. 10).

Scripture Memory 11

2 Corinthians 5:10

For we must all appear before the judgment seat of Christ, so that each one may receive what is due for what he has done in the body, whether good or evil.

Commentators differ on whether this "judgment" will take place earlier than the general resurrection and judgment of the wicked (the premillennial view) or rather if it will coincide with that "great white throne" judgment (amillennial and postmillennial views).[43] Regardless of the timing, Scripture is clear that believers will be judged by Christ—however, not to determine their eternal destinies but for the displaying of their eternal rewards.[44]

(12) *1 Thessalonians 4:13–5:11:* Resurrection and Rapture

The word *rapture* comes from the Latin *rapere,* which means "to snatch." The Latin translation of the New Testament renders the Greek term *harpazo*, in 1 Thessalonians 4:17, as *rapere*. This is the word used for the end-times "catching up" to heaven of the church—those who will experience bodily resurrection and have their condition transformed from mortal to immortal (1 Cor. 15:51–52).

For orthodox believers, the question is not *if* the church will be raised and caught up to meet the Lord in the air; this is the passage's straightforward teaching.[45] Disagreement centers on *when* this will happen in relation to a day of the Lord or tribulation period. Further, those believers who do not expect a literal period of judgment upon the earth prior to Christ's return have no question about the event's timing—for them, the resurrection and rapture will obviously occur when Christ returns to judge the living and the dead.

Simple, right?

Yet those who do expect a distinct period of tribulation leading up to the second coming have asked and answered the question of the rapture's timing in several ways. Among futurists, there are five basic approaches.

Pretribulation Rapture

The "pretrib" view holds that before the seven-year tribulation, true believers from the church age will be "caught up" (4:17) from earth to heaven and therefore be saved from God's wrath during the tribulation.

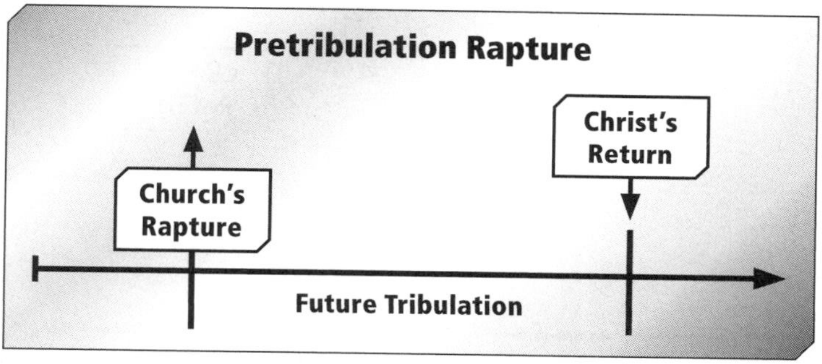

Midtribulation Rapture

The "midtrib" view maintains that in the middle of the seven-year tribulation, true believers will be "caught up" from earth to heaven and so be saved from God's direct wrath, which comes during the tribulation's last half.

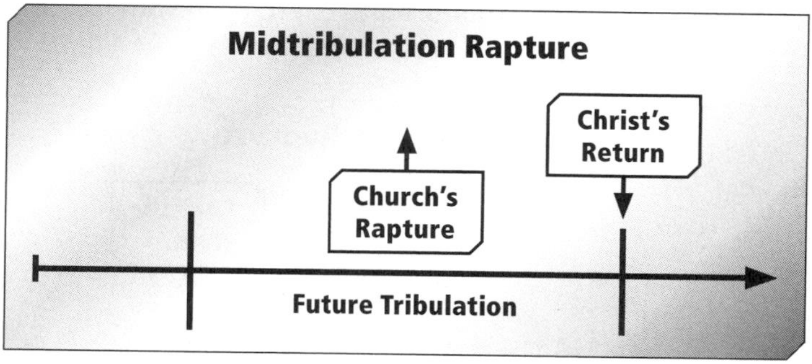

Pre-Wrath Rapture

The pre-wrath view is that before God pours out His direct wrath upon the earth (usually limited to the seven "bowls" of wrath; see

Rev. 15–16), He will rescue His faithful saints. This will occur very late in the tribulation but before Christ returns to earth. Thus the pre-wrath position places the rapture somewhere between the mid-tribulation and post-tribulation perspectives.

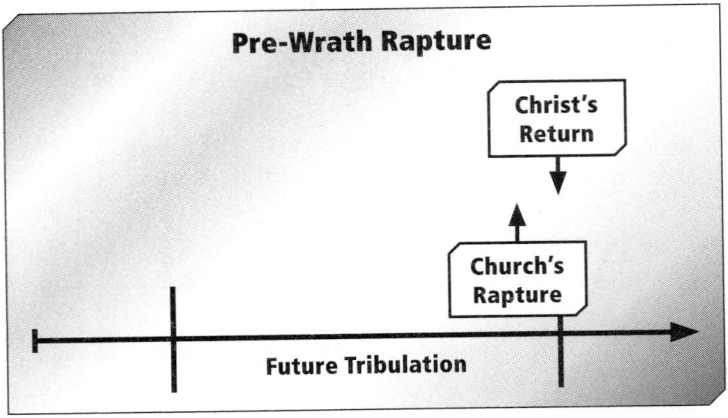

Post-Tribulation Rapture

The "post-trib" view says that after the seven-year tribulation, believers who survived its persecution and martyrdom will be "caught up" from earth to heaven, either to immediately return to earth to reign with Christ during the millennium or to reign with Christ over the earth from the heavenly sphere.

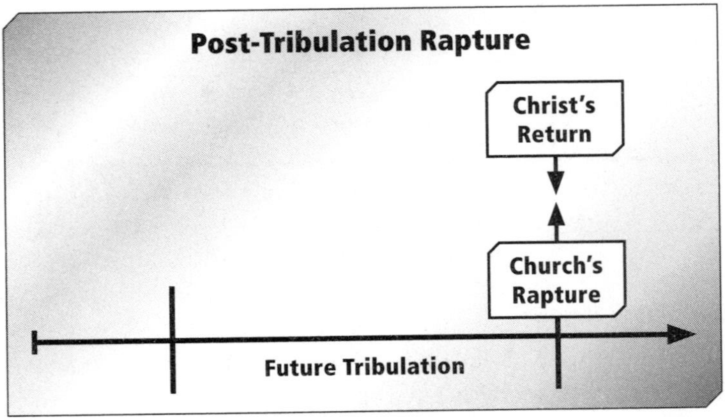

Partial Rapture

"Partial rapture" is the belief among futurists that only "spiritual Christians" will be raptured before the tribulation. Some proponents also hold that throughout the tribulation there will be repeated (multiple) raptures as various believers demonstrate faithfulness or overcome trials to their faith.

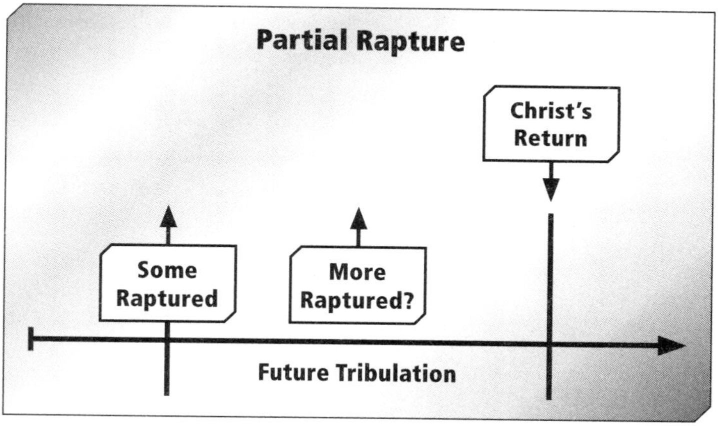

We should not let differences of opinion on the timing of the church's rapture distract us from Paul's main point in the passage. The truths are meant to strengthen us in the face of death and encourage us when we mourn the loss of a loved one. We do well to keep in mind the following four vital principles:

First, "*God will bring with him those who have fallen asleep*" (4:14): departed family members . . . friends . . . ancestors . . . heroes of old we've only read about. One glorious day, we'll be part of a grand reunion—the gathering of the saints of every generation!

Second, *all who are alive when Christ comes to raise the dead will also experience a sudden transformation from mortal bodies into immortal bodies without ever having to taste death* (4:16–17).[46] This means some of us alive today may never die—what a thrilling prospect! Yet Paul is quite clear that no one knows when this will happen (5:1); the day will come suddenly, like a thief (5:2), so we cannot know whether we'll receive our immortal bodies through resurrection after death or through transformation while still here.

Third, *the wrath of coming judgment is for unbelievers* (5:3–5, 9). God has not destined us for wrath but for salvation through Jesus (1 Thess. 5:9); there is no condemnation for those who are in Christ (Rom. 8:1). God will never pour out His wrath on His people—He will either rescue them from wrath, as with Lot in Sodom or Noah in the flood, or He will protect them through the wrath, as with Israel in Egypt or Daniel amid the lions. Though the day of the Lord is coming, it's not coming for anyone sealed by God's Spirit.

> **Scripture Memory 12**
>
> ***1 Thessalonians 4:13–18***
>
> 13 But we do not want you to be uninformed, brothers, about those who are asleep, that you may not grieve as others do who have no hope.
> 14 For since we believe that Jesus died and rose again, even so, through Jesus, God will bring with him those who have fallen asleep.
> 15 For this we declare to you by a word from the Lord, that we who are alive, who are left until the coming of the Lord, will not precede those who have fallen asleep.
> 16 For the Lord himself will descend from heaven with a cry of command, with the voice of an archangel, and with the sound of the trumpet of God. And the dead in Christ will rise first.
> 17 Then we who are alive, who are left, will be caught up together with them in the clouds to meet the Lord in the air, and so we will always be with the Lord.
> 18 Therefore encourage one another with these words.

Fourth, *the truth of our resurrection and transformation is to bring hope, encouragement, and sober living* (1 Thess. 4:18; 5:4–8, 11). Scripture may not include as many details about the resurrection and rapture as we would like or enough to answer all our questions. Yet God's Word gives us enough for His purposes—that we may be "equipped for every good work" (2 Tim. 3:17). Our certain hope of resurrection and eternal life with all the saints of every age should encourage us to look beyond death and see the glorious light of the age to come. Accordingly, we should live sober lives as citizens of that coming kingdom rather than allowing the wickedness of this age to intoxicate us with its appealing but destructive power.

(13) *2 Thessalonians 2:1–12:* The Man of Sin and the Day of the Lord

Makers of horror films aren't alone in fascination with the number 666, the antichrist figure, or satanic beings seeking ultimate control over the world. These and other apocalyptic themes have formed a fabric of folk theology for nearly two millennia, influencing virtually all of the fine arts—architecture, painting, song, theatre, sculpture, literature (poetry and prose of many genres), and dance . . . and, unfortunately, filling ill-informed minds with less-than-accurate or flat-out wrong ideas about the end times.

> **Scripture Memory 13**
>
> ***2 Thessalonians 2:7–8***
>
> 7 For the mystery of lawlessness is already at work. Only he who now restrains it will do so until he is out of the way.
>
> 8 And then the lawless one will be revealed, whom the Lord Jesus will kill with the breath of his mouth and bring to nothing by the appearance of his coming.

Though the title *antichrist* doesn't appear in 2 Thessalonians 2, as early as the second century the "man of lawlessness" (v. 3) was identified with the "beast rising out the sea" (Rev. 13:1–10), the "antichrist [who] is coming" (1 John 2:18; 4:3), and a great future apostasy just preceding the second coming. For example, Irenaeus of Lyons (c. AD 180) wrote:

> He [Antichrist], being endued with all the power of the devil, shall come, not as a righteous king, nor as a legitimate king, in subjection to God, but an impious, unjust, and lawless one; as an apostate, iniquitous and murderous; as a robber, concentrating in himself satanic apostasy, and setting aside idols to persuade that he himself is God, raising up himself as the only idol, having in himself the multifarious errors of the other idols. This he does, in order that they who do [now] worship the devil by means of many abominations, may serve himself by this one idol, of whom the apostle thus speaks in the second Epistle to the Thessalonians.[47]

This futurist expectation of an antichrist, a great apostasy, and deceiving signs and wonders has been a common view for much of the church's history.

Most *preterists* believe the events Paul describes in 2 Thessalonians 2 already took place in the years surrounding the destruction of the temple and the end of the age of Israel (between AD 66 and 73). That is, though the prophecy was still future when the epistle was written (c. AD 50), it pointed not to a long-future earthly reign of Antichrist but to later-first-century events.

However, if Paul's words do refer to a yet-future coming of an antichrist, as futurists believe, the following are some of his basic characteristics:

- He'll arrive before Christ's return and the day of the Lord (v. 2).
- He'll be associated with that apostasy or "rebellion" (v. 3).
- He'll be shown to be a man of sin or "lawlessness" (v. 3).
- He'll exalt himself against all faiths and God himself (v. 4).
- He'll sit in the temple of God, claiming to be God (v. 4).
- His coming is restrained until his time to be revealed (vv. 6–7).
- He'll be destroyed by Jesus at His return (v. 8).
- He'll be empowered by Satan with false signs and wonders (v. 9).
- He'll deceive the unsaved who have rejected the truth (v. 10).

(14) *2 Peter 3:1–18:* The Day of the Lord and the New Creation

Scoffers will come (v. 3)—this fact we're to get right from the start. Motivated by selfish desires, not wanting to be accountable to anybody but themselves, they will reject the idea that someday they'll be judged for their sins. Instead of living in light of the Lord's return, they mock those who order their lives with the future in mind. They live for this life's whims rather than hope in the glorious age to come. With arrogance they'll sneer: "Where is the promise of his coming? For ever since the fathers fell asleep, all things are continuing as they were from the beginning of creation" (v. 4).

The believer's worldview contrasts decisively with that of the unbeliever. The believer knows that the God who made this world is the God who judged it decisively with a flood (vv. 5–6). And the believer knows that the God who renewed the world after the flood will one day bring the world to a fiery judgment (v. 7). Though His hand presently is stayed by patience, at any moment His deserved wrath will be unleashed upon wickedness (vv. 8–10).

Considering that in verse 13 Peter punctuates his end-times description with the "new heavens and new earth" language of Isaiah 65:17, it seems most likely his inspiration for the judgment by fire comes from Isaiah 66:15–16, thus connecting Yahweh's coming judgment by fire with Christ's judgment of the world at His return.[48] This, then, would correspond to the "day of the Lord," when the current world system will be destroyed, just as the pre-flood world was demolished and then replaced by a new order. Peter warns that this judgment will come "like a thief" (3:10).[49]

The "current system" to be destroyed includes all evil and sin. It will also include the destruction of demons and a razing of the world's geography.[50] In fact, these fires (vv. 10, 12–13) are best interpreted as fire for purifying, likely drawn on metallurgical imagery—that is, of heating for the sake of cleansing and strengthening (Mal. 3:2–4; 4:1–3).[51]

The world established after Christ's return and His fiery judgment, Peter describes this way: "But according to His promise we are looking for new heavens and a new earth, in which righteousness dwells" (2 Peter 3:13 NASB). Jesus calls this the "regeneration" of the world (Matt. 19:28 NASB), which corresponds with the expectation to which Peter gave voice in Jerusalem:

> Therefore repent and return, so that your sins may be wiped away, in order that times of refreshing may come from the presence of the Lord; and that He may send Jesus, the Christ appointed for you, whom heaven must receive until the period of restoration of all things about which God spoke by the mouth of His holy prophets from ancient time. (Acts 3:19–21 NASB)

There is a relatively recent interpretation, cutting across premillennial, amillennial, and postmillennial lines, that says the destruction Peter describes in verses 10–13 refers to a total annihilation of the universe followed by a completely new creation "out of nothing" (*ex nihilo*).[52] The majority view of the ancient, medieval, and even protestant churches[53] (including most commentators throughout history) is that this language and imagery portends the destruction of the world system—its wickedness, and its godless religions and institutions—but not annihilation of the universe itself. The "new heavens and new earth," then, would be a completely new condition of this created realm, not a new creation out of nothing.[54] This view tries to harmonize Peter's language of the old world prior to the flood being destroyed by water, with that of the present world being destroyed by fire (vv. 5–7). As the waters of the flood wiped the world clean and prepared the way for a new world for Noah and his family, so the coming fire will purge and purify the world, preparing the way for a creation liberated from wickedness (Rom. 8:20–22).

Regardless, Peter's purpose in warning of coming judgment is not to thoroughly address the *where*, *what*, and *when* of the end times. Rather, he wants us to focus on the *who* and the *why*.

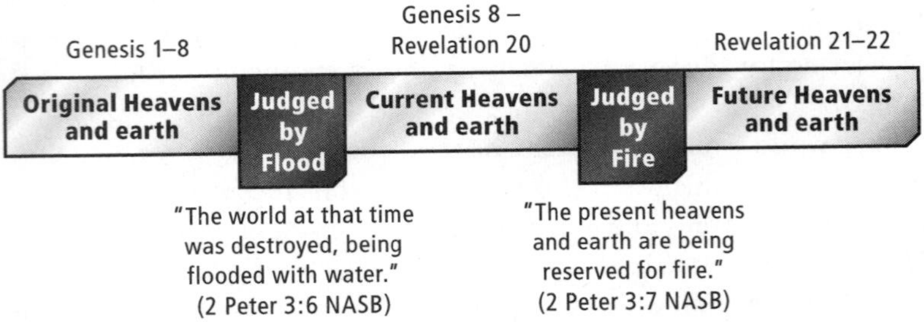

First, let's answer the *who* question: Whereas scoffers laugh at the notion of coming judgment, we should remember that what the holy prophets foretold already has been fulfilled, knowing that God's future judgment is as sure as His past creation and past judgments (3:1–7). All who reject God face unthinkable destruction if they don't take His merciful opportunity to repent while they still can (vv. 7–9). Believers continue to look forward to the fulfillment of God's great and glorious promise (v. 13).

Scripture Memory 14

2 Peter 3:13–14

13 But according to his promise we are waiting for new heavens and a new earth in which righteousness dwells. 14 Therefore, beloved, since you are waiting for these, be diligent to be found by him without spot or blemish, and at peace.

Second, how does Peter address the *why* question? He shares these teachings on judgment and renewal for a practical reason: to effect character change and spiritual growth in believers. As we wait for the new heavens and new earth, we ought to live in holiness and godliness (v. 11). We're to wait eagerly for the promise's fulfillment, preaching the gospel, living exemplary lives (vv. 11–12). We should be found "without spot or blemish, and at peace" (v. 14), avoiding the scoffing, ignorance, and unstable lives of false teachers (vv. 15–16). Instead of falling from a sure and stable faith, we must "grow in the grace and knowledge of our Lord and Savior Jesus Christ" (vv. 17–18).

(15) *Revelation 19–22:* The Return of Christ, Millennium, and New Creation

If Revelation presents the culmination of God's plan of redemption, then chapters 19–22 represent the *climax* of the climax—like the explosive cannons and resounding bells in Tchaikovsky's *1812 Overture* finale. Throughout the book we witness the undoing of earthly power. Orchestrated to call the wicked to repentance and punish those who persist in cursing their Creator, God's intensifying judgments remind us that one day He will vanquish all wickedness, and righteousness will enjoy ultimate victory.

The symbolic images stunningly portray this triumph over God's enemies at the return of Jesus (19:11–21). We witness the binding of Satan (20:1–3), the reign of Christ with His faithful saints and martyrs (20:4–6), the final defeat of Satan, sin, and death itself (20:7–15), and the ushering in of "a new heaven and a new earth," where God will dwell among His people and from which all death, mourning, crying, pain, and sinfulness will be banished (21:1–8). Finally, after an astounding tour of the magnificent destiny and breathtaking destination of redeemed humanity (21:9–22:5), the book ends with oaths, warnings, and a bold invitation:

> The Spirit and the Bride say, "Come." And let the one who hears say, "Come." And let the one who is thirsty come; let the one who desires take the water of life without price. (22:17)

The big picture of the final divine intervention in human history can be summed up in two words: "God wins." However, Bible-believing Christians understand the details of Revelation 19–22 in several different ways. Though all agree that Christ will one day return as Judge and King, one significant disagreement over end-times events is whether the second coming will occur *before* or *after* the thousand-year reign, described in 20:1–6. This question hinges on how one understands the nature of this reign. The variety of viewpoints on this specific issue can be divided into three tendencies.

Realized Millennialism

Those who hold to a *realized* millennial view believe the events or conditions symbolized in 20:1–6 (the millennium or "thousand years") already are being fulfilled either in heaven or through the church. This is often called "amillennialism" because it doesn't involve the expectation of a literal, future one-thousand-year earthly reign (the prefix "a-" meaning *no* or *not*).

Instead of reading Revelation 19–20 as one complete vision in which the millennial reign (chapter 20) chronologically follows the return of Christ (chapter 19), most amillennial interpreters see a completely new vision starting in chapter 20 that takes the reader back to the beginning of the church age.[55] Anthony Hoekema explains this well:

> That the millennial reign described in verses 4–6 occurs before the Second Coming of Christ is evident from the fact that the final judgment, described in verses 11–15 of this chapter, is pictured as coming after the thousand-year reign. Not only in the book of Revelation but elsewhere in the New Testament the final judgment is associated with the Second Coming of Christ. . . . This being the case, it is obvious that the thousand-year reign of Revelation 20:4–6 must occur *before* and *not after* the Second Coming of Christ.[56]

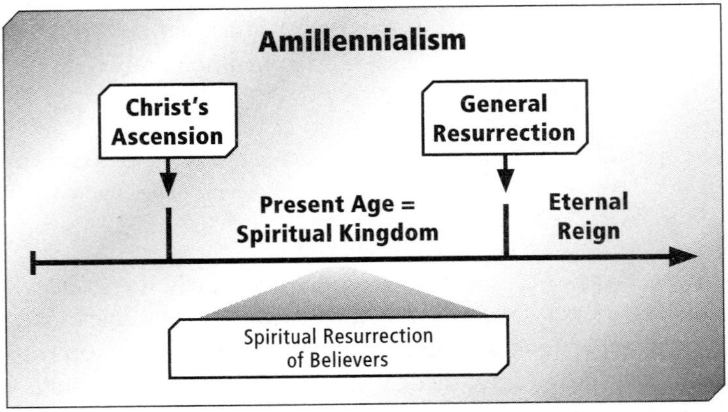

In the amillennial view, the "first resurrection" (20:5) doesn't refer to the bodily resurrection of both the righteous and the wicked at Christ's return.[57] Rather, it refers to the spiritual resurrection of believers saved during the present age of the church's mission (Eph. 2:5).

They reign spiritually with Christ as members of the kingdom of God today—either the church here on earth or the reigning saints already victorious in heaven (Eph. 2:6; Col. 1:13).

Anticipated Millennialism

Those who hold to an *anticipated* millennial view believe the events of Revelation 20:1–6 won't occur until after Christ physically returns to earth. This view is often called "premillennialism," as Christ is expected to return prior to ("pre-") the fulfillment of an actual thousand-year ("millennial") reign on this earth. Premillennial interpreters of Revelation 19–22 generally see this as a chronological unfolding of future history[58] and generally understand the period of one thousand years to be a literal number—or at least close enough to one thousand years for the number to be an accurate approximation.[59]

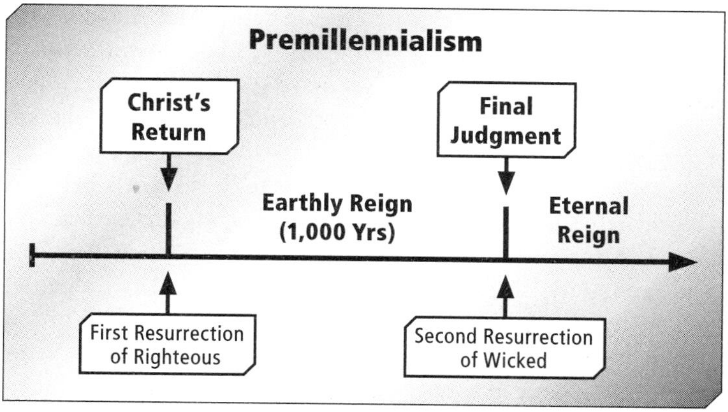

For premillennial readers, these events (Rev. 20) chronologically follow the vision of Christ's earthly return. So after His thousand-year reign over the earth, Satan will be released, a final rebellion will occur, and then the great white throne judgment—of the resurrected wicked from all of history—will usher in the eternal state (Rev. 21–22).[60] Craig Blaising summarizes this well:

> Premillennialists believe that when Jesus comes, he will raise the dead in two stages. First, he will raise some to participate with him in the millennial kingdom. After the Millennium (the thousand-year period) is

over, he will raise the rest of the dead and institute the Final Judgment. Then will come the final and eternal destinies of the saved and the lost. These future expectations are common to all premillennialists.[61]

Achievable Millennialism

Between these two vantages we might add a middle interpretation: the *achievable* millennial view. Proponents suggest that the conditions described in 20:1–6 are capable of gradual realization in this world through the efforts of God's people, prior to Christ's return as Judge and King. This view is often called "postmillennialism" because it expects that Jesus will return to earth after ("post") the world has enjoyed a long period of relative peace, justice, and prosperity through the worldwide success of the gospel.

Like premillennialists, many postmillennialists see the vision of Christ's return (Rev. 19) and the vision of the binding of Satan and the millennial reign (Rev. 20) as chronologically sequential, the millennium following the event of Christ's victory. Yet leading postmillennialists don't interpret Revelation 19 as a vision of the Lord's future physical return as Judge and King but as a symbolic picture of spiritual conflict between Jesus and His armies on the one side and the God-defying leaders of the earth on the other. This spiritual warfare is believed to have begun at Christ's ascension and has been raging for centuries.[62] His actual return, then, is not seen until the great white throne (Rev. 20:11), when all humanity is resurrected to stand before God as Judge. After this begins the eternal state, in which there will be no death or pain.

For postmillennialists, "a thousand years" is not to be taken as an exact period of ten centuries but as a symbolic number "indicating an indefinitely long period of time, a complete, perfect number of years."[63] As a middle position (between pre- and amillennialism), some postmillennialists describe the millennium as "the entire present age, between Christ's first and second advents, during which Satan is bound and the church is sharing in the victorious reign of Christ."[64] Others see the present age as a time during which the stage is being set for a future earthly golden age, after which Christ will return as Judge. Loraine Boettner writes:

> We have made much progress during the Christian era, but still, on postmillennial grounds, it hardly seems that even in the most advanced

> nations of the earth we have seen anything that is worthy of being called more than the early dawn of the Millennium. We might say that as yet we still are engaged primarily in laying the foundation rather than building the superstructure. . . . We believe, however, that while we are making progress we still have a long distance to go, and that the Millennium will be something much more advanced and glorious than anything that has yet been seen.[65]

In all postmillennial views, the ideals of the millennium (though not necessarily the full realization of the new heavens and new earth) are progressively achievable through the church's advancement of the gospel in this present world.

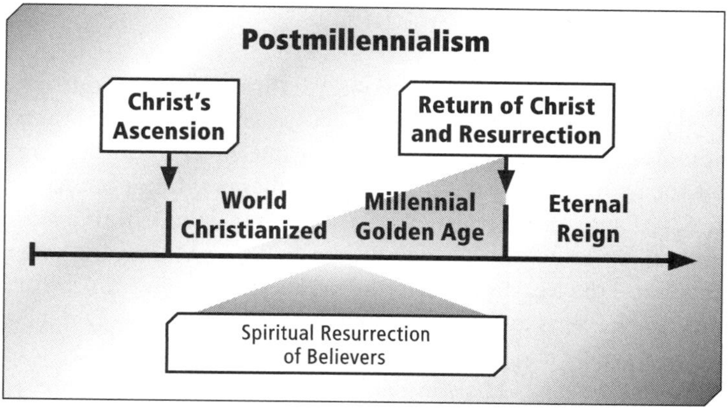

Reading Revelation 19–22 Together

Multiple distinctive ways of interpreting these symbolic visions (Rev. 19–22) prevail today. Though the differences in reading this biblical section are significant, we shouldn't forget Revelation's basic message. When the dust of our present and future spiritual and worldly warfare settles, Christ and His people will stand victorious forever. Sin, death, and pain will have been obliterated. Righteousness and peace will reign—forever and ever.

That's the story of Revelation 19–22, and that's an eternal aspect of our ultimate hope in Jesus.

THE END TIMES IN RETROSPECT

Probably no area of Christian theology has caused more controversy and led to more disunity among otherwise unified believers than eschatological doctrine. Debates raged during the early church period about the proper interpretation of the millennial kingdom in Revelation 20. Protestant reformers renewed that debate, some adding the identification of Antichrist: was it the Pope? Martin Luther? the Anabaptists? the Muslims? Still more detailed debates over the order of end-times events and the interpretation of symbols in Daniel and Revelation have divided evangelicals for decades.

However, if we step back and examine the major issues emphasized throughout church history, we discover that all Christians have sung the same basic tune without missing a note. All orthodox believers have anticipated the future, literal, bodily return of Christ as Judge and King. All have believed in the bodily resurrection of the righteous and the wicked—the one to everlasting life, the other to everlasting damnation. In 381, the Council of Constantinople represented the universal consensus despite their differences of opinion on lesser issues: "He [Jesus Christ] will come again in glory to judge the living and the dead, and his kingdom will have no end. . . . We look for the resurrection of the dead, and the life of the world to come."[1]

Not only have Christians always held to the bodily resurrection, they also have believed in an ultimate transformation and restoration of the created world—the renewed heavens and earth—in which only righteousness dwells. John of Damascus (c. 740), a theologian of the

Eastern Church, summarized the basic Christian teaching on future events this way:

> We shall therefore rise again, our souls being once more united with our bodies, now made incorruptible and having put off corruption. . . . Those who have done good will shine forth as the sun with the angels into life eternal, with our Lord Jesus Christ, ever seeing Him and being in His sight and deriving unceasing joy from Him, praising Him with the Father and the Holy Spirit throughout the limitless ages of ages.[2]

Believers of every denomination and tradition still hold without compromise to these truths. Yet throughout history the church has also known a wide spectrum of diversity regarding the details of end-times events. In short, while Christians from every age and every place have spoken in unison on core doctrines of eschatology, they have simultaneously disagreed on and debated less significant questions and concerns.

The Patristic Period (c. AD 100–500)

In the period immediately following the age of the apostles, who lived and taught together with their associates and immediate disciples between AD 30 and 100, the early church continued to anticipate the soon return of Jesus Christ. The persecutions they endured at the hands of pagans, Romans, and Jews represented for them the birth pangs of the end times. By persevering through these earthly trials, the faithful saints could expect to be rewarded in the coming kingdom. The basic expectation of early Christians is contained in the *Didache*, a very early summary of teaching for new converts.

> In the last days false prophets and corrupters shall be multiplied, and the sheep shall be turned into wolves, and love shall be turned into hate; for when lawlessness increaseth, they shall hate and persecute and betray one another, and then shall appear the world-deceiver as Son of God, and shall do signs and wonders, and the earth shall be delivered into his hands, and he shall do iniquitous things which have never yet come to pass since the beginning. Then shall the creation of men come into the fire of trial, and many shall be made to stumble and shall perish; but they that endure in their faith shall be saved from

> under the curse itself. And then shall appear the signs of the truth; first, the sign of an out-spreading in heaven; then the sign of the sound of the trumpet; and the third, the resurrection of the dead; yet not of all, but as it is said: The Lord shall come and all His saints with Him. Then shall the world see the Lord coming upon the clouds of heaven.[3]

Along with this imminent expectation of Christ's soon return as King and Judge, many early believers understood the thousand-year reign of Christ on earth (Rev. 20) as a future, literal event that would follow His return and the resurrection of the righteous (premillennialism). However, in the second century, orthodox Christians also explored other interpretations of end-times details, including a less literal millennial interpretation (amillennialism).[4]

In either case, early Christians expected a literal bodily resurrection of the dead. Just as Jesus Christ's body had been miraculously restored to life, gloriously transformed and rendered immortal, believers could look forward to when their own bodies would be raised, restored, and glorified. In a culture that tended to despise the physical body and the material world, the Christian doctrine of the bodily resurrection drew constant ridicule. Numerous early apologists defended the doctrine of the future resurrection against scoffers and critics, sometimes in whole treatises dedicated to the hope of resurrection.

Without abandoning the central focus on Christ's literal return, the real bodily resurrection, and future judgment of the world, many Christians' earlier expectations of an earthly thousand-year kingdom between the resurrection of the righteous and the final judgment of the wicked waned over time. By the fourth century this anticipation gave way to a widespread belief that Christ's kingdom had in some sense already commenced, requiring no future earthly millennial reign. Perhaps, some thought, the church itself was fulfilling kingdom prophecies and promises. Maybe the gospel's victory over paganism and the emperor's conversion to Christianity indicated that the expectations of the kingdom of God were being realized in history.[5]

The Medieval Period (500–1500)

If you were a medieval peasant eking out a living through constant labor, your eschatological expectations might be as simple as your daily life. An antichrist would one day appear, perhaps as the head of an army of Arabs or Turks . . . maybe an apostate emperor or king.[6] In any case, Jesus would ultimately return as Judge to destroy the wicked, raise the dead, and hold all accountable for their thoughts and deeds. The medieval Roman Catholic Mass for the dead shines light on the imagery with which the end times were portrayed:

> Day of wrath, that day,
> The world will dissolve in ashes
> As David and the Sibyl testified.
> Great trembling there is to be,
> When the Judge is to come,
> Everything will be judged strictly.[7]

What a dreadful picture! Of course, many believed they were at the brink of meeting their Maker at any moment through physical death, so fears about apocalyptic events in this world were overshadowed by the much more imminent fear of death by dagger, starvation, disease, or accident. In such a context, personal eschatology seemed more relevant than what might or might not happen to the world leading up to the second coming.

Official church doctrine emphasized the classic content of the creed, that is, "the resurrection of the dead and the life of the world to come."[8] Believers upheld the bodily resurrection. Anselm of Canterbury (1033–1109) reasoned,

> Human nature was ordained for this purpose, viz., that every man should enjoy a happy immortality, both in body and in soul; and that it was necessary that this design for which man was made should be fulfilled.[9]

Coupled with this expectation of resurrection unto immortal life was an enduring expectation of a renewed creation: "We believe that the material substance of the world must be renewed."[10] Yet increasingly the idea of the "world to come"—that is, the breaking of another world into this one—was replaced by the idea of each individual departing this world at death and "going to" another world—personal eschatology. Hugh of St. Victor (1097–1141) taught that there were five places in the universe created by God: "Heaven is the highest place;

after heaven, paradise; after paradise, the world; after the world, the purgatorial fire; and after purgatory, hell."[11]

A MEDIEVAL STRUCTURE OF THE UNIVERSE

Heaven	The abode of God and those who through merit of righteousness attained the highest degree of progress—the place of the blessed saints.
Paradise	The place of good (but not perfect) Christians who may still make progress toward perfection.
Earth	The "middle place" where both the good and evil dwell and can choose ascent upward through righteousness or descent downward through sin.
Purgatory	The fiery place of the evil who nevertheless have a second opportunity for correction since they did not take full advantage of the first opportunity on earth.
Hell	The abode of Satan and those who are confirmed in evil, having irreversibly rejected opportunities for repentance.

Many in this era expected that believers' glorification, heavenly ascent, and blessedness in God's presence awaited the future resurrection and renewal of the world.[12] However, that idea was displaced by many who taught that the "saints"—apostles, martyrs, and other "more perfect" Christians—were admitted into the highest heaven immediately, not having to await resurrection and final judgment.[13] A poem by Adam of St. Victor (c. 1080–1146) captures the extreme nature of an increasingly common "realized eschatology," in which, minimally, the church's true victorious "saints" were already experiencing end-times blessings in the afterlife:

Joy and triumph everlasting
Hath the heavenly Church on high;
For that pure immortal gladness
All our feast-days mourn and sigh

There the body hath no torment,
There the mind is free from care,
There is every heart rejoicing,
Every heart is loving there

Us, us too, when death hath freed us,
Christ of his good mercy lead us.[14]

Though it never completely died out, belief in a literal earthly millennial reign of Christ, held by many teachers of the earliest centuries, was for the most part now pushed into the doctrinal shadows and margins:[15] "Basing itself on the interpretations given by St. Augustine, it [the church] understood the thousand-year rule of the saints as the period of the church's present existence on earth, from its founding until judgment day."[16]

As both the church and society in Western Europe deteriorated in the late medieval period (1200–1500), apocalyptic expectations took on darker and more radical forms. Around 1200, Joachim of Fiore, an Italian monk, divided history into three distinct "ages" or "dispensations":

The Age of the Father—The Old Testament (Rule of Israel)
The Age of the Son—The New Testament (Rule of the Church)
The Age of the Spirit—The New Age (Rule of the Righteous)

Joachim predicted that the "Third Age" would begin in 1260. Even though no epochal event occurred in that year that could be identified as a fulfillment of this calculation, the sect known as the "Spiritual Franciscans" regarded themselves as the fulfillment of these predictions. In fact, when certain popes challenged the claims of the order, condemning them as false teachers, the Spirituals counter-labeled their papal opponents "Antichrists."[17] Jaroslav Pelikan writes, about this period of church history:

> What made late medieval apocalypticism important doctrinally was the growing belief in this period that "the man of sin, the son of perdition," the Antichrist whose coming was to be the principal sign of the end, was not some emperor (Nero or Frederick II) nor some false prophet (Arius or Mohammed), but the visible head of Christendom himself.[18]

This designation of the reigning Pope as Antichrist would be repeated throughout the late Middle Ages by such Reformation forerunners as John Wycliffe and John Hus.[19]

The Protestant Period (1500–1700)

Chances are if you lived in northern Europe between 1517 and 1550, you'd wonder whether the devil and his armies had somehow escaped hell and were marching across the earth. Muslim Turks threatened to blast through Eastern Europe into Austria. Martin Luther had gained the support of German princes to rebel not only against the Holy Roman Emperor but also against the Pope. Peasant mobs armed with pikes and pitchforks moved to riotously overthrow Church *and* State. Itinerant radical preachers sought to institute a utopian Christian society of the common people or even the kingdom of God on earth. Chaos prevailed; confusion ensued. Armies clashed, and cities burned.

The anxiety many felt in the waning years of the Middle Ages flared and exploded into outright warfare in the sixteenth century. Roman Catholic dogmas that had been rarely challenged were now open to reconsideration. Attempts to wind the church back to an earlier, purer age affected numerous realms of theology . . . even eschatology.

Most mainline reformers, like Martin Luther, Ulrich Zwingli, and John Calvin, maintained the amillennial perspective as well as the expectation of Christ's coming to judge the world.[20] They explicitly rejected an earthly, pre-day of judgment millennium, as expressed in the (Lutheran) Augsburg Confession of 1530: "They condemn others also, who now scatter Jewish opinions that, before the resurrection of the dead, the godly shall occupy the kingdom of the world, the wicked being everywhere suppressed."[21] Similarly, the (Reformed) Second Helvetic Confession of 1566 condemned "Jewish dreams that there will be a golden age on earth before the Day of Judgment, and that the pious, having subdued all their godless enemies, will possess all the kingdoms of the earth."[22]

At the same time, many of these leaders saw events of that day as fulfillments of end-times prophecies. In fact, so tumultuous and widespread were the Reformation events that many saw them as clear signs of Christ's soon return: "Virtually all Christians in the sixteenth century . . . were convinced that they were living in the last days, and that Christ was about to return."[23]

So, for example, Luther believed the Pope was the Antichrist.[24] In 1520 he outlined the false doctrines and practices of the Roman Catholic Church under the papacy and, in his irascible style, declared,

If there were nothing else to show that the Pope is Antichrist, this would be enough. Dost thou hear this, O Pope! not the most holy, but the most sinful? Would that God would hurl thy Chair headlong from heaven, and cast it down into the abyss of hell![25]

Calvin allowed that true churches continued to exist within the Roman Catholic dominion, but like Luther and other reformers he held the papacy as an institution of Antichrist: "Daniel and Paul foretold that Antichrist would sit in the temple of God (Dan. 9:27; 2 Thess. 2:4); we regard the Roman pontiff as the leader and standard-bearer of that wicked and abominable kingdom."[26]

After the dust settled following the Reformation's violent and tumultuous early days, rhetoric also died down, leaving only one key element of medieval eschatology greatly affected: the Roman Catholic doctrine of purgatory didn't survive the Reformation's purifying flames. The Church of England's Thirty-Nine Articles sum up the Protestant stance: "The Romish doctrine concerning Purgatory . . . is a fond thing, vainly invented, and grounded upon no warranty of Scripture, but rather repugnant to the Word of God."[27] Besides that element, the general contours remained intact: the return of Christ as Judge of the living and the dead, the resurrection of the body on judgment day, eternal life for believers, and eternal hell for unbelievers. These views became settled and dogmatized in the various protestant denominational confessions of faith and continue to prevail as such to the present day.

Like a well-tuned orchestra, the mainline magisterial reformers—such as Luther, Zwingli, Calvin, Bucer, Bullinger, Cranmer—mostly complemented each other's eschatological anthems. However, other dissonant performances resounded that would challenge many eschatological themes. Early in the sixteenth century, several politically and doctrinally radical figures sparked controversy and conflict with a militant form of millennialism.

Anabaptists like Melchior Hoffman and self-proclaimed prophets like Jan Matthys insisted that end-times prophecies were being fulfilled before their eyes and they had been entrusted with the duty of establishing the millennial kingdom on earth—if necessary, by force.[28] Their utopian dreams ended as apocalyptic nightmares. The tragic events in Münster (Germany) in the 1530s illustrate how out of control twisted eschatology can get. Jan Beukelsz took control of the city in 1534, attempting to institute a polygamous society governed by twelve apostle-like elders. He declared himself the end-times "King of Righteousness" and intended to reign over the millennial kingdom from Münster. Within a year he and his co-regents were captured and/or killed, putting an end to extreme millennial madness among radical reformers.

In the calm after the storm, in the next several decades many level-headed Protestants continued reexamining end-times doctrine in light of Scripture, history, and, yes, current events. Some Presbyterians, Congregationalists, Lutherans, and even Anglicans began to entertain postmillennial views, envisioning a spiritual golden age of universal peace and righteousness prior to a final rebellion and the return of Jesus. This, likely the predominant view of Puritan leaders like John Owen,[29] influenced Colonial America's religious, social, and political thinking in the eighteenth century.

The ancient view of premillennialism also experienced resurgence in the Reformation's aftermath, taking on a number of forms. However, not until the modern era would the expectation of a literal earthly reign of Christ become a force with which to be reckoned in protestant eschatology.

The Modern Period (1700–Present)

With modernism's rise, doctrines that had been held everywhere, always, and by (nearly) all were dragged into court and put on trial. The "Enlightened" stance toward traditional beliefs and practices affected core doctrines, including the Trinity, the incarnation and virgin birth, and the resurrection of Jesus. Liberal theologians and critical scholars reduced the Christian faith to an ethical philosophy centered on Christ's moral teaching about brotherly love and social justice. In such a reformulation (*not* reformation) of the Christian faith and message, little room was given to classic doctrines like the second coming, the resurrection of the body, or even eternal life. Even those believing scholars who retained some vestiges of a judgment day regarded the concept of hell to smack of superstition, a notion no longer tolerable to the sophisticated and scientific mind.[30]

In other liberal circles, the spiritual postmillennialism of the seventeenth and eighteenth centuries—manifested especially among New

England Puritan theologians—underwent a transformation.[31] Amid increased secularism, the Christ-centered spiritual and moral dimensions of the achievable millennium gave way to hope for global social and economic transformation. As Alister McGrath notes, "The idea of a cataclysmic end of history was set to one side, in favor of a doctrine of hope which was grounded in the gradual evolution of humanity towards moral and societal perfection."[32]

For an illustration of such despiritualizing among liberal Christians, consider Walter Rauschenbusch, who attempted to reinterpret classic eschatology in light of his "social gospel":

> The social gospel seeks to develop the vision of the Church toward the future and to co-operate with the will of God which is shaping the destinies of humanity. It would be aided and reinforced by a modern and truly Christian conception about the future of mankind. At present no other theological influence so hampers and obstructs the social as that of eschatology.[33]

In his mind, a premillennial view of eschatology that expects Jesus himself to step into history and usher in God's kingdom apart from human effort stands as an obstacle to true progress. The solution?

> Our chief interest in any millennium is the desire for a social order in which the worth and freedom of every last human being will be honoured and protected; in which the brotherhood of man will be expressed in the common possession of the economic resources of society; and in which the spiritual good of humanity will be set high above the private profit interests of all materialistic groups. We hope for such an order for humanity as we hope for heaven for ourselves.[34]

While people living in the 1800s might interpret advances in science, psychology, and technology as a sign that the world would only get better and better, it's an understatement to note that optimism in humanity's progress would suffer in the twentieth century. In regard to first dampening and then destroying these hopes, someone born in the early 1900s might live to witness (for example) World War I, the Great Depression, World War II, the Holocaust, the atomic bomb, other mass exterminations and genocides through various instruments and methods of horror, environmental disasters, economic crashes and crises, global terrorism, starvation by hundreds of millions, the arms race, ethnic "cleansings," the appearance and spread of incurable diseases, and capitalist greed beyond comprehension.

The positive thinking that fueled liberal theology's confidence in human achievement gave way to pessimism and despair, which powered a new kind of expectation about the future. In the late 1800s and early 1900s, a movement known as dispensationalism emphasized a futurist premillennial eschatology. Dispensationalists tended to see the world not as getting better through human effort but as spiraling further and further toward self-destruction. Ultimately, after the tribulation commenced, the Antichrist would establish a worldwide empire that would be destroyed only at the second coming.

THE END TIMES THROUGH THE AGES

Patristic Period (100–500)	Medieval Period (500–1500)	Protestant Period (1500–1700)	Modern Period (1700–Present)
• Expectation of Christ's soon return (30–100) • Persecution and martyrdom seen as signs of the end and Antichrist's coming (100–325) • Cessation of persecution (313) • Premillennialism declines, amillennialism rises (150–500) • Apologists defend a literal bodily resurrection (150–500)	• Fear of future judgments gives way to fear of fiery judgment in the afterlife • Roman Catholic doctrine of purgatory develops and dominates (600–1500) • Rise of Islam (622–700) increases fear of Antichrist's coming • Prevalence of disease, war, and heresy leads many to believe the end times had arrived	• Reformers label the Pope the Antichrist and the Roman Church his anti-Christian kingdom (1517–1700) • Reformers believe they're living in the last days • Most maintain Augustine's amillennial views • Minority (and often radical) premillennial views rejected • Doctrine of purgatory rejected	• Classic doctrines (return of Christ, bodily resurrection, and hell) rejected by liberal theologians (1700–2000) • New England Puritans advocate a postmillennial eschatology (1700–1800) • Premillennial theology has resurgence among mainline theologians (1700–1900) • Rise of dispensational premillennialism (1850–1900)

A renewed emphasis on the end times often led students of the Bible to seek signs of the end in current events and sometimes to speculate on the date of Christ's return. Spurred by radical changes in global politics, culture, and religion, this focus led to the publication of countless books on prophecy, the founding of numerous ministries promoting eschatological viewpoints, and the increase in evangelistic and missionary efforts to win as many to Christ as possible before His return.

The sometimes fanatical obsession with the world's end often led more traditional Protestants of an amillennial or postmillennial bent to respond very negatively to popular premillennial excitement. The result was increasing disunity among churches, pastors, theologians, and laypersons over details of end-times events and practical implications with regard to the church's role in society. Should believers continue to work at progressively improving society to bring about lasting peace and justice (per some postmillennialists and amillennialists)? Or is it better that Christians focus on saving as many souls as possible prior to the inevitable coming of the earth's cataclysmic judgment (per premillennialists)? Such differences among evangelicals continue to the present day.

Facts to Never Forget

Teachers often tell their students, "Even if you retain nothing else from this lesson, remember *this*." In any field of study we find basic fundamental truths that form the foundation upon which we can build. Without these "first principles" or "axioms" firmly in place, the entire structure will be unstable.

The following seven facts function like steel piers that hold up the study of eschatology. We may construct a floor, walls, and a roof on them, filling out our doctrine of the end times with more details. We may even paint, furnish, and decorate. In time some of these details and cosmetic changes can be altered . . . but the piers can never change without the building itself going down. Commit these facts to memory! Keep them front and center in your thinking and you'll save yourself and perhaps others from distorted teaching.

Fact 1: Jesus Christ is coming back as Judge and King.

As the disciples stared into the skies while their resurrected Lord ascended, two angels appeared and said, "Men of Galilee, why do you stand looking into heaven? This Jesus, who was taken up from you into heaven, will come in the same way as you saw him go into heaven" (Acts 1:11). Since that moment, faithful followers have always kept one eye on the skies, so to speak—expecting and longing for the Lord's physical return.

Christ's second coming will bring both judgment (for the wicked, living and dead—2 Tim. 4:1; 1 Peter 4:5; 2 Thess. 1:5–10) and a glorious kingdom, which will have no end (Rev. 11:15).

This expectation of His arrival as Judge and King has been a central part of the Christian faith from the very beginning. Not only does God's Word clearly teach it, it also has been faithfully believed by all genuine believers of every denomination and tradition since. We must never lose sight of this truth.

Fact 2: Nobody knows when Christ will return.

The testimony of Scripture and all well-balanced believers has always been that nobody can possibly know when Jesus will come back. No vision, dream, or clever calculation can change this reality. Though His coming as Judge and King is certain, its timing is not. Consider these straightforward statements:[1]

- Of that day and hour no one knows, not even the angels of heaven, nor the Son, but the Father alone. (Matt. 24:36)
- You do not know on what day your Lord is coming. (Matt. 24:42)
- Of that day or hour, no one knows. . . . Take heed, keep on the alert; for you do not know when the appointed time will come. . . . What I say to you I say to all, "Be on the alert!" (Mark 13:32–33, 37)
- As to the times and the epochs, brethren, you have no need of anything to be written to you. For you yourselves know full well that the day of the Lord will come just like a thief in the night. (1 Thess. 5:1–2)
- The day of the Lord will come like a thief. (2 Peter 3:10, emphasizing the suddenness of Christ's coming in judgment)
- I will come like a thief, and you will not know at what hour I will come to you. (Rev. 3:3)
- Behold, I am coming like a thief. Blessed is the one who stays awake and keeps his clothes, so that he will not walk about naked and men will not see his shame. (Rev. 16:15)

That Christ is returning is an unbreakable promise. *When* He is coming is completely unknown. Those false teachers who've presumed to have figured out the timing have always been wrong, and they always will be. We must never forget that it's impossible to know when Jesus Christ will return.

Fact 3: God will redeem our bodies through physical resurrection.

One day as we were visiting a historic family cemetery in Mesquite, Texas, my boys, Lucas and Nathan, were running to and fro over century-old graves. I called them to me and passed on to them the instruction that had been given to me as a little boy: "We don't walk on graves."

Lucas looked puzzled. "Why not?"

Good question. I realized I'd never thought about it. "Because . . . er . . ." I struggled and fumbled for a reasonable answer. Chances are I was just relaying some relic of superstition my mother herself had received. But somehow I just couldn't break the chain and say, *Oh, go ahead, then, stomp all over them. Doesn't matter—they're deader than dead anyway.*

I threw together the best ad hoc reply I could conjure: "Because," I said, "if the resurrection were to happen you'd get knocked over!"

It's true. At some point, the graves themselves will burst open. Whatever remains of the dead that had been in the ground will be changed and restored into a glorious new body that shares the characteristics of Jesus' own. Nothing of the old will remain in the grave; all things will be made new. That decomposed matter in the ground has a future in God's plan of redemption.

Sadly, far too many Christians believe their bodies are mere shells that contain the real "me," as if God never intended us to have a physical presence, a bodily existence, a permanent means of interacting with the creation He fashioned for us. The promise of bodily resurrection completely contradicts this notion! Belief in the redemption of our physical bodies has always been a central tenet of the faith (Rom. 8:23). When Christ returns, He "will transform our lowly body to be like his glorious body" (Phil. 3:21), no longer subject to aging and death. But note that this is a *transformation* of our present body, not a creation of an entirely different body. Jesus did not leave His old body in the grave when He rose—that old body was raised and transformed into the glorious body of His resurrection. Our change will follow the same pattern.

Why, though? Why would God bother restoring what's been laid to rest? Can't He just create a fully new body for our spirits out of nothing? Of course! However, by opening the graves and tombs and transforming our dead and decomposed bodies into glorious, incorruptible ones, He declares once for all: "O death, where is your victory"! (1 Cor. 15:55). As Paul explains, "When the perishable puts on the imperishable, and the mortal puts on immortality, then shall come to pass the saying that is written: 'Death is swallowed up in victory'" (v. 54). By snatching up our mortal dust and ashes and transforming them into something eternal and glorious, God will demonstrate that Satan's attempt at destroying humanity failed. Humans, who've been created with body and spirit in God's image, not only will be rescued from death and restored to life but also crowned with glory and honor (Ps. 8:5). Because God's victory over death is central to His promises and to our hope, we should never forget that God will redeem our bodies through physical resurrection.

Fact 4: God will utterly eradicate sin, suffering, and death.

The majestic Christmas carol "Joy to the World" expresses the magnificent hope of ultimate cosmic redemption this way:

> No more let sins and sorrows grow
> Nor thorns infest the ground:
> He comes to make His blessings flow
> Far as the curse is found.[2]

When Christ returns, He will bring power to liberate all creation from its bondage to corruption (Rom. 8:21). As far as the dark stains of sin and death, suffering and pain, evil and tragedy have infected this universe, the cleansing blessings of His life will wash it all away—forever. Though we struggle today with the excruciating pain of a dying world, one day that death will be vanquished permanently by the invincible force of Life itself (Rev. 21:4).

In the restored creation, there will be no more death, mourning, or pain. The terrible things that characterize this present world under the reign of sin and death will be eradicated under the reign of Jesus Christ (v. 3). Yet in the meantime it's so easy to let the darkness drag us down, to rob our joy, our hope, our contentment, and our patience. This is why we must never forget that one day God *will* forever do away with sin, suffering, and death.

Fact 5: We all must give an account for our lives before God.

"There is therefore now no condemnation for those who are in Christ Jesus" (Rom. 8:1). This truth should shine brightly in the minds of those who are "in Christ," piercing the darkness of doubt and driving out the shadows of despair. During His first coming, Christ didn't come to judge the world but to save it (John 12:47). Those who enter into a relationship with Him between then and His second coming have received His saving grace.

Yet this doesn't let us off the hook entirely. It's not that God has granted a "license to kill." We can't do whatever we want without repercussions. God warns of loving discipline for His children in this life (Heb. 12:5–11; Rev. 3:19). In fact, when during this life we as His children are judged by His loving hand, "we are disciplined so that we may not be condemned along with the world" (1 Cor. 11:32). Scripture also points to a time in the future—at Christ's return—when even believers will be subject to His judgment:

> We will all stand before the judgment seat of God; for it is written, "As I live, says the Lord, every knee shall bow to me, and every tongue shall confess to God." So then each of us will give an account of himself to God. (Rom. 14:10–12)

> We must all appear before the judgment seat of Christ, so that each one may receive what is due for what he has done in the body, whether good or evil. (2 Cor. 5:10)

Paul notes too that the work we do in building Christ's church will be judged on its quality, resulting in either reward or loss of reward when we are judged (1 Cor. 3:12–15).

Regardless of who we are, when we lived, how much we've had to contribute, or how little we've been given, the Lord expects us to live lives worthy of our calling in Him (Eph. 4:1). Though it's not our only motivation to live holy, blameless, and fruitful lives, we must always remember that one day each one of us, before God, must give an account for our life.

Fact 6: All of God's plans and promises will be fulfilled.

Even the most well-meaning people with the best intentions can let us down miserably. Whenever people make plans, we need to recognize that they may not manage to follow through. When somebody makes a promise, he or she may one day fail to keep it. Sometimes people just flake out. Other times they lack integrity. Oftentimes, circumstances beyond their control prevent them from meeting their goal or doing what they said they'd do.

But *God* isn't flaky, fickle, *or* feeble. His Word assures us again and again that *all* His plans and promises will be fulfilled—He will *never* break His word: "God is not man, that he should lie, or a son of man, that he should change his mind. Has he said, and will he not do it? Or has he spoken, and will he not fulfill it?" (Num. 23:19). He himself assures us, "My counsel shall stand, and I will accomplish all my purpose" (Isa. 46:10). In light of God's character as a promise-keeper, Paul notes that "the gifts and the calling of God are irrevocable" (Rom. 11:29).

The Old Testament contains countless prophecies and promises relating to God's redemption of humanity and creation. He promised He would fix what's been broken. The story that began with creation and the fall will be completed when He restores and renews creation. Though now we don't see all things subject to God's sovereign rule (Heb. 2:8), when Christ returns, God will fulfill all His ancient plans and enduring promises through His Son. At the proper time, which only He knows, He will remove all wickedness from the world so that "times of refreshing may come"—when He sends Jesus to reign (Acts 3:20). At long last will arrive "the time for restoring all the things about which God spoke by the mouth of his holy prophets long ago" (v. 21).

In our world of broken promises, breached contracts, and failures to follow through, it's easy to blame our disappointments on God.

This is why we must never forget: *every* plan and promise of God will be fulfilled.

Fact 7: Christ's kingdom will endure forever and ever.

December 21, 2012. Remember it? It was the day some believed the world would come to an end. Mostly, New Age prophets thought that when the long cycle of the ancient Mayan calendar closed on that fateful date, one cycle of world history would conclude and usher in a new beginning.

The Mayan mythology of creation included the operation of numerous gods and endless conflict between heavenly powers that affected the lives of earth-dwellers in significant ways. The Mayan worldview presented a dualistic existence—a constant struggle between darkness and light, good and evil, happiness and disaster. Within this living narrative various heroic figures—both mythical and historical—played a vital role at moving the story forward, battling evil forces, redeeming the world from chaos to order, or casting a vision for the future.

The complex calendar, with connections to the stars, seasons, gods, and past or future events, helped that society cope in an otherwise unpredictable and chaotic world. The Mayan story, then, was played out in endless cycles—illustrated vividly by their famous circular calendar. Though the current world would one day come to an end, that conclusion would become the beginning of another age that would then run its own circular course.

Nonetheless, in a cyclical story where each ending becomes a new start, history is ultimately going nowhere. The Mayan calendar can be projected into eternity past or eternity future, with endless cycles in which every event, individual, and generation is lost on an endless loop of recycled time.

Certainly this mythology isn't the only attempt at making sense of our place in the world through endless cycles of death and rebirth. Countless alternate narratives of the world's origin and destiny have competed for attention and allegiance. For example, Egyptian tales of the world's creation also were typically set on a cycle of daily repetitions. Each morning the gods would re-create the world, and the Egyptians made little distinction between their deities and what they represented—sun, sky, sea, river, earth . . . all of these were themselves manifestations of the gods,[3] and in the world's endless cycles of sunrise and sunset, the universe ultimately went nowhere.

Fast-forward to modern theories of the universe's origin and destiny. Many scientists today believe our universe is stuck in an eternal cycle of expansion and contraction, each collapse followed by another Big Bang, which ultimately is followed by another collapse.[4] Such a paradigm has no room for the notion of the universe reaching a state of unending perfection.

When contrasted with these cyclical plot lines, the story of the Bible looks radically different. God's Word presents a future in which all things will be restored under the reign of Christ, the God-man. In Him all things hold together (Col. 1:17). He upholds the entire universe by His powerful word (Heb. 1:3). And when He returns to reign, this universe will be made the way it always was meant to be. Far from being a temporary reign after which things again fall apart, the reign of Jesus Christ will be "forever and ever" (Rev. 11:15). His kingdom will have no end (Luke 1:33; cf. Dan. 2:44).

Seven Facts to Never Forget

1. Jesus Christ is coming back as Judge and King.
2. Nobody knows when Christ will return.
3. God will redeem our bodies through physical resurrection.
4. God will utterly eradicate sin, suffering, and death.
5. We all must give an account for our lives before God.
6. All of God's plans and promises will be fulfilled.
7. Christ's kingdom will endure forever and ever.

Think of it! The cycle of failed governments, corrupt administrations, declining societies, and the entire deteriorating cosmos will be replaced by a perfect universe and perfect kingdom of righteousness (2 Peter 3:13). We must never forget: *Christ's kingdom will endure forever and ever.*

Dangers to Avoid

In the last section we explored seven facts of eschatology to never forget. If we keep those main points at the center of our understanding, they will serve as essential guideposts for our interaction with peripheral, less crucial issues in the study of biblical prophecy. Now, let's look at seven dangers to avoid. These are the warning signs that tell us travelers when we're approaching precarious precipices or predator-laden swamplands that can harm or destroy those who wander off paths of safety.

Danger 1: Heinous Heresy

Heresy is knowingly, willfully, and unrepentantly believing or teaching doctrines that directly contradict the core tenets of orthodoxy as handed down throughout church history. And let me say up front that a person needs to go far out of their way to be an eschatological heretic. The shape of orthodox eschatology is painted with broad strokes, for the matters that constitute it have always been limited to the anticipation of Christ's physical return as Judge, the bodily resurrection of the dead unto either eternal life or eternal condemnation, and the eternal reign of Christ as King.

These doctrines are so foundational that they're directly related to the gospel message itself.[1] *Still*, a couple of heresies have developed over the centuries. How could any believer possibly reject such central elements?

Well, some believe Jesus "returned" in a purely spiritual sense with the coming of the Spirit on Pentecost.[2] Others believe He "returns" in a personal sense to each individual when he or she becomes a believer

(Acts 9:3–5; Col. 1:27). Still others have reinterpreted the second coming as His "coming" to take each believer to heaven when he or she dies (John 14:3). Though all these can be true in a sense, when they are maintained *instead of* a literal future return of Jesus Christ, they are heresies. From the very start, Christians have looked forward to His physical return as Judge and King. As Judge, He will consign the wicked to eternal punishment and reward the righteous with eternal life. As King, He will reign over all creation with justice forever.

Besides false teaching concerning Christ's return, throughout history heretics have occasionally challenged aspects of the future bodily resurrection. Some have said the resurrection is *only spiritual,* referring exclusively to the new birth and eternal life. Therefore, *resurrection* means "being saved"; after a saved person dies, he or she will instantly receive the full inheritance of salvation apart from a future literal resurrection of the body.

This was the view of the ancient Gnostic heretics, who despised the physical body as essentially evil and unredeemable. The so-called *Gospel of Philip* says, "Some are afraid lest they rise naked. Because of this they wish to rise in the flesh, and [they] do not know that it is those who wear the [flesh] who are naked."[3] Similarly, the Gnostic *Treatise on the Resurrection* says the resurrection occurs for believers when they are "drawn to heaven by him like beams by the sun, not being restrained by anything. This is the spiritual resurrection which swallows up the psyche in the same way as the flesh."[4]

In the area of final judgment, a variety of views are regarded as fringe, peculiar, or even dangerous. The Roman Catholic doctrine of purgatory teaches that after death, baptized Christians undergo a further purging of sins that were not satisfied in this life. Purgatory is not a means for all people to be eventually saved (universalism), but for only baptized Christians who died with unresolved sin and guilt. Purgatory is a later development, historically, that neither the Eastern Orthodox nor Protestants accept as orthodox.

According to another erroneous view, "conditional immortality," human souls (like their bodies) are mortal. There's no conscious existence beyond physical death—only at the resurrection will humans again experience conscious existence. This is similar to the notion of soul sleep, in which the dead are thought to rest in an unconscious state until the day of judgment.

Annihilationism, also a marginal view, says the fires of hell symbolize the utter destruction (not eternal suffering) of the wicked. Such perspectives are typical of Jehovah's Witnesses, Seventh-day Adventists, and a few otherwise orthodox Christians who hold to minority views on the subject.[5]

One other view related to personal eschatology that doesn't measure up against orthodox protestant evangelical faith is universalism. By this vantage, all people will ultimately be saved; no one can face eternity without God. Some believe universal salvation may be achieved through something like purgatory, in which all sinners will purge their wickedness and thus merit heaven. Others believe God's loving mercy will prevail when He simply chooses to forgive and save everybody. Like conditional immortality and annihilationism, universalism is not a classic Christian perspective, but has been (and continues to be) held by a minority of otherwise orthodox believers.

In sum, classic orthodox faith doesn't require widespread agreement on all kinds of details about end-times events. It does expect that all true Christians stand in full agreement with Scripture as it has been understood throughout history—that Jesus will return as perfect Judge and eternal King and that He will resurrect both the saved unto eternal life and the unsaved unto eternal condemnation.

Danger 2: My Way or the Highway

Several years ago I was chatting with a Bible scholar at a social gathering. To my surprise our conversation moved quickly from run-of-the-mill small talk to details of eschatology. To be specific, he asked if I believed Jesus Christ was currently reigning on the throne of David in His present session at the right hand of the Father or if His reign as King was reserved for His future return. Not a topic you'd expect to come up at a birthday party, but there it stood, like a belligerent guest threatening to crash a perfectly uneventful event.

I quickly replied with my view on the matter and he sighed with relief. I obviously answered the question his way, because a few minutes later when one of his colleagues turned our twosome into a trio, he introduced me as "one of us." Was I glad he didn't go on to grill me—I suspected that when he *did* find an aspect of dissent, then it would be no cake for me!

Actually, that particular friend was kind and gracious. In this case it was all harmless shop talk. But I've endured numerous not-so-friendly encounters with overly passionate preterists, foaming-at-the-mouth futurists, diehard dispensationalists, and armed-to-the-hilt amillennialists. Several were poised for battle royal to defend their mole-hill doctrine against "evil opponents" who saw things differently. And all of them failed to distinguish between the central doctrines of the faith worth fighting for (Jude 3) and the less critical end-times details on which differences of opinion have always prevailed.

R. C. Sproul writes, "Trying to understand all the details of what is set forth in the New and Old Testaments about future things taxes us beyond perhaps any other dimension of biblical understanding."[6] No doubt, beyond the big-picture events of Christ's return, the resurrection, and eternal glory, obsession with eschatological details can lead to a my-way-or-the-highway mentality. There's nothing wrong with firm convictions about the details of biblical prophecy. In fact, I encourage my students to settle even the minor issues in their own minds before going into ministry and further confusing already confused parishioners. But when such convictions become the standard by which a preacher, teacher, church, school, or ministry is rejected as less (or un-) orthodox, they become obstacles to the paramount virtues of love, peace, patience, humility, and unity.

Danger 3: End-Times Agnosticism

I frequently meet people who'd rather clean the streets of New York City with a toothbrush than read a book on the end times. It's not that they're scared, confused, or lazy . . . *they just don't care*. Perhaps in reaction to overemphasis on end-times teaching in some churches or denominations, many today feel repulsed by eschatology. Sometimes this stems from inability to see any practical or "real life" value in the various views. Or they've witnessed too many my-way-or-the-highway debates that ended with harsh words and hard feelings. Or they once went off the deep end with end-times obsession, were infected by this-is-that syndrome, or even played along with the dating game (see below). Such experiences can lead otherwise faithful Bible-believers to simply shrug their shoulders whenever the subject of the end times surfaces.

An "I don't care" attitude can be costly for several reasons.

First, it leads to neglecting portions of God's Word that point to the world's future. That can't be healthy, for Paul said, "*All* Scripture is inspired by God and profitable" (2 Tim. 3:16 NASB). This includes Isaiah, Jeremiah, Ezekiel, Daniel, Joel, Zechariah, the Gospels, 1 Corinthians, 1 Thessalonians, 2 Thessalonians, 2 Peter, Jude, and Revelation, to name a few.

Second, an ignorance of basic end-times tenets can affect other aspects of vital doctrine—the work of Christ as Judge and King (Christology), the future aspect of our salvation (Soteriology), God's redemptive plan and purpose for humanity (Anthropology), the ultimate answer to the problem of evil in the world (Theodicy), the plan for the church in the future (Ecclesiology), and the role of hope in spiritual growth (Sanctification). *A well-balanced theology requires eschatology.*

Third, if due to disinterest or neglect we aren't equipped to handle issues of basic eschatology, we'll be unable to respond to sincere questions posed by younger believers about the end times. When we miss such opportunities, they won't drop their queries and suddenly become as detached as we are. Instead, they'll find answers somewhere else—maybe through reliable sources, maybe not. Wouldn't you rather be involved and take an active role in what, and who, influences and teaches them?

Apathy and agnosticism in any area of theology is at least unhealthy and often downright hazardous. Though the details of the end times don't rank with the doctrines of the Trinity, the person and work of Christ, or salvation, eschatology is a vital part of the Christian faith.

Danger 4: This-Is-That Syndrome

Some of the first books I read as a young believer had to do with eschatology. Okay, that's an understatement. I didn't just *read*—I consumed them. And they weren't just *about* the end times; they made it sound like we were surely on the brink of that climactic world crisis that would usher in the end itself.

Those books had red, yellow, and/or black covers. They usually featured atomic blasts, fire, smoke, dragons, and/or demons. All of them said we should read the Bible alongside the newspaper because current events were fulfilling the prophecies of the Apocalypse nearly every day.

Some nuanced treatments said things like "So-and-so *could* be the Antichrist" or "This technology *may* be used in the tribulation as the mark of the beast" or "These events in Europe [or the Middle East, or Russia, or China] *might* be setting the stage for the rise of Antichrist's one-world government." Authors, TV preachers, pastors, and general enthusiasts sought everywhere after signs that would point to the imminent end. In fact, I was once told not to bother with seminary because "There isn't time."

I began to grow weary (and distrustful) of sign-seeking when some teachers kept changing their identifications. First the ten-nation confederacy (Rev. 13) was the European Union . . . then it was a Mediterranean alliance that included the Middle East . . . then it was a Middle Eastern and Asian conglomerate. Some suggested Antichrist would be a New Age guru . . . others a European politician . . . others a Muslim dictator. And the mark of the beast—social security numbers? bar codes? GPS devices? smartphones? . . .

Besides looking foolish, sign-seekers can do damage to people's faith and to the cause of Christ. When "fulfillments" don't pan out, weak believers, unbelievers, skeptics, critics, and scoffers may conclude one of two things: (1) Christianity and the Bible are untrustworthy, leading to the question "What else does the Bible teach that isn't true?" Or more likely, (2) The Bible is hopelessly ambiguous, for if careful interpreters can wrongly read into it so many different current events, then Scripture apparently can be interpreted to say anything people want it to say. In either case, *nothing* good comes from sign-seeking as sport. Those who engage in it make authentic believers get lumped together with thrill-chasers and cast us as both dim and misguided.

Danger 5: The Dating Game

Over the last few decades we've endured abundant attempts by high-profile leaders at predicting Christ's return or the rapture of the church. Several claimed we wouldn't make it out of the 1980s. Another set the rapture in 1993, with the second coming in 2000. Another pointed at 1994 . . . then 2011. And it doesn't matter on what side of the denominational or theological table one sits. Premillennialists and amillennialists alike have tried the "dating game."

The truth is, for almost twenty centuries, misguided Christians have been studying prophecies with the Bible in one hand and a calculator, abacus, or chalk slate in the other.[7] Every time they've "set the date" they've been wrong. And of course there's a good reason for this: the Bible guarantees that anybody who plays this game will lose.

Jesus, Paul, Peter, and the entire early church knew that nobody can know the timing of Christ's return. Jesus himself said, "Of that day and hour no one knows, not even the angels of heaven, nor the Son, but the Father alone" (Matt. 24:36 NASB); "Be on the alert, for you [the disciples] do not know which day your Lord is coming" (v. 42 NASB). And to underscore that no one who lived later could know either, He said, "Take heed, keep on the alert; for you do not know when the appointed time will come. . . . What I say to you I say to all, 'Be on the alert!'" (Mark 13:33, 37 NASB).

Paul later reiterated that nobody knows the time but that all believers of every generation must remain alert and ready for judgment at any moment: "As to the times and the epochs, brethren, you have no need of anything to be written to you. For you yourselves know full well that the day of the Lord will come just like a thief in the night" (1 Thess. 5:1–2 NASB). Believers, however, will not be overtaken by the suddenness of this coming (v. 4), not because they will know before it happens, but because they will be ready for Christ's return regardless of when it does. Peter echoes the same thought: "The day of the Lord will come like a thief" (2 Peter 3:10 NASB).

Finally, a very early document called *The Didache* (c. AD 50–70), written for instruction of new Gentile believers, included a brief account of Christian expectations of the end times. The author wrote, "Watch over your life: do not let your lamps go out, and do not be unprepared, but be ready, for you do not know the hour when our Lord is coming" (16.1). The pattern of teaching in the early orthodox church was the same as that of Jesus and the apostles: we do not (and cannot) know the time of Christ's return. It could happen any day. So we're to be ready for it every day and every moment of our lives.

Even so, these facts don't stop those high-risk gamblers playing the game. Instead, they suggest that these warnings are for unbelievers, or that God has chosen to progressively illuminate His church to discover secret knowledge long hidden in Scripture, or they use verses like Amos 3:7 to mean that God wouldn't suddenly judge the world without adequate warning.

God's Word teaches (and history has taught us) that whenever we play the dating game, we lose. The solution: *don't play.*

Danger 6: End-Times Obsession

One of the greatest things about the advent of digital music is that MP3s don't skip. At least I've never heard one skip. On the other hand, I have childhood memories of scratched vinyl records playing the same words over and over and over and over: "On a train bound for nowhere, I met up with the with the with the with the with the . . ." A gentle nudge of the record player might correct the problem, but sometimes after a couple of turntable rotations the needle would find its way back to the scratch: "We were both too tired to—met up with the with the with the with the . . ."

Over the years I've encountered well-meaning Christians who are obsessed with the end times. Like with a broken record, it seems every conversation returns to discussing eschatology. Every book they read handles prophecy. They attend conferences on Bible prophecy, tune in to programs on prophecy, watch current events through the lens of prophecy. If you haven't already encountered such a person, you will. They exhibit a fascination with details, charts, scenarios, and speculations—often in reaction against a perceived lack of attention to eschatology among other believers or churches.

Though it's unhealthy to avoid eschatology or to give the book of Revelation a cold shoulder, it's also unhealthy to neglect the other vital doctrines of the faith in order to devote oneself to Bible prophecy. The core convictions of Christianity center on the gospel concerning the person and work of Jesus Christ (Rom. 1:1–4; 1 Cor. 15:1–4). This gospel does include His second coming as Judge (Rom. 2:16), but we must never exaggerate one element of the gospel message. We must avoid end-times obsession in our own lives and discourage it as we disciple others in a balanced faith walk.

Danger 7: Fearful Fretting

I wish I'd saved an article from the late 1990s. Astronomers had calculated that a catastrophically large asteroid was on a collision course for the Big Blue. I can't recall the exact date it was supposed to annihilate the earth, but I remember it was likely to be within my lifetime.

My wife asked, "Do you think it's true?"

I thought for several seconds, running through all the viable Christian perspectives on the end times, and said something like, "No. I don't believe it. I'm not a scientist, and I can't possibly challenge their conclusions, but the whole world being obliterated by an asteroid doesn't fit with Scripture. So I'm not going to worry about it."

A few days later the same source ran a follow-up article correcting the first announcement. After rerunning the numbers, the experts determined the asteroid would *not* collide with the earth—it would pass "astronomically close" to our planet. (Which probably means we still wouldn't be able to see it with a strong telescope!)

Had my understanding of biblical eschatology been less firm, I could have hastily junked its portrayal of the end times and believed the scientists instead. Or I could have taken the report's version of the world's end as fact and reinterpreted Scripture to fit with its bleak outlook. But because there was a conflict, I chose to believe God's Word and reject the wisdom of man.

Seven Dangers to Avoid

1. Heinous Heresy
2. My Way or the Highway
3. End-Times Agnosticism
4. This-Is-That Syndrome
5. The Dating Game
6. End-Times Obsession
7. Fearful Fretting

A solid knowledge of the doctrine's essentials and an awareness of related possibilities will drive out fears and diminish anxieties. Though most Christian understandings of the end times involve a period of increased warfare, disease, and destruction, *none* involve a man-made catastrophe *or* a natural disaster that would obliterate the human race or vaporize the world. And, some scenarios—say, a sudden global nuclear war or an unavoidable asteroid impact—simply don't fit the Bible's version of end-times events.

Principles to Put Into Practice

"How does that affect how I'm going to live my life today?"

That brief, blunt response by a co-worker hit me like a slap in the face. I had shared with her some intriguing, prophecy-related fact I'd just learned at a Bible study, and whatever it was (this was many years ago), it had me fired up—it had made me think the Lord might well return before this shift at the supermarket deli was over. I was a college student; I'd only been a believer for a couple of years and, like many newbies, I spent quite a bit of time poring over prophecy. And I thought everybody would be equally interested.

But when she gave that response, I didn't know how to take it. She claimed to be a believer too. In fact, she'd been a Christian much longer than I had. Why wouldn't she be as thrilled about prophetic ins and outs as I was? *How does that affect how I'm going to live my life today?* What a silly reply!

It wasn't, though.

Since that time, my interest in biblical prophecy has not ceased, though I've put it in its proper place, that is, balanced it with and by other vital areas of belief and practice. And since that question, I've had many years to think about how I should have answered. God has given us a glimpse into the future for a reason: to change our minds, our hearts, our priorities, our attitudes, and our actions. *Promises and prophecies about what lies ahead are intended to transform (not merely inform) us.*

Let me share five principles of eschatology to put into practice—not on the eve of Christ's return, not in the perfect world we'll enjoy after He comes back, but right now . . . today . . . and for the rest of our lives.

Principle 1: Wait eagerly for Christ's return with a life lived in holiness.

The main purpose of all Scripture is to equip believers for "every good work" (2 Tim. 3:16–17). This is no less true for prophetic Scripture. In fact, in one of the Bible's most intense apocalyptic passages, where the apostle Peter contrasts this world's destruction with the establishment of the world to come, he turns our attention from the prophetic to the practical.

In Light of Coming Judgment	In Light of Coming Blessing
"Since all these things are thus to be dissolved, what sort of people ought you to be in lives of holiness and godliness!" (2 Peter 3:11)	"Therefore, beloved, since you are waiting for these, be diligent to be found by him without spot or blemish, and at peace." (2 Peter 3:14)

On the negative side, as we anticipate the certain judgment of this world, we ought to align ourselves with the side of holiness and godliness rather than wickedness and faithlessness. On the positive side, as we contemplate the glorious blessings of the world to come, we ought to live pure and peaceful lives rather than dirty and disagreeable ones. When you read a passage of Scripture that refers to the future or study themes of biblical prophecy, don't forget to ask, "*What sort of person should I be in light of this truth?*"

Principle 2: Invest in eternity, not in temporalities.

We live in a culture obsessed with economics, finances, investments, profits, dividends, and interest. For many, economic priorities rather than spiritual or moral concerns drive everyday decisions. Yet the Bible emphasizes investment in the eternal rather than the temporal—in the heavenly instead of the earthly. In a blunt rebuke of obsession with material possessions, Jesus denounces the misappropriation of time, energy, and other resources:

> Do not lay up for yourselves treasures on earth, where moth and rust destroy and where thieves break in and steal, but lay up for yourselves treasures in heaven, where neither moth nor rust destroys and where thieves do not break in and steal. For where your treasure is, there your heart will be also. (Matt. 6:19–21)

The next time you review your retirement plan or peruse your investment portfolio, take some time to weigh the amount of time, energy, and money you spend on your present "holdings" in eternal accounts. These might include:

- Supporting your local church's ministry
- Giving to alleviate suffering and injustice
- Contributing to evangelism and discipleship
- Donating to worldwide mission efforts
- Spending some of your "off" time on a missions trip
- Volunteering at a homeless shelter
- Giving up "me" time to share Christ's love with others
- Asking your leaders where they need you most and diving in!

Principle 3: Focus on foundational facts, not incidental opinions.

The author of Hebrews encourages his readers to "hold fast the confession of our hope without wavering, for he who promised is faithful" (10:23). This confession refers to the simple truths of the Christian faith related to the person and work of Jesus Christ as the center of the triune God's plan of creation and redemption. It's the "confession of the gospel of Christ" (2 Cor. 9:13), which Paul describes as "of first importance" (1 Cor. 15:3–4): "that Christ died for our sins in accordance with the Scriptures, that he was buried, that he was raised on the third day in accordance with the Scriptures." This gospel even includes the reality of the coming day of judgment (Rom. 2:16).

In 1 Timothy Paul summarizes some elements of this confession of Christ's saving work of incarnation, proclamation, and ascension:

> Great indeed, we confess, is the mystery of godliness: He was manifested in the flesh, vindicated by the Spirit, seen by angels, proclaimed among the nations, believed on in the world, taken up in glory. (3:16)

In another "trustworthy saying," he touches on eschatological elements that must form our doctrine's foundation: "If we died with Him, we will also live with Him; If we endure, we will also reign with Him" (2 Tim. 2:11–12 NASB). Perhaps associated with a charge to new believers at baptism, these words emphasize our belief in the resurrection and eternal reign with Jesus.

It's so easy to get carried away by enthralling details and stimulating end-times trivia—for instance, potential *whens, wheres,* and *hows.* But if we're to keep the gospel itself central in our preaching and teaching, we must remain focused on those elements of eschatology that are part of the confession of faith—our future resurrection as a result of Christ's resurrection, our reign with Christ the King, and the reality of Christ's coming judgment.

Principle 4: Don't be crushed by present suffering; be comforted by future splendor.

When I was only five, my eleven-year-old brother succumbed to a long bout with childhood leukemia. That experience confused my younger brother and me, but it *crushed* my mom and dad. No clever theological explanations, no frame-worthy Bible verses on pastel paper, no warm embraces or encouraging pats on the back could lighten the emotional suffering they endured at the loss of their eldest son.

Years later, when my mother was facing another family medical crisis, I asked, "How are you going to get through this?"

With a shake of her head, she answered matter-of-factly, "When you've buried a son, you can get through anything."

The horror of losing a child is the worst-case scenario of parenthood. It's hard to imagine a more heart-rending or life-changing experience. Many marriages don't survive it, and for those that do, the scars of suffering never fully heal. But even in the face of such extreme anguish, believers in Christ can confess this truth: *our present burdens DO pale when compared to our future splendor*. We may not be able to fully comprehend this truth either intellectually or emotionally, but we can fully embrace it.

Paul says, "I consider that the sufferings of this present time are not worth comparing with the glory that is to be revealed to us" (Rom. 8:18). When we read these words, we shouldn't imagine, for example, a balancing scale with a glowing treasure chest on one side that droops below a bin of putrid rubbish on the other. He doesn't say our future glory *outweighs* our current suffering—he says the two aren't even comparable. It's like measuring the universe against a speck of sand, or all the water in all the oceans against a single drop. The difference is so vast as to be inexpressible.

Now, the fact of an immeasurable future glory doesn't change the reality of today's agony.

It doesn't ease the pain . . . it promises a future without pain.

It doesn't save our sick children from death . . . it promises to bring them back from the dead.

It doesn't lessen this life's tears of sorrow . . . it promises that God himself will wipe away every tear and all sorrow in the next.

When we embrace by faith the assurance of the wondrous things to come, the Lord God will give us a hope that enables us to survive in our struggle with this world's very real suffering.

Equip yourself now with a concrete hope of future glory, so that when the inevitable storms of suffering blow in, you won't be washed away in the flood. As Christ promised, "In the world you will have tribulation. But take heart; I have overcome the world" (John 16:33).

Principle 5: Gather often to exhort one another to love and good works.

To the question, "How can we apply the coming of Christ to our lives today?" very few would say, "Go to church often." In fact, I've never had a student in either the church or seminary answer in that way. But God's Word does!

The author of Hebrews urges us to "consider how to stir up one another to love and good works, not neglecting to meet together, as is the habit of some, but encouraging one another" (10:24–25). Then, to firm up this exhortation, he adds, "and all the more as you see the Day drawing near" (v. 25). As we anticipate the coming day of judgment, we should respond by gathering together frequently, exhorting each other to lives lived in holiness.

Five Principles to Put Into Practice

1. Wait eagerly for Christ's return with a life lived in holiness.
2. Invest in eternity, not in temporalities.
3. Focus on foundational facts, not incidental opinions.
4. Don't be crushed by present suffering; be comforted by future splendor.
5. Gather often to exhort one another to love and good works.

Also, as the church gathers for regular participation in sharing the bread and cup as Christ's body and blood, we "proclaim the Lord's death until he comes" (1 Cor. 11:26). This observance represents our oneness in His body as we partake together of the one loaf (10:17)—not only in memory of Him and in celebration of His abiding presence but also in anticipation of His return.

Want to do something easy and practical in light of the return of Jesus Christ? It's as easy as joining together for worship, prayer, praise, exhortation, and accountability, as the members of the body live together in anticipation of the coming day of judgment and of everlasting life in the Lord's presence.

Voices From the Past and Present

In the fifth century, St. Vincent of Lérins described orthodox doctrine as those truths that have been believed "everywhere, always, by all." This theological content has been called by a number of terms: fixed elements, central truths, normative dogmas, foundational doctrines, fundamentals of the faith, essential marks. These core doctrines mark a person or church as truly "Christian."

While evangelicals have done well to defend these doctrines through faithful biblical interpretation, they often have lacked a strong historical perspective on the faith's essential truths. By looking through the rearview mirror, so to speak, we gain better ability to discern core truths from marginal teachings, central dogmas from peripheral matters, orthodox essentials from ancillary opinions. At the same time, looking backward helps us to fathom, appreciate, and critique the diverse opinions that also have been a part of the fabric of Christian history. This dual exploration of its unity and diversity will help us reckon with our own place in the history of doctrine.

In the following pages we provide a selection of quotations related to eschatology from each of the four periods of church history: Patristic, Medieval, Protestant, and Modern. Again, these can help students of doctrine to observe some of the constant themes that unite the history of Christianity as well as the diverse opinions that have enriched it. Pastors and teachers may find them to add historical perspective to their own preaching, teaching, and writing.[1]

The Patristic Period (pre- AD 100–500)

The Didache (c. 50–70)

"Watch over your life: do not let your lamps go out, and do not be unprepared, but be ready, for you do not know the hour when our Lord is coming. . . . For in the last days the false prophets and corrupters will abound, and the sheep will be turned into wolves, and love will be turned into hate. For as lawlessness increases, they will hate and persecute and betray one another. And then the deceiver of the world will appear as a son of God and will perform signs and wonders, and the earth will be delivered into his hands, and he will commit abominations the likes of which have never happened before. Then all humankind will come to the fiery test, and many will fall away and perish; but those who endure in their faith will be saved by the accursed one himself. And then there will appear the signs of the truth: first the sign of an opening in heaven, then the sign of the sound of a trumpet, and third, the resurrection of the dead—but not of all; rather, as it has been said, 'The Lord will come, and all his saints with him.' Then the world will see the Lord coming upon the clouds of heaven."[2]

Irenaeus of Lyons (c. 180)

"All these and other words were unquestionably spoken in reference to the resurrection of the just, which takes place after the coming of Antichrist, and the destruction of all nations under his rule; in the times of which resurrection of the righteous shall reign in the earth, waxing stronger by the sight of the Lord: and through Him they shall become accustomed to partake in the glory of God the Father, and shall enjoy in the kingdom communion with the holy angels, and union with spiritual beings; and with respect to those whom the Lord shall find in the flesh, awaiting Him from heaven, and who have suffered tribulation, as well as escaped the hands of the Wicked one. For it is in reference to them that the prophet says: 'And those that are left shall multiply upon the earth.'[3]

"But when this present fashion of things passes away, and man has been renewed, and flourishes in an incorruptible state, so as to preclude the possibility of becoming old, then there shall be the new heaven and the new earth, in which the new man shall remain continually, always holding fresh converse with God."[4]

Tertullian of Carthage (c. 200)

"The whole human race shall be raised again, to have its dues meted out according as it has merited in the period of good or evil, and thereafter to have these paid out through the immeasurable ages of eternity. Therefore after this there is neither death nor repeated resurrections, but we shall be the same that we are now, and still unchanged—the servants of God, ever with God, clothed upon with the proper substance of eternity; but the profane, and all who are not true worshippers of God, in like manner shall be consigned to the punishment of everlasting fire."[5]

Origen of Alexandria (c. 220)

"These subjects, indeed, are treated by us with great solicitude and caution, in the manner rather of an investigation and discussion, than in that of fixed and certain decision. For we have pointed out in the preceding pages those questions which must be set forth in clear dogmatic propositions, as I think has been done to the best of my ability when speaking of the Trinity. But on the present occasion our exercise is to be conducted, as best we may, in the style of a disputation rather than of strict definition. The end of the world, then, and the final consummation, will take place when everyone shall be subjected to punishment for his sins; a time which God alone knows, when He will bestow on each one what he deserves. We think, indeed, that the goodness of God, through His Christ, may recall all His creatures to one end, even His enemies being conquered and subdued."[6]

"If the heavens are to be changed, assuredly that which is changed does not perish, and if the fashion of the world passes away, it is by no means an annihilation or destruction of their material substance that is shown to take place, but a kind of change of quality and transformation of appearance. . . . And if any one imagine that at the end material, i.e., bodily, nature will be entirely destroyed, he cannot in any respect meet my view, how beings so numerous and powerful are able to live and to exist without bodies, since it is an attribute of the divine nature alone—i.e., of the Father, Son, and Holy Spirit—to exist without any material substance, and without partaking in any degree of a bodily adjunct."[7]

Commodianus (c. 240)

"From heaven will descend the city in the first resurrection; this is what we may tell of such a celestial fabric. We shall arise again to Him, who have been devoted to Him. And they shall be incorruptible, even already living without death. And neither will there be any grief nor any groaning in that city. They shall come also who overcame cruel martyrdom under Antichrist, and they themselves live for the whole time, and receive blessings because they have suffered evil things; and they themselves marrying, beget for a thousand years."[8]

Council of Constantinople (381)

"[He] will come again with glory to judge the living and dead. His Kingdom shall have no end. . . . We look forward to the resurrection of the dead and the life of the world to come."[9]

The Medieval Period (500–1500)

Boethius (c. 520)

"This teaching . . . promises that in the end of the age our bodies shall rise incorruptible to the kingdom of heaven, to the end that he who has lived well on earth by God's gift should be altogether blessed in that resurrection, but he who has lived amiss should, with the gift of resurrection, enter upon misery. And this is a firm principle of our religion, to believe not only that men's souls do not perish, but that their very bodies, which the coming of death had destroyed, recover their first state by this bliss that is to be."[10]

Gregory the Great (c. 601)

"Now that this End of the world is approaching, many things are at hand which previously have not been; to wit, changes of the air, terrors from heaven, and seasons contrary to the accustomed order of times, wars, famine, pestilences, earthquakes in diverse places. Yet these things will not come in our days, but after our days they will all ensue. You therefore, if you observe any of these things occurring in your land, by no means let your mind be troubled, since these signs of the End of the world are sent beforehand for this purpose, that we should be solicitous about our souls, suspectful of the hour of death, and in our good deeds be found prepared for the coming Judge."[11]

John of Damascus (c. 740)

"We shall therefore rise again, our souls being once more united with our bodies, now made incorruptible and having put off corruption. . . . Those who have done good will shine forth as the sun with the angels into life eternal, with our Lord Jesus Christ, ever seeing Him and being in His sight and deriving unceasing joy from Him, praising Him with the Father and the Holy Spirit throughout the limitless ages of ages."[12]

Anselm of Canterbury (c. 1077, 1078, 1100)

"From this the future resurrection of the dead is clearly proved. For if man is to be perfectly restored, the restoration should make him such as he would have been had he never sinned. . . . Therefore, as man, had he not sinned, was to have been transferred with the same body to an immortal state, so when he shall be restored, it must properly be with this, that as man, had he continued in holiness, would have been perfectly happy for eternity, both in body and soul; so, if he perseveres in wickedness, he shall be likewise completely miserable forever."[13]

"If beauty delights thee, there shall the righteous shine forth as the sun (Matt. xiii. 43). If swiftness or endurance, or freedom of body, which naught can withstand, delight thee, they shall be as angels of God—because it is sown a natural body; it is raised a spiritual body (1 Cor. xv. 44)–in power certainly, though not in nature. If it is a long and sound life that pleases thee, there a healthful eternity is, and an eternal health."[14]

Bernard of Clairvaux (c. 1150)

"But in the spiritual and immortal body, the body perfected, at peace and unified, the body made in all things subject to the spirit, there she may hope to reach the fourth degree of love—or, rather, to be taken into it, for it is not attained by human effort but given by the power of God to whom he will. . . . But souls loosed from their bodies, we believe, will be immersed completely in that sea of endless light and bright eternity."[15]

Francis of Assisi (c. 1220)

"Thy Kingdom come; that thou shouldst reign within us with thy grace and let us come to thy Kingdom, where we will see thee face to face, and have perfect love, blessed company, and sempiternal joy."[16]

Thomas Aquinas (c. 1265, 1270)

"Although the reward or punishment of the body depends upon the reward or punishment of the soul, nevertheless, since the soul is changeable only accidentally, on account of the body, once it is separated from the body it enters into an unchangeable condition, and receives its judgment. But the body remains subject to change down to the close of time: and therefore it must receive its reward or punishment then, in the last Judgment."[17]

"The details mentioned in the Gospels and Epistles in connection with the last advent are not sufficient to enable us to determine the time of the judgment, for the trials that are foretold as announcing the proximity of Christ's coming occurred even at the time of the Early Church, in a degree sometimes more sometimes less marked; so that even the days of the apostles were called the last days (Acts 2:17) when Peter expounded the saying of Joel 2:28, 'It shall come to pass in the last days,' etc., as referring to that time. Yet it was already a long time since then: and sometimes there were more and sometimes less afflictions in the Church. Consequently it is impossible to decide after how long a time it will take place, nor fix the month, year, century, or thousand years. . . . And even if we are to believe that at the end these calamities will be more frequent, it is impossible to fix what amount of such calamities will immediately precede the judgment day or the coming of Antichrist, since even at the time of the Early Church persecutions were so bitter, and the corruptions of error were so numerous, that some looked forward to the coming of Antichrist as being near or imminent."[18]

Thomas à Kempis (c. 1470)

"Why for a little pleasure which ye love, haste ye to eternal torments?

"Have ye no horror of hell, ye who shrink from a little penance?

"And ye who quiver at the death of the flesh, why be ye not in instant prayer against the eternal death of the soul? For unless ye be converted and repent, ye will not (when God judges) escape these fearful evils, and fiery torments. I tremble as I think of the last day and hour; when God may no longer be entreated in prayer, but be the just Judge of all."[19]

The Protestant Period (1500–1700)

The Augsburg Confession (1530)

"In the consummation of the world, Christ shall appear to judge, and shall raise up all the dead, and shall give unto the godly and elect eternal life and everlasting joys; but ungodly men and the devils shall he condemn unto endless torments."[20]

John Calvin (1559)

"We must hold . . . that the body in which we shall rise will be the same as at present in respect of substance, but that the quality will be different; just as the body of Christ which was raised up was the same as that which had been offered in sacrifice, and yet excelled in other qualities, as if it had been altogether different. . . . The corruptible body, therefore, in order that we may be raised, will not perish or vanish away, but, divested of corruption, will be clothed with incorruption. . . . But a distinction must be made between those who died long ago, and those who on that day shall be found alive. For as Paul declares, 'We shall not all sleep, but we shall all be changed' (1 Cor. 15:51); that is, it will not be necessary that a period should elapse between death and the beginning of the second life, for in a moment of time, in the twinkling of an eye, the trumpet shall sound, raising up the dead incorruptible, and, by a sudden change, fitting those who are alive for the same glory. So, in another passage, he comforts believers who were to undergo death, telling them that those who are then alive shall not take precedence over the dead, because those who have fallen asleep in Christ shall rise first (1 Thess. 4:15)."[21]

The Second Helvetic Confession (1566)

"Now Christ shall return to redeem his, and to abolish Antichrist by his coming, and to judge the quick and the dead (Acts xvii. 31). For the dead shall arise, and those that shall be found alive in that day (which is unknown unto all creatures) 'shall be changed in the twinkling of an eye' (1 Cor. xv. 51, 52). And all the faithful shall be taken up to meet Christ in the air (1 Thess. iv. 17); that thenceforth they may enter with him into heaven, there to live forever (2 Tim. ii. 11); but the unbelievers, or ungodly, shall descend with the devils into hell, there to burn forever, and never to be delivered out of torments (Matt. xxv. 41)."[22]

Mennonite Dordrecht Confession (1632)

"Regarding the resurrection of the dead, we confess with the mouth, and believe with the heart, that according to the Scriptures all men who shall have died or 'fallen asleep,' will, through the incomprehensible power of God, at the day of judgment, be 'raised up' and made alive; and that these, together with all those who then remain alive, and who shall be 'changed in a moment, in the twinkling of an eye, at the last trump,' shall 'appear before the judgment seat of Christ,' where the good shall be separated from the evil, and where 'every one shall receive the things done in his body, according to that he hath done, whether it be good or bad'; and that the good or pious shall then further, as the blessed of their Father, be received by Christ into eternal life, where they shall receive that joy which 'eye hath not seen, nor ear heard, nor hath entered into the heart of man.' Yea, where they shall reign and triumph with Christ for ever and ever. . . .

"And that, on the contrary, the wicked or impious, shall, as the accursed of God, be cast into 'outer darkness'; yea, into eternal, hellish torments; 'where their worm dieth not, and the fire is not quenched'; and where—according to Holy Scripture—they can expect no comfort nor redemption throughout eternity."[23]

Westminster Confession (1646)

"At the last day, such as are found alive shall not die, but be changed: and all the dead shall be raised up, with the self-same bodies, and none other (although with different qualities), which shall be united again to their souls forever."[24]

The Modern Period (1700–Present)

Jonathan Edwards (c. 1750)

"At the sound of the last trumpet, the dead shall rise, and the living shall be changed. As soon as Christ is descended, the last trumpet shall sound, as a notification to all mankind to appear; at which mighty sound shall the dead be immediately raised, and the living changed. . . . There will be some great and remarkable signal given for the rising of the dead, which it seems will be some mighty sound, caused by the angels of God, who shall attend on Christ.

"Upon this all the dead shall rise from their graves; all both small and great, who shall have lived upon earth since the foundation of the world; those who died before the flood, and those who were drowned in the flood, all that have died since that time, and that shall die to the end of the world. There will be a great moving upon the face of the earth, and in the waters, in bringing bone to his bone, in opening graves, and bringing together all the scattered particles of dead bodies. The earth shall give up the dead that are in it, and the sea shall give up the dead that are in it.

"However the parts of the bodies of many are divided and scattered; however many have been burnt, and their bodies have been turned to ashes and smoke, and driven to the four winds; however many have been eaten of wild beasts, of the fowls of heaven, and the fishes of the sea; however many have been consumed away upon the face of the earth, and a great part of their bodies have ascended in exhalations; yet the all-wise and all-powerful God can immediately bring every part to his part again.

"Of this vast multitude some shall rise to life, and others to condemnation. . . . When the bodies are prepared, the departed souls shall again enter into their bodies, and be re-united to them, never more to be separated. The souls of the wicked shall be brought up out of hell, though not out of misery, and shall very unwillingly enter into their bodies, which will be but eternal prisons to them. . . . They shall lift their eyes full of the utmost amazement and horror to see their awful Judge. And perhaps the bodies with which they shall be raised will be most filthy and loathsome, thus properly corresponding to the inward, moral turpitude of their souls.

"The souls of the righteous shall descend from heaven together with Christ and his angels. . . . They also shall be re-united to their bodies, that they may be glorified with them. They shall receive their bodies prepared by God to be mansions of pleasure to all eternity. They shall be every way fitted for the uses, the exercises, and delights of perfectly holy and glorified souls. They shall be clothed with a superlative beauty, similar to that of Christ's glorious body. . . . Their bodies shall rise incorruptible, no more liable to pain or disease, and with an extraordinary vigour and vivacity, like that of those spirits that are as a flame of fire. . . . With what joy will the souls and bodies of the saints meet, and with what joy will they lift up their heads out of their graves to behold the glorious sight of the appearing of Christ! And it will be a glorious sight to see those saints arising out of their graves, putting off their corruption, and putting on incorruption and glory.

"At the same time, those that shall then be alive upon the earth shall be changed. Their bodies shall pass through a great change, in a moment, in the twinkling of an eye. . . . The bodies of the wicked then living will be changed into such hideous things, as shall be answerable to the loathsome souls that dwell in them, and such as shall be prepared to receive and administer eternal torments without dissolution. But the bodies of the righteous shall be changed into the same glorious and immortal form in which those that shall be raised will appear."[25]

John Wesley (1758)

"And then shall be heard the universal shout, from all the companies of heaven, followed by the 'voice of the archangel,' proclaiming the approach of the Son of God and Man, 'and the trumpet of God,' sounding an alarm to all that sleep in the dust of the earth (1 Thess. 4:16). In consequence of this, all the graves shall open, and the bodies of men arise. The sea also shall give up the dead which are therein (Rev. 20:13), and every one shall rise with 'his own body': his own in substance, although so changed in its properties as we cannot now conceive. 'For this corruptible will' then 'put on incorruption, and this mortal put on immortality' (1 Cor. 15:53). Yea, 'death and hades,' the invisible world, shall 'deliver up the dead that are in them' (Rev. 20:13). So that all who ever lived and died, since God created man, shall be raised incorruptible and immortal.

"At the same time, 'the Son of Man shall send forth his angels' over all the earth; 'and they shall gather his elect from the four winds, from one end of heaven to the other' (Matt. 24:31). And the Lord himself shall come with clouds, in his own glory, and the glory of his Father, with ten thousand of his saints, even myriads of angels, and shall sit upon the throne of his glory. 'And before him shall be gathered all nations; and he shall separate them one from another, and shall set the sheep,' the good, 'on his right hand, and the goats,' the wicked, 'upon the left' (25:31ff.). Concerning this general assembly it is, that the beloved disciple speaks thus: 'I saw the dead,' all that had been dead, 'small and great, stand before God; and the books were opened' (a figurative expression, plainly referring to the manner of proceeding among men), 'and the dead were judged out of those things which were written in the books, according to their works'" (Rev. 20:12).[26]

***New Hampshire Baptist Confession** (c. 1833)*

"[We believe] that the end of this world is approaching: that at the last day, Christ will descend from heaven, and raise the dead from the grave to final retribution; that a solemn separation will then take place; that the wicked will be adjudged to endless punishment, and the righteous to endless joy; and that this judgment will fix forever the final state of men in heaven or hell, on principles of righteousness."[27]

***The Evangelical Alliance** (1867)*

"[We believe in] the immortality of the soul, the resurrection of the body, the judgment of the world by our Lord Jesus Christ, with the eternal blessedness of the righteous, and the eternal punishment of the wicked."[28]

***Charles Hodge** (c. 1870)*

"The Apostle teaches that our vile bodies are to be fashioned like unto the glorious body of Christ, and that a similar change is to take place in the world we inhabit. There are to be new heavens and a new earth, just as we are to have new bodies. Our bodies are not to be annihilated, but changed. . . . The result of this change is said to be the introduction of a new heavens and a new earth. This is set forth not only in the use of these terms, but in calling the predicted change 'a regeneration,' 'a restoration,' a deliverance from the bondage of corruption and an introduction into the glorious liberty of the Son of God. This earth, according to the common opinion, that is, this renovated earth, is to be the final seat of Christ's kingdom. This is the new heavens; this is the New Jerusalem, the Mount Zion in which are to be gathered the general assembly and church of the first-born, which are written in heaven; the spirits of just men made perfect; this is the heavenly Jerusalem; the city of the living God; the kingdom prepared for his people before the foundation of the world."[29]

Charles H. Spurgeon (c. 1890)

"Can all the saints put together fully measure the greatness of the promise of the Second Advent? This means infinite felicity for saints. What else has he promised? Why, that because he lives we shall live also. We shall possess an immortality of bliss for our souls; we shall enjoy also a resurrection for our bodies; we shall reign with Christ; we shall be glorified at his right hand."[30]

Millard J. Erickson (1998)

"All human beings (except those still alive when the Lord returns) must undergo physical death, at which time they go to an intermediate state appropriate to their spiritual condition. Those who have trusted themselves to the saving work of Jesus Christ will go to a place of bliss and reward; those who have not, will go to one of punishment and torment. At some future time Christ will return bodily and personally. Then all the dead will be resurrected and consigned to their ultimate destination—heaven or hell. There they will remain eternally in an unalterable condition."[31]

Baptist Faith and Message (2000)

"God, in His own time and in His own way, will bring the world to its appropriate end. According to His promise, Jesus Christ will return personally and visibly in glory to the earth; the dead will be raised; and Christ will judge all men in righteousness. The unrighteous will be consigned to Hell, the place of everlasting punishment. The righteous in their resurrected and glorified bodies will receive their reward and will dwell forever in Heaven with the Lord."[32]

SHELF SPACE: *Recommendations for Your Library*

This book provides central themes, essential passages, and a basic orientation to major Christian doctrines from a broadly orthodox protestant evangelical perspective. One could spend several lifetimes exploring these topics in greater detail; for help with delving deeper into some of them we've provided the following recommendations for your library. We've included brief notes describing the content and orientation of each book as well as a general rating (beginner, intermediate, or advanced). You should find representative voices from a variety of evangelical perspectives.

General Books on Eschatology and Hope

Benware, Paul N. *Understanding End Times Prophecy: A Comprehensive Approach.* Chicago: Moody, 1995. Overview of eschatology from a premillennial dispensational perspective. [INTERMEDIATE]

Chia, Roland. *Hope for the World: A Christian Vision of the Last Things.* Downers Grove, IL: InterVarsity Press, 2005. Traces hope as a biblical theme. [BEGINNER]

Erickson, Millard J. *A Basic Guide to Eschatology: Making Sense of the Millennium.* Grand Rapids: Baker, 1998. A balanced presentation and evaluation of various end-times views from a historical premillennial perspective. [BEGINNER]

Lightner, Robert P. *Last Days Handbook: A Complete Guide to the End Times.* Nashville: Thomas Nelson, 1998. An overview of end-times positions from a premillennial dispensational perspective. [BEGINNER]

Wright, N. T. *Surprised by Hope: Rethinking Heaven, the Resurrection, and the Mission of the Church.* New York: HarperCollins, 2008. Defends bodily resurrection and the re-created earth as the locus of the eschatological hope. [INTERMEDIATE]

Yancey, Philip. *Rumors of Another World.* Grand Rapids: Zondervan, 2003. Popular-level discussion of eschatological implications. [BEGINNER]

Books on the History of Eschatology

Boyer, Paul. *When Time Shall Be No More: Prophecy Belief in Modern American Culture*. Cambridge: Belknap of Harvard, 1992. This survey, which emphasizes eschatological interests in modern culture, also gives a broad historical survey of apocalyptic expectations. [ADVANCED]

Daley, Brian. *The Hope of the Early Church: A Handbook of Patristic Eschatology*. Grand Rapids: Baker, 2002. Surveys patristic eschatology, arguing for a unity of beliefs, noting diverse opinions. [ADVANCED]

Gumerlock, Francis X. *The Day and the Hour: Christianity's Perennial Fascination with Predicting the End of the World*. Powder Springs, GA: American Vision, 2000. Chronicles the failed attempts at anticipating the world's end (first through twentieth centuries). [INTERMEDIATE]

Hill, Charles E. *Regnum Caelorum: Patterns of Millennial Thought in Early Christianity*. 2nd ed. Grand Rapids: Eerdmans, 2001. A study of patristic views of the millennium arguing for very early emergence of both millennial and non-millennial eschatological forms. [ADVANCED]

Kromminga, Diedrich H. *The Millennium in the Church: Studies in the History of Christian Chiliasm*. Grand Rapids: Eerdmans, 1945. A classic and influential history of millennialism, though somewhat outdated in its research and conclusions. [ADVANCED]

Murray, Iain H. *The Puritan Hope: Revival and the Interpretation of Prophecy*. Edinburgh: Banner of Truth, 1971. Explores Puritan postmillennial hopes. [ADVANCED]

Viviano, Benedict T. *The Kingdom of God in History*. Eugene, OR: Wipf and Stock, 2002. Surveys the variety of views of the kingdom in the Christian tradition. [INTERMEDIATE]

Books on the Tribulation and the Antichrist

Gentry, Kenneth L. Jr. *Perilous Times: A Study in Eschatological Evil*. Fountain Inn, TX: Victorious Hope, 2012. Presents the classic preterist interpretation of key biblical passages. [ADVANCED]

Pink, Arthur. *The Antichrist*. Grand Rapids: Kregel, 1988. Classic presentation of the Antichrist from a biblical perspective. [ADVANCED]

Sproul, R. C. *The Last Days According to Jesus*. Grand Rapids: Baker, 1998. A defense of the partial-preterist interpretation of the Olivet Discourse and other passages. [INTERMEDIATE]

Books on Millennial Views

Blomberg, Craig L., and Sung Wook Chung, eds. *A Case for Historic Premillennialism: An Alternative to "Left Behind" Eschatology*. Grand Rapids: Baker, 2009. A collection of essays defending historic premillennialism. [INTERMEDIATE]

Bock, Darrell, ed. *Three Views on the Millennium and Beyond*. Grand Rapids: Zondervan, 1999. Defenses and rejoinders of premillennialism, amillennialism, and postmillennialism. [INTERMEDIATE]

Boettner, Loraine. *The Millennium*. Phillipsburg, PA: P & R, 1957. A biblical argument for the postmillennial interpretation. [INTERMEDIATE]

Clouse, Robert, ed. *The Meaning of the Millennium: Four Views*. Downers Grove, IL: InterVarsity Press, 1977. Defenses and rejoinders of historic premillennialism, dispensational premillennialism, postmillennialism, and amillennialism. [INTERMEDIATE]

Grenz, Stanley J. *The Millennial Maze: Sorting Out Evangelical Options*. Downers Grove, IL: InterVarsity Press, 1992. A survey and critique of contemporary views. [INTERMEDIATE]

Hoekema, Anthony. *The Bible and the Future*. Grand Rapids: Eerdmans, 1979. A defense of amillennial eschatology from a Reformed perspective. [INTERMEDIATE]

Kik, J. Marcellus. *The Eschatology of Victory*. Phillipsburg, PA: P & R, 1992. A classic defense of postmillennialism. [INTERMEDIATE]

Ladd, George Eldon. *The Presence of the Future: The Eschatology of Biblical Realism*. Reprint ed. Grand Rapids: Eerdmans, 1996. A biblical defense of historic premillennialism. [INTERMEDIATE]

Mathison, Keith A. *Postmillennialim: An Eschatology of Hope*. Phillipsburg, PA: P & R, 1999. A contemporary defense of postmillennialism. [INTERMEDIATE]

Riddlebarger, Kim. *A Case for Amillennialism: Understanding the End Times*. Grand Rapids: Baker, 2003. A biblical and theological defense of amillennialism. [INTERMEDIATE]

Walvoord, John F. *The Millennial Kingdom: A Basic Text for Premillennial Theology*. Grand Rapids: Zondervan, 1959. A biblical defense of dispensational premillennialism. [INTERMEDIATE]

Books on the Rapture

Govett, Robert G. *The Saints' Rapture to the Presence of the Lord Jesus*. London: Nisbet, 1852. A classic defense of the partial-rapture theory. [INTERMEDIATE]

Hultberg, Alan, ed. *Three Views on the Rapture: Pretribulation, Pre-Wrath, or Post-Tribulation*. 2nd ed. Counterpoints: Bible and Theology. Grand Rapids: Zondervan, 2010. A defense of each major view of the rapture with counterarguments from contributors. [INTERMEDIATE]

Rosenthal, Marvin. *The Pre-Wrath Rapture of the Church*. Grand Rapids: Zondervan, 1990. A defense of the pre-wrath rapture from a premillennial vantage. [INTERMEDIATE]

Books on Prophetic Scripture

Anderson, Robert. *The Coming Prince*. London: Hodder & Stoughton, 1894. Classic work on a futurist chronology of Daniel 9:24–27. [ADVANCED]

Barnhouse, Donald Grey. *Revelation: An Expositional Commentary*. Grand Rapids: Zondervan, 1971. An exposition of the book of Revelation from a premillennial perspective. [INTERMEDIATE]

Bauckham, Richard. *The Theology of the Book of Revelation*. Cambridge: Cambridge University Press, 1993. Commentary on Revelation from an idealist perspective. [ADVANCED]

Beale, G. K. *The Book of Revelation*. New International Greek Testament Commentary. Grand Rapids: Eerdmans, 1999. An idealist amillennial take that provides excellent Old Testament background and Greek exegetical information. [ADVANCED]

Charles, R. H. *A Critical and Exegetical Commentary on the Revelation of St. John*. International Critical Commentary. 2 vols. New York: Scribners, 1920. An exegetical commentary on Revelation from a premillennial viewpoint. [ADVANCED]

Darby, John Nelson. *Notes on the Apocalypse*. London: Morrish, c. 1850. A classic work by the pioneer of the dispensational, pretribulational, premillennial perspective. [INTERMEDIATE]

Gregg, Steve. *Revelation: Four Views*. Nashville: Thomas Nelson, 1997. Presented in a four-column parallel commentary format. [ADVANCED]

Pate, Marvin, ed. *Four Views on the Book of Revelation*. Counterpoints. Grand Rapids: Zondervan, 1998. Surveys contemporary views of the Apocalypse. [INTERMEDIATE]

Pentecost, J. Dwight. *Things to Come*. Findlay, OH: Dunham, 1962. Comprehensive survey of biblical prophecy from a dispensational premillennial perspective. [INTERMEDIATE]

Poythress, Vern S. *The Returning King: A Guide to the Book of Revelation.* Phillipsburg, PA: P & R, 2000. A practically oriented overview of the Revelation from an amillennial vantage, focusing on the big picture rather than details. [INTERMEDIATE]

Thomas, Robert L. *Revelation 1–7: An Exegetical Commentary*. Chicago: Moody, 1992. Often regarded as the most thorough contemporary presentation of the futurist interpretation of Revelation from a premillennial dispensational perspective. [ADVANCED]

Thomas, Robert L. *Revelation 8–22: An Exegetical Commentary*. Chicago: Moody, 1995. See description of volume 1, above. [ADVANCED]

Walvoord, John F. *Major Bible Prophecies: 37 Crucial Prophecies That Affect You Today*. Grand Rapids: Zondervan, 1991. A survey of Old Testament and New Testament prophecies from a premillennial and pretribulational understanding. [BEGINNER]

Notes

Part Two: "When He Returns: Resurrection, Judgment, and the Restoration" by Michael J. Svigel

High-Altitude Survey

1. William Shakespeare, *Measure for Measure,* Act III, Scene 1.

2. Janet M. Soskice, "The Ends of Man and the Future of God" in *Postmodern Theology* (Oxford: Basil Blackwells, 2001), 78.

3. John Polkinghorne, *The God of Hope and the End of the World* (New Haven, CT: Yale, 2002), 47.

4. Isa. 53; cf. Luke 24:27; Acts 17:2–3; Rom. 1:1–4; 1 Cor. 15:1–5

Passages to Master

1. See, e.g., Isa. 9:6–7; 11:1–7; 32:1–8; 35:1–10; 42:1–9; 52:13–15; 61:1–11.

2. See Heb. 8:8–12; 10:16–17; Rom. 11:27.

3. See, e.g., Isa. 43:25; Jer. 24:7; 30:22; 32:38; Ezek. 36:26; 37:27; Zech. 8:8.

4. See Matt. 26:28; Mark 14:24; Luke 22:20; 1 Cor. 11:25.

5. See, e.g., Isa. 42:6–7; Mal. 3:1.

6. See, e.g., Luke 22:20; 1 Cor. 11:25; Heb. 8:6–13; 9:15; 12:24.

7. Oswald T. Allis, *Prophecy and the Church* (Philadelphia: P & R, 1945), 42.

8. Charles Hodge, *Commentary on the Epistle to the Romans* (New York: Armstrong, 1909), 589.

9. Keith A. Mathison, *Postmillennialism: An Eschatology of Hope* (Phillipsburg, NJ: P & R, 1999), 90.

10. George Eldon Ladd, *Crucial Questions about the Kingdom of God* (Grand Rapids: Eerdmans, 1952), 137.

11. John Nelson Darby, *Synopsis of the Books of the Bible*, vol. 5 (London: Morrish, n.d.), 286.

12. C. I. Scofield, ed., *The Scofield Reference Bible* (New York: Oxford, 1917), 1297–1298.

13. Lewis Sperry Chafer, *Systematic Theology*, vol. 4 (Dallas: DTS, 1947), 105–107.

14. Craig A. Blaising and Darrell L. Bock, *Progressive Dispensationalism* (Grand Rapids: Bridgepoint, 1993), 208–211.

15. The image can be found in various forms at commons.wikimedia.org/wiki/File:127.Ezekiel's_Vision_of_the_Valley_of_Dry_Bones.jpg.

16. Mathison, *Postmillennialism*, 91–92.

17. J. Dwight Pentecost, *Things to Come* (Grand Rapids: Zondervan, 1958), 517–519.

18. See, e.g., Dan. 7:13 and Rev. 1:7; also, Dan. 9:2; 11:31; 12:11 and Matt. 24:15–16.

19. Mathison, *Postmillennialism*, 93–94.

20. See, e.g., Matt. 8:20; 9:6; 12:32, 40; 13:41; 16:27; 19:28; 24:30; 25:31; 26:64.

21. H. W. Wolff, *Joel and Amos,* Hermeneia (Philadelphia: Fortress, 1977), 66; Duane A. Garrett, Vol. 19A, *Hosea, Joel.* The New American Commentary (Nashville: Broadman & Holman, 1997).

22. Mathison, *Postmillennialism*, 97–98.

23. D. A. Carson, *The Expositor's Bible Commentary,* vol. 8, *Matthew*, ed. Frank E. Gaebelein (Grand Rapids: Zondervan, 1984), 488.

24. Mathison, *Postmillennialism*, 115.

25. Ibid., 117.

26. Again, see also Mark 13 and Luke 21.

27. The individual Gospel writers each emphasized one aspect of the teaching. Mark appears to balance near and far fulfillments; Matthew emphasizes the distant future; Luke focuses on events that would be fulfilled in the disciples' lifetimes.

28. Charles C. Ryrie, *The Ryrie Study Bible*, note at Mark 13:4 (Chicago: Moody, 1978), 1530.

29. C. E. B. Cranfield, *The Gospel According to St. Mark*, The Cambridge Greek Testament (New York: Cambridge, 1983), 402.

30. See Joel 2:28–32.

31. Walvoord, *The Millennial Kingdom*, 117–118.

32. Derek W. H. Thomas, *Acts* (Phillipsburg, NJ: P & R, 2011), 11.

33. See Ex. 19:9, 16; Ex. 13:21–22; 1 Kings 8:10–11; Matt. 17:5 (cf. Mark 9:7; Luke 9:34–35).

34. *The Epistle to the Romans*, vol. 1, The International Critical Commentary, eds. J. A. Emerton, C. E. B. Cranfield, and G. N. Stanton (Edinburgh: T. & T. Clark, 1975), 413–414.

35. From the Apostles' Creed.

36. A few commentators have suggested that Paul has in mind only a resurrection of the saved, not the unsaved; e.g., see C. K. Barrett, *The First Epistle to the Corinthians*, Harper's New Testament Commentaries (New York: Harper & Row, 1968), 355–356; George E. Ladd, *A Theology of the New Testament*, rev. ed. (Grand Rapids: Eerdmans, 1993), 610. However, Scripture is clear that there will be a bodily resurrection of both the righteous and the unrighteous.

37. John Jefferson Davis, *Christ's Victorious Kingdom: Postmillennialism Reconsidered* (Grand Rapids: Baker, 1986), 56–59.

38. Millard J. Erickson, *Christian Theology*, 2nd ed. (Grand Rapids: Baker, 1998), 1223.

39. F. F. Bruce, *1 & 2 Corinthians*, The New Century Bible Commentary (Grand Rapids: Eerdmans, 1971), 152. See also C. K. Barrett, *First Epistle to the Corinthians*, 372–373.

40. 1 Cor. 15:51–52; see also 1 Thess. 4:16–17.

41. See also 1 John 5:12–13 and 2 Tim. 4:8, where the present tense likewise is used to indicate the certainty of future reward.

42. There are two major views regarding Paul's emphasis in 2 Corinthians 5:1–10. The first is that he mainly has in mind a future bodily resurrection; the second is that he's focusing on the experience of believers immediately after they die. The former seems to be his primary focus, though here he also addresses the question of what happens to a person's spirit when he or she dies before Christ's return. See Paul Barnett, *The New International Commentary on the New Testament: The Second Epistle to the Corinthians* (Grand Rapids: Eerdmans, 1997), 247.

43. See Rev. 20:11–15.

44. See 1 Cor. 3:12–15.

45. Premillennialists, amillennialists, and postmillennialists, whether they're futurists or preterists, all acknowledge the basic teaching of the future resurrection and catching up of the saints (though some see 1 Thessalonians 4 as referring to the end-times coming of Christ and 1 Thessalonians 5 as referring to Israel's first-century destruction; see Mathison, *Postmillennialism,* 223–226). Only full preterists, who hold that all such prophecies were fulfilled in the first century, maintain that even the resurrection and rapture were fulfilled in the past. We do not regard full preterism as either evangelical or orthodox (see brief but helpful critique in ibid., 235–248).

46. See also 1 Cor. 15:51–53; 2 Cor. 5:4.

47. Irenaeus, *Against Heresies* 5.25.2.

48. Louis A. Barbieri, *First and Second Peter* (Chicago: Moody, 1977), 122.

49. See also Matt. 24:42–43; 1 Thess. 5:2; Rev. 3:3; 16:15.

50. Harry Ironside, *Lectures on the Book of Revelation* (New York: Loizeaux, 1930), 344.

51. See excellent discussion in Blaising, "The Day of the Lord Will Come," 395–399.

52. John MacArthur Jr., *2 Peter and Jude,* The MacArthur New Testament Commentary (Chicago: Moody, 2005), 125; Grant R. Osborne, *Revelation*, Baker Exegetical Commentary on the New Testament, ed. Moisés Silva (Grand Rapids: Baker, 2002), 730.

53. See Daniel Keating, *First and Second Peter, Jude*, Catholic Commentary on Sacred Scripture, eds. Peter S. Williamson and Mary Healy (Grand Rapids: Baker, 2011), 185.

54. Wayne Grudem, *Bible Doctrine: Essential Teachings of the Christian Faith*, ed. Jeff Purswell (Grand Rapids: Zondervan, 467); Joseph A. Seiss, *Lectures on the Apocalypse*, vol. 3 (Philadelphia: Philadelphia School of the Bible, 1865), 371.

55. William Hendriksen, *More Than Conquerors* (Grand Rapids: Eerdmans, 1940), 221–223; Kim Riddlebarger, *A Case for Amillennialism: Understanding the End Times* (Grand Rapids: Baker, 2003), 200–206.

56. Anthony A. Hoekema, "Amillennialism" in Robert G. Clouse, ed., *The Meaning of the Millennium: Four Views* (Downers Grove, IL: InterVarsity, 1977), 160. Also see a fuller treatment in Anthony A. Hoekema, *The Bible and the Future* (Grand Rapids: Eerdmans, 1979), 223–238.

57. See Dan. 12:2; John 5:28–29; Rev. 20:11–15.

58. Harold W. Hoehner, "Evidence from Revelation 20" in Donald K. Campbell and Jeffrey L. Townsend, *A Case for Premillennialism: A New Consensus* (Chicago: Moody, 1992), 247.

59. Hoehner, "Evidence from Revelation 20," 235; George E. Ladd, *Crucial Questions about the Kingdom of God* (Grand Rapids: Eerdmans, 1952), 135–150.

60. John F. Walvoord, *The Millennial Kingdom* (Grand Rapids: Zondervan, 1959), 5–6.

61. Craig A. Blaising, "Premillennialism" in Darrell L. Bock, ed., *Three Views on the Millennium and Beyond,* Counterpoints: Exploring Theology, ed. Stanley N. Gundry (Grand Rapids: Zondervan, 1999), 157.

62. Loraine Boettner, *The Millennium* (Phillipsburg, NJ: P & R, 1984), 69; John Jefferson Davis, *Christ's Victorious Kingdom: Postmillennialism Reconsidered* (Grand Rapids: Baker, 1986), 92–93; David Chilton, *The Days of Vengeance* (Fort Worth, TX: Dominion, 1987), 485; Mathison, *Postmillennialism*, 154. Other postmillennialists see Christ's coming (Rev. 19) as a symbol for the judgment against Israel that took place in AD 70 (Kenneth L. Gentry Jr., "A Postmillennial Response to Craig A. Blaising" in Darrell L. Bock, ed., *Three Views on the Millennium and Beyond*, 244–250).

63. Boettner, *The Millennium*, 64.

64. Mathison, *Postmillennialism*, 158.

65. Boettner, *The Millennium,* 60.

The End Times in Retrospect

1. Second Ecumenical Council at Constantinople, The Constantinopolitan Creed (381).

2. John of Damascus, *An Exact Exposition of the Orthodox Faith* 4.27 (NPNF 2.9:101).

3. *Didache* 16.3–8. The *Didache* was written in the second half of the first century, with many scholars today placing it more narrowly between AD 50 and 70.

4. Scholars have debated whether premillennialism represents the church's earliest widespread view or whether the earliest fathers held both amillennial and premillennial interpretations. See Charles E. Hill, *Regnum Caelorum: Patterns of Millennial Thought in Early Christianity*, 2nd ed. (Grand Rapids: Eerdmans, 2001).

5. See J. N. D. Kelly, *Early Christian Doctrines* (New York: HarperCollins, 1978), 459–489.

6. See Adriaan H. Bredero, *Christendom and Christianity in the Middle Ages: The Relations between Religion, Church, and Society*, trans. Reinder Bruinsma (Grand Rapids: Eerdmans, 1994), 97–98.

7. Translated by the author from the Latin text, composed c. mid-thirteenth century (H. T. Henry, "Dies Irae" in *The Catholic Encyclopedia*, vol. 4, *Cland–Diocesan*, ed. Charles G. Herbermann et al. [New York: Encyclopedia, 1913], 787).

8. The Constantinopolitan Creed.

9. Anselm, *Why God Became Man*, preface (trans. Sidney Norris Dean, *St. Anselm: proslogium; Monologium; An Appendix in Behalf of the Fool by Gaunilon;* and *Cur Deus Homo*, reprint ed. [Chicago: Open Court Publishing, 1926], 177–178).

10. Anselm, *Why God Became Man* 1.18 in Dean, *St. Anselm*, 217.

11. Hugh of St. Victor, *On the Sacraments of the Christian Faith* 1.8.2 in Eugene R. Fairweather, *A Scholastic Miscellany: Anselm to Ockham*, The Library of Christian Classics, eds. John Baillie, John T. McNeill, and Henry P. Van Dusen (Louisville, KY: Westminster John Knox, 1956), 100.

12. Louis Berkhof, *The History of Christian Doctrines* (Carlisle, PA: Banner of Truth Trust, 1969), 259–260.

13. Jaroslav Pelikan, *The Christian Tradition: A History of the Development of Doctrine*, vol. 3, *The Growth of Medieval Theology (600–1300)* (Chicago: U. of Chicago, 1978), 33–34.

14. Adam of St. Victor, *Sequence for a Saint's Day* in *A Scholastic Miscellany*, 332–333.

15. Cf. Berkhof, *History of Christian Doctrine*, 263; Pelikan, *The Christian Tradition*, 3:43.

16. Bredero, *Christendom and Christianity*, 97.

17. See Timothy George, *Theology of the Reformers* (Nashville: Broadman & Holman, 1988), 37–38.

18. Pelikan, *The Christian Tradition*, 3:38.

19. Ibid., 4:109.

20. Berkhof, *History of Christian Doctrines*, 263, 268.

21. Philip Schaff, *The Creeds of Christendom*, 4th rev. ed. (Grand Rapids: Baker, 1977), 3:18.

22. Ibid., 3:257.

23. C. Arnold Snyder, *Anabaptist History and Theology* (Kitchener: Pandora, 1997), 154.

24. Bernard McGinn, *Antichrist: Two Thousand Years of the Human Fascination with Evil* (San Francisco: HarperCollins, 1994), 202–203.

25. Martin Luther, *To the Christian Nobility of the German Nation Respecting the Reformation of the Christian Estate*, 3.23 in Henry Wace and C. A. Buchheim, eds. and trans., *First Principles of the Reformation or the Ninety-five Theses and the Three Primary Works of Dr. Martin Luther* (London: Murray, 1883), 73.

26. John Calvin, *Institutes of the Christian Religion* 4.2.12 in Henry Beveridge, trans. 2 vols. in 1 (Grand Rapids: Eerdmans, 1989), 2: 313–314.

27. *Thirty-Nine Articles* 22 in Schaff, *Creeds of Christendom*, 3:501.

28. Crawford Gribben, *Evangelical Millennialism in the Trans-Atlantic World, 1500–2000* (New York: Palgrave Macmillan, 2011), 20–22.

29. See Gary L. Nebeker, "John Nelson Darby and Trinity College, Dublin: A Study in Eschatological Contrasts" in *Fides et Historia* 34.2 (2002): 94.

30. cf. McGrath, *Christian Theology: An Introduction*, 469.

31. See Berkhof, *History of Christian Doctrines*, 264.

32. McGrath, *Christian Theology: An Introduction*, 469.

33. Walter Rauschenbusch, *A Theology for the Social Gospel* (New York: Macmillan, 1922), 210.

34. Ibid., 224.

Facts to Never Forget

1. All from the following list are quoted from the NASB.

2. "Joy to the World" in *The Hymnal for Worship and Celebration* (Waco: Word Music, 1984).

3. See Gordon H. Johnston, "Genesis 1 and Ancient Egyptian Creation Myths" in *Bibliotheca Sacra* 165 (April–June 2008): 183.

4. Roger Penrose, *Cycles of Time: An Extraordinary New View of the Universe* (London: Bodley Head, 2010); Paul J. Steinhardt and Neil Turok, *Endless Universe* (New York: Doubleday, 2007).

Dangers to Avoid

1. See, e.g., Rom. 2:16; 1 Cor. 15:13–14.

2. John 14:16–20; Matt. 28:20; Acts 2

3. *Gospel of Philip* (Nag Hammadi Library II.3.56, 26–30).

4. *Treatise on the Resurrection (Epistle to Rheginos)* (Nag Hammadi Library I.4.45, 14–46.2).

5. See, e.g., Clark Pinnock, "The Destruction of the Finally Impenitent" in *Criswell Theological Review* 4:2 (1990): 246–247.

6. R. C. Sproul, *1–2 Peter*, St. Andrew's Expositional Commentary (Wheaton, IL: Crossway, 2011), 282.

7. For a detailed account of attempts, see Francis X. Gumerlock, *The Day and the Hour: A Chronicle of Christianity's Perennial Fascination with Predicting the End of the World* (Atlanta: American Vision, 2000).

Voices From the Past and Present

1. Unless otherwise noted, patristic-era quotations come from the *Ante-Nicene Fathers* (ANF) or the *Nicene and Post-Nicene Fathers* (NPNF). Each parenthetical citation points to volume and page number. For example, ANF 3:34 refers to *The Ante-Nicene Fathers* volume 3, page 34. The *Nicene and Post-Nicene Fathers* span two series; for these I indicate the series (1 or 2), then volume within that series, then page within that volume. (So, e.g., NPNF 1.3:34 refers to the first series, volume 3, page 34.) Though there are more recent translations of some of these writings, I've chosen to use these because they're in the public domain and are easily accessible online at www.ccel.org.

2. *The Didache* 16.1, 3–8 in Michael W. Holmes, ed., *The Apostolic Fathers: Greek Texts and English Translations of Their Writings*, 3rd ed. (Grand Rapids: Baker, 2007), 367, 369.

3. Irenaeus, *Against Heresies* 5.35. (ANF 1:565).

4. Ibid., 5.36.1 (ANF 1:566).

5. Tertullian, *The Apology* 48 (ANF 3:54).

6. Origen, *On First Principles* 1.6.1 (ANF 4:260).

7. Ibid., 1.6.4 (ANF 4:262).

8. Commodianus, *Instructions* 44 (ANF 4:212).

9. The Constantinopolitan Creed in John H. Leith, ed., *The Creeds of Christendom: A Reader in Christian Doctrine from the Bible to the Present*, 3rd ed. (Louisville, KY: John Knox, 1982), 33.

10. Boethius, "On the Catholic Faith" in *The Theological Tractates, The Consolation of Philosophy*, trans. H. F. Stewart and E. K. Rand (London: Heinemann, 1918), 69, 71.

11. Gregory the Great, *Epistles* 11.66 (NPNF 2:13:82).

12. John of Damascus, *An Exact Exposition of the Orthodox Faith* 4.27 (NPNF 2.9:101).

13. Anselm, *Why God Became Man* (*Cur Deus Homo*) 2.3 (Dean, *St. Anselm*, 241–242).

14. Anselm, *Proslogion* 25 (Dean, *St. Anselm*, 30).

15. Bernard, *On the Love of God* 10 in Ray C. Petry, ed., *Late Medieval Mysticism*, The Library of Christian Classics (Louisville, KY: Westminster John Knox, 1957), 65.

16. Francis of Assisi, *Exposition of the Lord's Prayer* in ibid., 120–121.

17. Thomas Aquinas, *Summa Theologica* 3.59.5 in *Volume 4* (Part 3, First Section), trans. Fathers of the English Dominican Province (New York: Benziger, 1915), 2335.

18. Thomas Aquinas, *Summa Theologica*, 3[Supp].88.3 in ibid., 18.

19. Thomas à Kempis, *Soliloquy of the Soul* 2.4 (London: Suttaby, 1883), 16.

20. *Augsburg Confession of Faith* 17 in Philip Schaff, ed., *The Creeds of Christendom*, vol. 3, *The Evangelical Protestant Creeds*, 4th ed. (New York: Harper & Row, 1877), 17.

21. John Calvin, *Institutes of the Christian Religion*, ed. and trans. Henry Beveridge (Grand Rapids: Eerdmans, 1989), 2:271.

22. *The Second Helvetic Confession* 11 in Schaff, *The Creeds of Christendom*, 3:852.

23. *The Dordrecht Confession*, 18, in Leith, *Creeds of the Churches*, 307–308.

24. Westminster Confession, 32.2 in Schaff, *The Creeds of Christendom*, 3:671.

25. Jonathan Edwards, *The Final Judgment* 4.2 in *The Works of Jonathan Edwards*, vol. 2, rev. ed. (Edinburgh: Banner of Truth, 1974), 194–195.

26. John Wesley, *Sermon 15: The Great Assize* 1.1–2 in *Sermons on Several Occasions.*

27. *The New Hampshire Baptist Confession* 18 in Leith, *Creeds of the Churches*, 339.

28. *The Doctrinal Basis of the Evangelical Alliance*, adopted by the American Branch of the Evangelical Alliance (Jan. 1867) in Schaff, *Creeds of Christendom*, 3:828.

29. Charles Hodge, *Systematic Theology,* vol. 3 (New York: Charles Scribner, 1871), 852, 854.

30. Charles Haddon Spurgeon, *According to Promise: The Lord's Method of Dealing with His Chosen People* (New York: Funk & Wagnalls, 1887), 66–67.

31. Millard J. Erickson, *A Basic Guide to Eschatology: Making Sense of the Millennium* (Grand Rapids: Baker, 1998), 12.

32. *The Baptist Faith and Message,* 10, available online at sbc.net/bfm/bfm2000.asp.

GLOSSARY OF TERMS
for the Church, Spiritual Growth, and the End Times

Amillennialism Held by most theologians since Augustine (fourth century), this view understands the millennium described in Revelation 20:4–6 as occurring presently and spiritually either through Christ's reign at God's right hand or through the righteousness of the church. Thus, those who maintain this view deny that Christ will reign over a literal earthly kingdom after His return. Amillennialists believe in a single, general resurrection of the righteous and the wicked for reward and punishment.

Annihilationism Regarding personal eschatology, annihilationism says that instead of sending condemned sinners to eternal, conscious torment in the lake of fire, God will simply annihilate them, wiping them out of existence. Though held by a relative handful of Christians throughout history, this view has never been broadly maintained as biblically defensible. Another form, "cosmic" annihilationism, suggests that prior to the final, eternal state, God will completely annihilate this present creation, essentially "un-creating" it, then re-creating all things by a second act of creation out of nothing. This also has been a minority view in the church's history; most scholars and theologians believe that God will redeem and renovate this present creation.

Antichrist Though the title *Antichrist* doesn't appear in 2 Thessalonians 2, as early as the second century the "man of lawlessness" (2 Thess. 2:3) was being identified with the "beast rising out of the sea" (Rev. 13:1–10), the "antichrist [who] is coming" (1 John 2:18; 4:3), and a future great apostasy just preceding the second coming.

Antinomianism From Greek *anti-* ("against") and *nomos* ("law"); the idea that Christians are freed from obeying God's commands. That is, by virtue of the grace available in Christ, believers can do as they please.

Apocalypse From Greek *apokalupsis*; refers to a revealing, or unveiling, of something previously hidden. The book of Revelation, or "The Apocalypse of John," is an unveiling of future events (Rev. 1:1). In popular usage, the terms *apocalypse* and *apocalyptic* can refer to theories of a looming, tragic ending of society or the world itself through natural or supernatural events.

Apostolic Fathers Persons in church history who form the first "generation" of leaders after the Lord's apostles and were directly or (in some cases) indirectly associated with them. Today this term can refer either to the persons or to their written works; for example, a collection of their writings itself might be called *The Apostolic* (or *The Early*) *Fathers.*

Baptism Water baptism is an ordinance or sacrament of the church in which water is applied as a symbol of identification with Christ (or, by extension, with the community of the faithful). While there are differences of perspective on qualifications for and modes of baptism, evangelicals are united in its practice.

Biblical Authority The view that final authority in all matters of faith and practice rests in Scripture alone, not in the pronouncements of the Pope (papal authority) or in the declarations of councils (conciliar authority). Though protestants acknowledge the contributions of church fathers, councils, and creeds in the interpretation of Scripture, they believe that God's Spirit spoke infallibly only through the Bible.

Bishop Ultimately derived from the Greek *episkopos,* originally *bishop* referred to the role of overseer. For all practical purposes, the New Testament considers overseers and elders to be equivalent, yet as the church developed historically, the term came to refer to one who oversees local pastors; thus, *bishop* now refers most commonly to a member of the ecclesial hierarchy.

Catholic See Church, Catholic.

Catholic, Eastern See Eastern Orthodox Church.

Catholic, Roman See Roman Catholic Church.

Chiliasm Pronounced "*kill*-ee-az-uhm"; derives from the Greek word for "one thousand" and often is used synonymously with premillennialism. The term *chiliasts* (proponents of chiliasm) is sometimes used negatively or derogatively by critics who point out the occasionally carnal character of millennial expectations and who believe the whole view is based upon misinterpretations of Scripture about the resurrection and Christ's return.

Church, Catholic A term derived from the Greek *katholikos,* meaning "throughout the whole," *catholic* originally was used as a synonym for "whole." So in early church history, *the catholic church* simply means "the whole church" or the "universal church" as distinguished from the "local church" (see Church, Local). Only much later did *catholic* come to be a shorthand way of referring to the Roman Catholic Church.

Church, Invisible The body of all believers, united to Christ by the ministry of the Holy Spirit; the company of true believers (whom some call "the elect"), ultimately known only by God. The term *invisible church* emphasizes the importance of the saving relationship in understanding what the church is and recognizes that every individual Christian is part of Christ's body no matter the spiritual state of the organized church and/or local church of which he or she is a part (see also Church, Visible).

Church, Local We owe a debt to John Calvin for the look and feel of his definition of a true church: "Wherever we see a group of believers with leadership willing to accept all biblically affirmed responsibilities for the spiritual care and feeding of that group, there, it is not to be doubted, a church of God exists." Often contrasted with the church catholic or "universal church," which comprises all local churches that exist or have existed globally, the local church is a distinct body of believers under local leadership organized to carry out the works of the ministry.

Church, Visible The body of church members professing faith in Christ and/or associating themselves with a local church or denomination. In the common view, not all members of the visible church are necessarily members of the invisible church (see Church, Invisible); "visible church" also sometimes refers to all church bodies that claim to follow Christian teaching.

In this sense, the "visible church" would include the Anglican Communion, the Roman Catholic Church in its entirety, all branches of Presbyterianism, and so on.

Conciliar Authority To be distinguished from Roman Catholicism's papal authority and Protestantism's biblical authority, the belief that final doctrinal and practical authority rests with a duly called council of the church's bishops, each of whom has equal authority at the council. The Eastern Orthodox Church holds to this view, regarding the creeds and acts of the seven ecumenical councils (between the fourth and eighth centuries) as bindingly authoritative. Conciliarists uphold the absolute authority of Holy Scripture but believe that God's Spirit interprets Scripture authoritatively through the councils.

Conditional Immortality The (non-classic-Christian) idea that human souls, like human bodies, are mortal. After physical death, only at the resurrection will humans again experience conscious existence. This is similar to the notion of soul sleep, in which the dead rest in an unconscious state until the day of judgment (see also day of the Lord).

Congregationalism A form of church government in which each local assembly recognizes no authority above that assembly (except, of course, for Christ, the head of the church). In practice, the authority of the assembly is delegated to ministers, elders, or some combination of both.

Consubstantiation A perspective on the Lord's Supper that suggests Christ's actual body and blood are mysteriously present *with* the elements of bread and wine; it does not suggest the elements are changed essentially. (The doctrine typically is associated with Martin Luther's teaching on this sacrament and so is linked with modern Lutheranism.)

Council of Trent A gathering of more than two hundred Roman Catholic bishops in the Italian city of Trento (also for a time in Bologna), on and off for eighteen years (1545–1563) during the reign of three different popes. The Council shaped what many call the *Counter-Reformation,* Rome's response to the challenges raised by the Protestants. Trent reaffirmed pre-Reformation Roman Catholic doctrines and practices while condemning what it termed Protestant abuse of those practices.

Covenant Premillennialism A view of the end times (usually distinguished from dispensational premillennialism) that holds to the tenets of covenant theology while also expecting a future millennial reign of Christ on earth.

Covenant Theology A theological system using the principle of divine covenants as its organizational motif. Many adherents find their central tenets built upon a series of three covenants: the *Covenant of Works,* between God and Adam, in which perfect obedience is enjoined with the promise of eternal life; the *Covenant of Redemption,* between God the Father and God the Son, in which all God's elect are promised to the Son on condition of His obedience in incarnation, death, and resurrection; and the *Covenant of Grace,* between God the Son and the elect person, in which eternal life is pledged on condition of faith. Covenant theologians often (though not exclusively or necessarily) hold to amillennialism or postmillennialism; covenant premillennialism almost always rejects a pretribulation rapture. In the twentieth century, covenant theology and dispensationalism became regarded as distinct protestant traditions.

Day of Pentecost See Pentecost, Day of.

Day of the Lord Refers to times of reckoning, when God has intervened to judge or bless nations based on their response to His Word. As God has many times intervened in human history, there have been many "days of the Lord," though the prophetic writings frequently point to an ultimate day of the Lord coinciding with Christ's return as Judge and King.

Denomination An officially organized association of churches usually with authority structures beyond the local-church level and normally bearing a distinct name. Well-known protestant examples include the Southern Baptist Church, Presbyterian Church of America, Lutheran Church (Missouri Synod), United Methodist Church, and Evangelical Free Church of America. "Denominationalism" often refers to a strong particular loyalty, often resulting in conflict between denominations. (See also Nondenominational and Interdenominational.)

Dispensationalism A system of theology built around *dispensations,* viewed as (1) periods of time during which God established different regulations governing human behavior or (2) distinct "administrations" by which He providentially governs humanity or parts of humanity. Despite diverse views on some details, all dispensationalists believe Israel (the people of God in a previous dispensation, with their unique promises) and the church (the people of God in the present dispensation, with their unique promises) are distinct. Therefore, the dispensations at least include a past Old Testament dispensation, present church age, and future millennium. Dispensationalists necessarily hold to premillennialism and almost always hold to a pretribulation rapture.

Dispensations The means by which God administers His governance of humanity throughout history. Some adherents view the dispensations as completely separate periods of time, each with a clear beginning and end; others view them as various means of administration that may overlap or progress toward a final and ultimate expression of God's administration under Jesus Christ in the future.

Eastern Orthodox Church Distinct from the Protestant and Roman Catholic branches, this tradition has often been dominated by the Greek Orthodox Church and the bishop of Constantinople. The Eastern Church subscribes to conciliar authority, believing that final doctrinal and disciplinary authority rests in the church's councils, especially the seven ecumenical councils that convened from the fourth through the eighth centuries.

Ecclesiastical Related to the church, typically in reference to its structure, leadership, and practical functions.

Ecclesiology From the Greek *ecclesia* ("church") and *logos* ("discourse"), the study of the church, including its origin, place, and purpose in God's plan of redemption, its organization, ordinances, and responsibilities.

Ecumenical From a Greek term meaning "the inhabited world"; originally referred to the "whole church" spread throughout the world, or the "church catholic." In more modern times *ecumenical* has come to mean "interdenominational," that is, churches of various ecclesiastical traditions cooperating in pragmatic matters. The word also has a broader sense in some circles, e.g., interfaith cooperation between such divergent religions as Christianity, Hinduism, and Islam.

Election God's act of choosing those who will form the community of the redeemed, or those humans whom He will save. Evangelicals typically form their understanding of election in response to their reading of passages such as Ephesians 1, Romans 8, and 2 Thessalonians 2.

Episcopalianism A form of church government characterized by a hierarchy of bishops (the Greek word for "bishop" is *episkopos*).

Erastianism Named after Thomas Erastus (1524–1583), a position on church-state relations that says the state has supremacy over the church even in church matters.

Eschatology From the Greek *eschatos* (last) and *logos* (discourse); the study of the culmination of God's plan for His creation and the completion of His work of redemption and re-creation. Eschatology includes study of Old and New Testament promises awaiting future fulfillment and perspectives related to the rapture, the tribulation, resurrection, and millennium. (On the question of individual life after death, see Personal Eschatology.)

Evangelicalism An interdenominational protestant movement that emphasizes a personal relationship with God through faith in the person and work of Jesus Christ, insists on the paramount place of inspired Scripture as the final authority in matters of faith and practice, adheres to essential doctrines relative to God, Christ, and salvation, and seeks to engage the world through evangelism and missions. Evangelicals align themselves with churches and organizations that adhere to these emphases.

Fathers (of the Church) The leaders (pastors, teachers, elders, bishops) who lived during the patristic period (from the generation after the apostles to about AD 500). Some traditions regard their testimony as having a greater weight of authority because of their proximity to the apostles and/or their presence during the most formative period of orthodoxy.

Flesh A translation of the Greek *sarx,* Paul uses the concept of "flesh" (see especially Romans 7) to describe the sinful tendencies and impulses arising from within. In Galatians 5 he portrays the tension between his desire as a believer to do good and his innate desire to do selfish things as a battle between flesh and spirit. As a result, the concept of "living after the flesh" is common in discussing the doctrine of sanctification.

Full Preterism Also called *hyper-preterism*; a form of preterism holding that *all* prophecies of end-times events, including the second coming, final judgments, final resurrection, fulfillment of the Great Commission, coming of the new heavens and new earth, Armageddon, and renewal of all things are already fulfilled. Regarded as heresy by almost every branch of Christian orthodoxy, past and present. Full preterism should not be confused with *classic preterism* or *partial preterism*, both of which are viable options in orthodox Christian eschatology (see Preterism).

Futurism The interpretive stance that the apocalyptic and prophetic writings in Revelation and elsewhere primarily refer to future events not only from the perspective of the original biblical authors and readers but also from ours. As such, though these documents use highly symbolic language, the symbols refer to actual events that will occur in the future.

Heaven In the Bible, the term *heaven* or *heavens* can refer to the visible sky, outer space, the invisible spirit realm, the place of departed spirits (also called *paradise*), or the presence of God. In popular usage, *heaven* simply means the eternal destination of the saved, the opposite of hell.

Hell Several terms in the Bible can sometimes be rendered as "hell": *hades,* a Greek term for the underworld or non-bodily afterlife; *sheol*, the Hebrew word for the physical grave or the mysterious place of departed spirits (righteous or wicked); *gehenna*, which refers to a place of eternal punishment for the wicked. In popular usage, it can also be applied to the lake of fire—the final destination for the unsaved described in Revelation. In most people's minds today, *hell* is where the wicked go either permanently or temporarily—the opposite of heaven.

Historicism The view that regards prophecies in Revelation, and other Old and New Testament books, to have been mostly fulfilled throughout the past two thousand years.

Historic Premillenialism A premillennialist form that proponents believe most accurately reflects that held by early church fathers, its main distinguishing factor is belief in the *post*-tribulation rapture (and, usually, no major role for ethnic Israel during the tribulation or millennium). Some adherents also have distinguished themselves as historicists rather than futurists with regard to their view on the fulfillment of biblical prophecy throughout church history. Many also hold to the tenets of covenant theology and sometimes call their position "covenant premillennialism." See also Premillennialism.

Holiness Tradition Descriptive term for that part of the Wesleyan movement that greatly emphasisizes the doctrine of entire sanctification. Followers typically affirm that in this life a believer can experience perfection.

Hyper-Preterism See Full Preterism and Preterism.

Idealism Primarily dealing with how to interpret the visions of Revelation (or of Daniel, Zechariah, and other "apocalypses"), idealists in this vein see such visions as symbolically portraying the constant conflict between good and evil. Any resemblance to historical, contemporary, or future events does not indicate any literal fulfillment in this world but conveys an identifiable instance of the general spiritual reality that there has been and is an ongoing clash between the kingdoms of God and of Satan.

Inaugurated Eschatology The eschatological perspective that emphasizes some prophetic aspects that already have been fulfilled without rejecting the idea that others still await a future fulfillment. On the spectrum of positions, this view usually stands between realized eschatology (amillennialism) and futurist eschatology (premillennialism).

Interdenominational A term used to describe intentional cooperation between churches of various denominations. Schools, missionary societies, publishers, etc., that cross denominational/nondenominational lines regard themselves as "interdenominational." See also Ecumenical.

Justification God's forensic (or legal) declaration that a person is acceptable (or righteous) in His sight. One major Reformation teaching is that this divine vindication occurs on the basis of faith alone in Christ alone.

Kingdom A broad, multi-faceted, sometimes ambiguous term used throughout the Bible; can refer to a reign, a realm, even a ruler. On understanding the biblical kingdom of heaven or kingdom of God: some believe it primarily refers to a present reality of Christ reigning in heaven or through the church (realized eschatology or amillennialism); others believe it awaits a mostly future fulfillment when Christ returns (futurism or premillennialism); others see some aspects of the kingdom present with other aspects awaiting the future (inaugurated eschatology).

Lord's Supper An ordinance or sacrament in which, in obedience to Scripture, the church takes bread and wine in imitation of the Lord's example at the Last Supper. According to Jesus' own words and Paul's reiteration of them, the church does this "in remembrance of [Him]."

Medieval Period The church history era from c. AD 500 to 1500, known for the increase of the Roman Catholic Church's papal authority, the split between the Eastern Orthodox and Roman Catholic Churches (1054), the rise of Islam and the launching of the Crusades, and the founding of numerous monastic orders and universities. This period also saw early attempts at reforming the church both doctrinally and practically.

Memorial View A perspective on the Lord's Supper that holds it to be a remembrance of Christ's sacrifice, typically associated with the teaching of Ulrich Zwingli. Some have erroneously argued that "Zwinglianism" teaches Christ is not present in the sacrament (or ordinance), but Zwingli affirmed Christ's presence therein; he objected strongly to the concept of Christ's *physical* presence (e.g., see the arguments of the Zwinglian party at the Marburg Colloquy of 1529).

Midtribulation Rapture A view of the rapture's timing that says in the middle of the future seven-year tribulation true believers will be "caught up" (1 Thess. 4:17) from the earth to heaven, saved from the direct wrath of God that comes during the tribulation's last half.

Millennium From the Latin *mille* (thousand) and *annus* (year); a thousand-year reign of Christ with His saints (see Revelation 20:1–5), during which Satan is bound. Some take this as a literal kingdom to be established in the future (premillennialism); others take it less literally, seeing a current or ideal spiritual or heavenly state (amillennialism). Some see it as referring to an earthly golden age of Christiandom preceding an apostasy and Christ's return (postmillennialism).

Modern Period The era of church history beginning around 1700 and extending to the present. The modern age is more of a mind-set characterized by the exchange of traditional authorities like the church, the creeds or confessions, and Scripture for the individual authority of human reason. In this period science, philosophy, and theology all moved from the Christian worldview toward a more secular worldview.

Nondenominational The designation of independent churches, or the independent church tradition, characterized by non-membership in an official association of local churches; the highest authority within a nondenominational church is that local church. Examples include many Bible churches, community churches, or independent Baptist churches.

Ordinance A practice, or rite, established as an authoritative part of church order by customary usage or a biblical command. For example, many consider Baptism and the Lord's Supper to be ordinances. Sometimes the word *ordinance* is contrasted with the word *sacrament* by distinguishing how the rite relates to divine grace: an ordinance has sacred significance, whereas a sacrament conveys divine grace to the recipient.

Paedobaptism A perspective on the sacrament of baptism that suggests infants are the proper recipients (*pais* or *paidos* is Greek for "child").

Papal Authority The view developed gradually throughout the patristic and medieval periods that final doctrinal authority rests with the Pope, who is held to have the right and responsibility of universal headship over all Christian churches. Ecclesiastical authority is often contrasted with conciliar authority and biblical authority, but Roman Catholics also believe in Scripture's unquestioned authority and the councils' doctrinal authority regarding the bishop of Rome as having final authority in calling and ratifying councils and rightly interpreting Scripture.

Paradise In many traditions, the place of the departed spirits of those saved in the Old Testament period (see Luke 23:43). Ancient Christians equated it with Eden, translated into the spiritual realm, where Abraham awaited the Messiah's coming (16:22). Some also believe it to be the place of Christ's current sojourn, where even departed Christians rest between their bodily death and bodily resurrection (2 Cor. 12:3; Rev. 2:7).

Partial Rapture The futurist belief that only "spiritual Christians" will be raptured before the tribulation. Sometimes proponents also hold that there will be repeated raptures throughout the tribulation as various believers demonstrate faithfulness or overcome trials to their faith.

Patristic Period The church age related to the early fathers, c. AD 100 to 500. A foundational era during which the canon of Scripture was settled, the major ecumenical councils met, major creeds were formulated, and the church emerged from a night of persecution into the dawn of a favored status of what became the Roman Empire's official religion.

Pentecost, Day of *Pentecost* is derived from a Greek word meaning "fiftieth." As such it became their term for the Jewish Feast of Weeks (one of three great Jewish feasts), which fell on the fiftieth day after Passover. The disciples were waiting in an upper room in Jerusalem, in obedience to Jesus, when the Holy Spirit came upon them (see Acts 2), thus making Pentecost the Christian symbol of the gift of the Spirit.

Pentecostal A term referring to the church renewal movement that sees its example or paradigm in the events of the day of Pentecost (Acts 2). The Pentecostal movement (started in January 1901) is characterized by an emphasis on the spiritual gifts—most notably (e.g.,) tongues, prophecy, healing, and miracles—and so also is called the Charismatic movement.

Personal Eschatology Division of eschatology dealing with the individual's destiny after death, including the idea of an intermediate state, the nature of a bodiless condition, the notion of purgatory, the differences between the Old and New Testament experiences of life after death, the future resurrections, and the judgments to eternal life or eternal damnation.

Postmillennialism Understands Christ's return to occur after the millennium, which is interpreted as His historically realized reign on earth through the gospel and the church's social and political influence. Often associated with the social gospel of liberal theology or with reconstructionism, which seeks to secure a Christian kingdom or government on the earth.

Post-Tribulation Rapture The view holding that after the future seven-year tribulation, true believers who survived its persecution and martyrdom will be "caught up" from the earth to heaven (1 Thess. 4:17), either to immediately return to earth to reign with Christ during the millennium or to reign with Christ over the earth from the heavenly sphere.

Predestination A concept related to election. Some see the terms as roughly synonymous; others say that election is simply God's choice, whereas predestination brings the purpose or goal of His choice into view.

Premillennialism Believes Christ's return to be before the millennium, which is understood as a literal reign of Christ and all true believers on earth after the tribulation. Adherents hold that the first resurrection will occur in two stages—the redeemed will be resurrected before the millennium; unbelievers will be resurrected and judged after the millennium.

Presbyterianism Form of church government characterized by the leadership of elders (*presbyteros* is Greek for "elder"). Elders usually are arranged in a hierarchy of courts: The *session* is the group that leads a single congregation, the *presbytery* is made up of representative elders from sessions in a local area, the *synod* is composed of representative elders from a larger region; the *General Assembly* is the representative elders from across a nation. Churches that have a presbyterian form may not be part of a Presbyterian denomination; Reformed churches also exemplify presbyterian government. Further, many Reformed churches use different names for hierarchical levels: the *consistory* is the local church court; the *classis* represents an area, while the *synod* and *General Assembly* usually refer to the same organizational levels as in Presbyterian churches.

Preterism Regards most biblical prophecies (including visions in Revelation) to have been fulfilled in the first- to fifth-century persecutions, wars, and ultimate victory of Christianity over paganism. *Classic* preterists believe Jesus will still return as Judge of the living and the dead, and hold to a final resurrection unto eternal life or death. *Hyper-* (or *full*) preterists tend to deny any future judgment, reducing all eschatological judgments to personal eschatology.

Pretribulation Rapture The view of the rapture's timing that before the tribulation, true believers from the church age will be "caught up" from earth to heaven (1 Thess. 4:17) and so be saved from God's wrath.

Pre-Wrath Rapture The view of the rapture's timing (see 1 Thess. 4:17) that before God pours out His direct wrath upon the earth (usually limited to the seven "bowls" of Rev. 15–16), He will rescue His faithful saints. This will occur late in the tribulation but before Christ's return, so the rapture would happen somewhere between the midtrib and post-trib views.

Prophecy The message of a prophet that applies both to forth-telling (a moral message to the present generation, usually warning of judgment if repentance does not follow) and to foretelling (a prediction of future events). Also regarded as a biblical genre (similar to apocalyptic).

Protestant Reformation A church movement, beginning in 1517 with Martin Luther's declaration, that resulted in several church groups breaking from the authority of the Roman Catholic Church. Since they were formed from protests against practices found in the Roman Church, these were called *Protestants*; some of the most well-known are the Lutheran, Presbyterian, Anabaptist, and Anglican groups. The "Protestant Period" is generally regarded to extend from about 1500 to 1700.

Purgatory In the Roman Catholic tradition, where baptized Christians go to experience "purging" of sin in preparation for their eternal destiny. Neither the Eastern Orthodox nor Protestants accept this doctrine. *Not* a means for all people to be eventually saved (universalism), but only for baptized Christians who died with unresolved sin and guilt.

Rapture The "catching up" to heaven of all dead (upon resurrection) and living (upon transformation) believers. Different views on its timing in relation to the tribulation include pretribulation, midtribulation, post-tribulation, pre-wrath, and partial rapture. (See 1 Thess. 4:17.)

Realized Eschatology The eschatological perspective that holds most end-times-related prophecies to be in the process of unfolding in the church's present age, especially those regarding the kingdom. Popularly called *amillennialism,* though many reject that term for this one or *realized millennialism,* both more accurate and perhaps less derogatory.

Reformed A theological approach most associated with the followers of John Calvin and particularly with the Calvinistic form arising from the Synod of Dort (1618). Features an emphasis on God's sovereignty, especially as it shapes an understanding of His plan of salvation (e.g., typically affirms predestination and the human inability to choose to follow God).

Regeneration A ministry of the Holy Spirit in which the gift of spiritual life is bestowed upon a sinful human being. This rebirth results in a new nature for the person, so many evangelicals call those who believe in Christ "born again." One central biblical passage on regeneration is John 3.

Resurrection As a Christian doctrine, it refers to the restoration of physical life to those once dead. It applies first to Jesus Christ, raised in the same body that had been crucified and buried, though that body was miraculously glorified and made immortal and incorruptible, fit for eternal life. Jewish and Christian theologies have always held to two resurrections: the resurrection of the saved (righteous) and of the unsaved (wicked). The first resurrection includes all true believers throughout history, beginning with the resurrection of Christ and concluding with all of the elect. The second includes all the unsaved from history for judgment according to their works and eternal suffering in the lake of fire (Rev. 20:11–15).

Roman Catholic Church A term describing those in communion with the Roman Church headed by the Pope. A number of doctrinal distinctives set it apart from various Protestant churches and the Eastern Orthodox Church, including papal authority, purgatory, and transubstantiation.

Sacrament A practice, or rite, established as an authoritative part of church order by customary usage or biblical command. In Roman Catholicism there are seven *sacraments:* Baptism, Confirmation, Penance, Eucharist, Marriage, Extreme Unction, and Holy Orders. Sometimes the word is contrasted with *ordinance* by distinguishing how the rite is related to divine grace: an ordinance has sacred significance, whereas a sacrament conveys divine grace to the recipient; e.g., the *Catechism of the Council of Trent for Parish Priests* (Part II) says, "[A sacrament] is a sensible object which possesses, by divine institution, the power not only of signifying, but also of accomplishing holiness and righteousness."

Sanctification From the Latin *sanctus* ("holy") and *facere* ("to make"); can refer to the act of setting objects or persons apart for a special purpose. In Christian theology, refers especially to the process by which God's grace leads to a progressive growth in holiness for believers.

Sanctification, Final Also called "complete" or "perfect" sanctification; an aspect of the biblical teaching on the believer's growth in holiness. Scripture suggests that his or her experience of being taken to be with the Lord will coincide with a divinely given freedom from sin's very presence—i.e., sin will no longer be a part of his or her experience.

Second Coming The coming of Christ in glory (see Rev. 19:11–21) to judge the nations, to complete the first resurrection (of the righteous saints), and to establish the millennium. Those who hold to a pretribulation rapture distinguish between Christ's coming "in the air" to rapture the church and His second coming to earth in judgment to reign as King.

Soul Sleep The belief within personal eschatology that a person's soul does not consciously exist between physical death and resurrection but rests in an unconscious state until judgment. Not a classic Christian view.

Spiritual Presence View A perspective on the Lord's Supper that says Christ is actually present in the elements of bread and wine but spiritually, not physically. Typically associated with John Calvin's teaching on the ordinance and, hence, often represented as "the Reformed view."

Transubstantiation Stance on the Lord's Supper that says the bread and wine become Christ's body and blood. Does not suggest that the elements no longer taste like bread and wine but instead teaches that the substances' accidental characteristics remain the same—the flavor, texture, color, etc., do not change. Rather, there is a change in *essence*; the actual body and blood of Jesus are present in a form that looks and tastes like bread and wine. Typically associated with Roman Catholic teaching.

Tribulation Besides referring to the general troubles, trials, and persecutions all Christians endure through the church age (John 16:33), in reference to the end times the term specifies the final period of judgments described in Revelation. Historicists and idealists often view it as a condition more or less prevalent throughout the church's history. Futurists see it as a future fulfillment of certain passages (e.g., Dan. 9:27; Matt. 24:1–28; Rev. 11–13), often designating it to a period of seven years; some use the term *great tribulation* to refer specifically to the last three and a half years of the seven-year period leading up to the second coming.

Universalism In personal eschatology, the view that ultimately all people will be eternally saved and no one will be condemned to hell. This exhaustive salvation may be achieved either (1) through a universal purgation in which wicked sinners suffer sufficiently in hell to pay for their sins, or (2) through the loving mercy of God, who determines by His free choice to save everybody equally. Not a classic Christian perspective.

Scripture Index

Ezekiel

Daniel

Joel

Amos

Zechariah

Malachi

Matthew

Mark

Luke

Nathan D. Holsteen, ThM, PhD, is associate professor of Theological Studies at Dallas Theological Seminary, where he teaches all areas of systematic theology. Trained as an engineer, he is awed by systems of theology that exhibit internal coherence. He and his wife, Janice, have two children and live in Fort Worth, Texas.

Michael J. Svigel, ThM, PhD, is associate professor of Theological Studies at Dallas Theological Seminary. He has written numerous Bible study guides, articles, and papers, and is the author of *Retro-Christianity.* He lives in Garland, Texas, with his wife, Stephanie, and their three children. Learn more at www.retrochristianity.com.